OPPOSING
VIEWPOINTS ®

Other Books of Related Interest in the Opposing
Viewpoints Series:

OPPOSING VIEWPOINTS ®

David L. Bender & Bruno Leone, *Series Editors*

Matthew Polesetsky, *Book Editor*

OPPOSING VIEWPOINTS SERIES ®

Greenhaven Press, Inc.   PO Box 289009   San Diego, CA 92198-0009

Library of Congress Cataloging-in-Publication Data

Global resources : opposing viewpoints / Matthew Polesetsky,
book editor.
    p.   cm. — (Opposing viewpoints series)
    Includes bibliographical references and index.
    Summary: Sets out differing views on the nature and extent
of depletion of the Earth's resources and whether development
has caused environmental and population crises.
    ISBN 0-89908-152-5 (pbk.). — ISBN 0-89908-177-0 (lib. bdg.)
    1. Economic development—Environmental aspects. 2. Natural
resources—Management.   [1. Conservation of natural resources.]
I. Polesetsky, Matthew, 1968-   . II. Series: opposing viewpoints
series (Unnumbered)
HD75.6.G56   1991
333.7—dc20
                                                                   90-24088

"Congress shall make no law . . . abridging the freedom of speech, or of the press."

First Amendment to the U.S. Constitution

The basic foundation of our democracy is the first amendment guarantee of freedom of expression. The Opposing Viewpoints Series is dedicated to the concept of this basic freedom and the idea that it is more important to practice it than to enshrine it.

Contents

Why Consider Opposing Viewpoints?

"It is better to debate a question without settling it than to settle a question without debating it."

Joseph Joubert (1754-1824)

The Importance of Examining Opposing Viewpoints

The purpose of the Opposing Viewpoints Series, and this book in particular, is to present balanced, and often difficult to find, opposing points of view on complex and sensitive issues.

Probably the best way to become informed is to analyze the positions of those who are regarded as experts and well studied on issues. It is important to consider every variety of opinion in an attempt to determine the truth. Opinions from the mainstream of society should be examined. But also important are opinions that are considered radical, reactionary, or minority as well as those stigmatized by some other uncomplimentary label. An important lesson of history is the eventual acceptance of many unpopular and even despised opinions. The ideas of Socrates, Jesus, and Galileo are good examples of this.

Readers will approach this book with their own opinions on the issues debated within it. However, to have a good grasp of one's own viewpoint, it is necessary to understand the arguments of those with whom one disagrees. It can be said that those who do not completely understand their adversary's point of view do not fully understand their own.

A persuasive case for considering opposing viewpoints has been presented by John Stuart Mill in his work *On Liberty*. When examining controversial issues it may be helpful to reflect on this suggestion:

The only way in which a human being can make some approach to knowing the whole of a subject, is by hearing what can be said about it by persons of every variety of opinion, and studying all modes in which it can be looked at by every character of mind. No wise man ever acquired his wisdom in any mode but this.

Analyzing Sources of Information

The Opposing Viewpoints Series includes diverse materials taken from magazines, journals, books, and newspapers, as well as statements and position papers from a wide range of individuals, organizations, and governments. This broad spectrum of sources helps to develop patterns of thinking which are open to the consideration of a variety of opinions.

Pitfalls to Avoid

A pitfall to avoid in considering opposing points of view is that of regarding one's own opinion as being common sense and the most rational stance, and the point of view of others as being only opinion and naturally wrong. It may be that another's opinion is correct and one's own is in error.

Another pitfall to avoid is that of closing one's mind to the opinions of those with whom one disagrees. The best way to approach a dialogue is to make one's primary purpose that of understanding the mind and arguments of the other person and not that of enlightening him or her with one's own solutions. More can be learned by listening than speaking.

It is my hope that after reading this book the reader will have a deeper understanding of the issues debated and will appreciate the complexity of even seemingly simple issues on which good and honest people disagree. This awareness is particularly important in a democratic society such as ours where people enter into public debate to determine the common good. Those with whom one disagrees should not necessarily be regarded as enemies, but perhaps simply as people who suggest different paths to a common goal.

Developing Basic Reading and Thinking Skills

In this book, carefully edited opposing viewpoints are purposely placed back to back to create a running debate; each viewpoint is preceded by a short quotation that best expresses the author's main argument. This format instantly plunges the reader into the midst of a controversial issue and greatly aids that reader in mastering the basic skill of recognizing an author's point of view.

A number of basic skills for critical thinking are practiced in the activities that appear throughout the books in the series. Some of the skills are:

Evaluating Sources of Information. The ability to choose from among alternative sources the most reliable and accurate source in relation to a given subject.

Separating Fact from Opinion. The ability to make the basic distinction between factual statements (those that can be demonstrated or verified empirically) and statements of opinion (those that are beliefs or attitudes that cannot be proved).

Identifying Stereotypes. The ability to identify oversimplified, exaggerated descriptions (favorable or unfavorable) about people and insulting statements about racial, religious, or national groups, based upon misinformation or lack of information.

Recognizing Ethnocentrism. The ability to recognize attitudes or opinions that express the view that one's own race, culture, or group is inherently superior, or those attitudes that judge another culture or group in terms of one's own.

It is important to consider opposing viewpoints and equally important to be able to critically analyze those viewpoints. The activities in this book are designed to help the reader master these thinking skills. Statements are taken from the book's viewpoints and the reader is asked to analyze them. This technique aids the reader in developing skills that not only can be applied to the viewpoints in this book, but also to situations where opinionated spokespersons comment on controversial issues. Although the activities are helpful to the solitary reader, they are most useful when the reader can benefit from the interaction of group discussion.

Using this book and others in the series should help readers develop basic reading and thinking skills. These skills should improve the reader's ability to understand what is read. Readers should be better able to separate fact from opinion, substance from rhetoric, and become better consumers of information in our media-centered culture.

This volume of the Opposing Viewpoints Series does not advocate a particular point of view. Quite the contrary! The very nature of the book leaves it to the reader to formulate the opinions he or she finds most suitable. My purpose as publisher is to see that this is made possible by offering a wide range of viewpoints that are fairly presented.

David L. Bender
Publisher

Introduction

"Within the limits of the physical laws of nature, we are still masters of our individual and collective destiny, for good or ill."

E.F. Schumacher
Small Is Beautiful: Economics as if People Mattered

Paul R. Ehrlich, a biologist at Stanford University, tells a story of two brothers who inherit portions of their parents' property. One brother invests the property intelligently, withdrawing only the income generated by the investment. He is able to pass the inheritance on to his children. The other brother takes a completely different path. He uses all of the property in his own lifetime, not thinking about his children. Ehrlich warns that society, like the wasteful brother, has treated its inheritance, the earth, without regard for future generations. Society is destroying the rich diversity of life on earth, reducing the amount of fertile soil, and even endangering the climate in pursuit of immediate gains, he believes. It cannot be long before our negligence results in dire consequences for all of humanity, Ehrlich concludes.

Some experts believe that Ehrlich's views are no more than pessimistic bluster. For example, critics such as Julian L. Simon, an economist and professor at the University of Maryland in College Park, argues that human ingenuity and technology have solved natural resource problems in the past and will continue to solve them in the future. Despite many previous warnings that humanity was depleting the earth's resources and thereby endangering its own survival, for example, such a disaster has not occurred. Technology has steadily improved living standards and life expectancy throughout history and is likely to continue to do so, says Simon.

The split between these two opposing views can be seen in the debate over the greenhouse effect. For example, Al Gore Jr., a U.S. senator, worries that greenhouse pollutants generated by fossil fuels and factories are pushing the planet toward higher temperatures and ecological disaster. He warns that "Global climate change is real. It is the single most serious manifestation of a larger problem: the collision course between industrial civilization and the ecological system that supports life as we know it." Environmentalist Michael Oppenheimer agrees, arguing that civilization has already produced so much greenhouse pollution that substantial warming is inevitable. Unless we act immediately, society will face hotter temperatures and fewer options in the years ahead, these critics agree. Those on this side of the issue believe our global resources are seeping away from us, depleting at a frightening rate.

On the other side, researchers Jane S. Shaw and Richard L. Stroup believe that the greenhouse theory is inadequately substantiated and that calls for immediate, drastic countermeasures are misguided. Shaw, Stroup, and others emphasize the ability of humans to cope with problems as they develop. Even if scientists accumulate enough evidence to verify the greenhouse theory, our technologically advanced society will be able to prevent or adapt to the new situation, they believe. Just as people replaced traditional farming methods with modern agriculture and discovered the potential of fossil fuels to replace wood, they will continue to develop new technologies and ways to use natural resources when faced with global resource problems.

The debate over global resources is a debate over faith in technology. Can science, technology, and industry surmount all future natural resource problems? Or will unfettered growth exact a toll on the planet which science cannot correct? Will humanity have to redefine progress to ensure the continuance of the earth and its species? The viewpoints in *Global Resources: Opposing Viewpoints* address these questions. The following issues are debated: Are Global Resources Becoming More Scarce? Is the Greenhouse Effect a Serious Threat? Are Population Control Measures Needed to Protect Global Resources? How Can Rain Forests Be Saved? How Can Sustainable Agriculture Be Promoted? What Policies Would Help Conserve Global Resources? Whether humanity can be wise guardians of the earth is a question inherent in all of these issues.

Are Global Resources Becoming More Scarce?

Chapter Preface

The status of global resources is the focus of much concern on the part of politicians, the media, and the general public. These concerns are reflected by reports of the rain forests disappearing, species becoming extinct, the global climate changing, and population exploding.

Lester Brown, president of the environmental organization Worldwatch Institute, agrees with these conclusions. According to Brown and others, as human numbers increase, the planet's resources may prove too limited to meet the increased demands. At some point, these critics argue, global resources will become so scarce that living standards in the United States and the rest of the world will actually decline. For example, as the population expands, Brown warns, society will lose ever more valued cropland to soil erosion, housing, and industry. He concludes that this overuse of the land may cause food production to fall, leading to widespread hunger.

Yet not everyone is convinced that global resources are being exhausted. Writer Warren Brookes, for example, argues that while many environmental problems may be worthy of investigation, the media and politicians have inflated concerns, unduly alarming the public. James Bovard, an analyst for the Competitive Enterprise Institute, a public policy research organization, believes that Lester Brown's pessimistic predictions were wrong in the past and will be wrong in the future. According to Bovard, the prices of wheat, sugar, and other agricultural products have declined substantially in the past sixty years, reflecting the continuing success of modern agriculture. Despite Brown's claims, Bovard says, soil erosion and starvation are not likely to occur.

Are global resources becoming more scarce? The viewpoints in the following chapter debate this question.

"The world has lost nearly one fifth of the topsoil from its cropland, a fifth of its tropical rain forests, and tens of thousands of its plant and animal species."

Global Resource Scarcity Is a Serious Problem

Lester R. Brown

In the following viewpoint, Lester R. Brown warns that several forms of environmental destruction, including global warming, soil erosion, and deforestation, are depleting the earth's biological abundance. This trend, Brown argues, is showing up in the declining supplies and rising prices of agricultural products. With population growth accelerating into the nineties, the author concludes, the earth's life-supporting systems may crumble under the pressure. Brown is the president of Worldwatch Institute, a research center on environmental issues located in Washington, D.C.

As you read, consider the following questions:

1. What has been the history of world grain production since 1950, according to Brown?
2. Why is Brown concerned about future food production?
3. In the author's opinion, what three biological systems form the foundation for the world economy?

Excerpted, with permission, from "The Illusion of Progress," by Lester R. Brown, in *State of the World 1990,* edited by Linda Starke. Copyright © 1990 Worldwatch Institute.

For most of the nearly four fifths of humanity born since World War II, life has seemed to be a period of virtually uninterrupted economic progress. Since mid-century, the global economic product has nearly quintupled. On average, the additional economic output in each of the last four decades has matched that added from the beginning of civilization until 1950.

Illusion of Progress

World food output during this period also grew at a record pace. Soaring demand fueled by population growth and rising affluence provided the incentive, and modern technology the means, to multiply the world's grain harvest 2.6 times since mid-century. No other generation has witnessed gains even remotely approaching this.

Such gains would seem to be a cause for celebration, but instead there is a sense of illusion, a feeling that they overstate progress. The system of national accounting used to measure economic progress incorporates the depreciation of plant [factories] and equipment, but not the depletion of natural capital. Since mid-century, the world has lost nearly one fifth of the topsoil from its cropland, a fifth of its tropical rain forests, and tens of thousands of its plant and animal species.

During this same period, atmospheric carbon dioxide (CO_2) levels have increased by 13 percent, setting the stage for hotter summers. The protective ozone layer in the stratosphere has been depleted by 2 percent worldwide and far more over Antarctica. Dead lakes and dying forests have become a natural accompaniment of industrialization. Historians in the twenty-first century may marvel at this economic performance—and sorrow over its environmental consequences.

Reversal of Trends

Throughout our lifetimes, economic trends have shaped environmental trends, often altering the earth's natural resources and systems in ways not obvious at the time. Now, as we enter the nineties, the reverse is also beginning to happen: environmental trends are beginning to shape economic trends.

The environmental degradation of the planet is starting to show up at harvest time. The cumulative effects of losing 24 billion tons of topsoil each year are being felt in some of the world's major food-producing regions. Recent evidence indicates that air pollution is damaging crops in both auto-centered economies of the West and coal-burning economies of the East. Meteorologists cannot yet be certain, but the hotter summers and drought-reduced harvests of the eighties may be early indications of the greenhouse effect.

Environmental degradation undoubtedly contributed to the

slower growth in world grain output during the eighties. The 2.6-fold gain in world grain output just mentioned occurred between 1950 and 1984; since then, there has been no appreciable increase. The 1989 estimated harvest (1.67 billion tons) was up only 1 percent from that of 1984, which means that grain output per person is down nearly 7 percent. Some two thirds of this fall in production has been offset by drawing down stocks, reducing them to a precariously low level; the remainder, by reducing consumption. Although five years is obviously not enough time to signify a long-term trend, it does show that the world's farmers are finding it more difficult to keep up with growth in population.

© Christian/Rothco. Reprinted with permission.

Nowhere is this more clear than in Africa, where the combination of record population growth and widespread land degradation is reducing grain production per person. A drop of 20 percent from the peak in 1967 has converted the continent into a grain importer, fueled the region's mounting external debt, and left millions of Africans hungry and physically weakened, drained of their vitality and productivity. In a 1989 report sketching out several scenarios for this beleaguered continent, World Bank analysts termed the simple extrapolation of recent trends the "nightmare scenario."

In both Africa and Latin America, food consumption per person is lower today than it was when the decade began. Infant mortality rates—a sensitive indicator of nutritional stress—appear to have turned upward in many countries in Africa and Latin America, reversing a long-term historical trend. Nations in which there are enough data to document this rise include Brazil, the Dominican Republic, El Salvador, Ghana, Madagascar, Mexico, Peru, Uruguay, and Zambia.

Lack of Progress

On the two most important fronts in the race to save the planet —stopping population growth and stabilizing climate—the world is losing ground. Some progress has been made in slowing the rate of population growth since 1970, but the decline has been so gradual that the annual increment grows larger each year. During the eighties, world population increased by 842 million, an average of 84 million a year. During the next 10 years it is projected to grow by 959 million, the largest increment ever for a single decade. As the annual excess of births over deaths continues to widen, the date of population stability is pushed ever further into the future.

Progress in stabilizing climate is equally disappointing. Carbon emissions from fossil fuel use declined for several years as countries invested heavily in energy efficiency measures. But in the last few years they have started to rise again. Leading industrial economies, such as the United States and Japan, are the primary contributors to this unfortunate global upturn. In 1987, global carbon emissions from fossil fuels rose 1.5 percent and in 1988, 3.7 percent, reaching a record total of 5.7 billion tons.

Reading the daily newspapers gives the impression that changes in economic indicators such as the gross national product (GNP), interest rates, or stock prices are the keys to the future. But it is changes in the biological product that are shaping civilization. It is changes in the size of the photosynthetic product that determine ultimately how many of us the earth can support and at what level of consumption.

Biological Foundations

Three biological systems—croplands, forests, and grasslands—support the world economy. Except for fossil fuels and minerals, they supply all the raw materials for industry; except for seafood, they provide all our food. Forests are the source of fuel, lumber, paper, and numerous other products. Grasslands provide meat, milk, leather, and wool. Croplands supply food, feed, and an endless array of raw materials for industry such as fiber and vegetable oils.

Common to all these biological systems is the process of photosynthesis, the ability of plants to use solar energy to combine water and carbon dioxide to produce carbohydrates. Although an estimated 41 percent of photosynthetic activity takes place in the oceans, it is the 59 percent occurring on land that underpins the world economy. And it is the loss of terrestrial photosynthesis as a result of environmental degradation that is undermining many national economies.

The biological activity that supplies the bulk of our food and raw materials takes place on the nearly one third of the earth's surface that is land, some 13 billion hectares. According to a United Nations Food and Agriculture Organization tabulation, 11 percent of this—nearly 1.5 billion hectares—is used to produce crops. Roughly 25 percent is pasture or rangeland, providing grass or other forage for domesticated livestock and wild herbivores. A somewhat larger area (31 percent) is in forests, including open forests or savannahs only partly covered with trees. The remaining 33 percent of the world's land supports little biological activity. It is either wasteland, essentially desert, or has been paved over or built on.

The Earth's Declining Productivity

The share of land planted to crops increased from the time agriculture began until 1981, but since then the area of newly reclaimed land has been offset by that lost to degradation and converted to nonfarm uses. The grassland area has shrunk since the mid-seventies, as overgrazing slowly converts it to desert. The forested area has been shrinking for centuries, but the losses accelerated at mid-century and even more from 1980 onward. The combined area of these three biologically productive categories is shrinking while the remaining categories—wasteland and that covered by human settlements—are expanding.

Not only is the biologically productive land area shrinking, but on part of it productivity is falling. In forests, for example, output is being lowered on some remaining stands, apparently by air pollution and acid rain. Evidence of this damage in industrial countries is now widespread. In the United States, it can be found throughout much of the country, and in Europe it stretches from the Atlantic coast in the west to the remote reaches of Siberia in the east.

Even an experienced forester often cannot see any changes in the trees that would indicate slower growth; only careful measurements over time show how much pollutants are stressing trees. A Forest Inventory Analysis conducted regularly by the U.S. Forest Service reports that the annual growth of yellow pines, a major species covering some 42 million hectares in the Southeast, declined by 30-50 percent between 1955 and 1985. From 1975 to 1985, the dead pines increased from 9 percent of all trees to 15 percent. Soviet foresters report a decline in tree growth rates in central Siberia over the last few decades that is remarkably similar.

Diminishing Grasslands

While forest productivity is being diminished by chemical stress, that of grasslands is being reduced by the physical stress of overgrazing. Widespread grassland degradation can now be seen on every continent. Although the data for grassland degradation are even more sketchy than for forest clearing, the trends are no less real. This problem is highly visible throughout Africa, where livestock numbers have expanded nearly as fast as the human population. In 1950, 238 million Africans relied on 272 million livestock. By 1987, the human population had increased to 604 million, and the livestock to 543 million.

Stressing the Planet

One of the simplest ways to evaluate human pressure on the biosphere is to calculate the proportion of total biological productivity that we consume directly, waste, or co-opt (as in clearing pastures). Like all organisms that lack the ability to capture energy from the sun directly (as do plants or algae), we depend directly on this energy for our survival. Although we are just one of the estimated 5-10,000,000 species on Earth, our use of world resources now amounts to some 40% of the total. As our numbers double by the middle of the next century, will we be able to use the world's productivity even more extensively and in a stable manner? Moreover, can individual and national standards of living be increased?

Peter H. Raven, *USA Today,* May 1989.

In a continent where grain is scarce, 183 million cattle, 197 million sheep, and 163 million goats are supported almost entirely by grazing and browsing. Everywhere outside the tsetse-fly belt, livestock are vital to the economy, but in many countries their numbers exceed grassland carrying capacity by half or more. A study charting the mounting pressures on grasslands in nine southern African countries found that the capacity to sustain livestock is diminishing. As grasslands deteriorate, soil erosion accelerates, further reducing the carrying capacity and setting in motion a self-reinforcing cycle of ecological degradation and deepening human poverty.

Fodder needs of livestock in nearly all developing countries now exceed the sustainable yield of grasslands and other forage resources. In India, the demand by the end of the decade is expected to reach 700 million tons, while the supply will total just 540 million. The National Land Use and Wastelands Development Council there reports that in states with the most serious land degradation, such as Rajasthan and Karnataka, fodder supplies satisfy only 50-80 percent of needs, leaving large numbers of emaciated cattle. When drought occurs, hundreds of thousands of these animals die. . . .

Overgrazing is not limited to the Third World. In the United States, where the Bureau of Land Management (BLM) is responsible for 66 million hectares of government-owned grazing land, overgrazing is commonplace. A 1987 survey found that only 33 percent of the BLM's rangeland was in good to excellent condition; 58 percent was fair to poor.

As the deterioration of grazing lands continues, some of it eventually becomes wasteland, converted to desert by the excessive demands of growing livestock populations. And as the forage available to support animals diminishes, pressure shifts to croplands to produce more grain to feed livestock, thus intensifying the competition between humans and animals for scarce food supplies.

Paving Over the Future

The loss of productive woodland, grassland, and cropland to nonfarm uses is also progressing on every continent, though at varying rates. Each year, millions of hectares of biologically productive land are paved over or built upon. Growth in the world's automobile fleet, though it has slowed dramatically over the last decade, is nonetheless leading to the paving of more and more of the earth's surface with streets, roads, and parking spaces. Each car added to the world fleet competes with farmers.

Stanford University biologist Peter M. Vitousek and his colleagues estimate that humans now appropriate close to 40 percent of the land's net primary biological product. In other words, nearly 40 percent of the earth's land-based photosynthetic activity is devoted to the satisfaction of human needs or has been lost as a result of human degradation of natural systems. As our own share continues to increase, it becomes more difficult for other species to survive. Eventually, life-supporting systems could begin to unravel.

To summarize, at a time when demand for various biological products is rising rapidly, the earth's biological production is shrinking. The even greater annual additions to world population in prospect for the nineties will further reduce the earth's ability to supply our food and raw materials. These two trends cannot continue indefinitely. At some point, the continuing decline in the photosynthetic product will translate into a decline in the economic product.

"It is reasonable to forecast. . .continued decline in resource prices and increase in availability."

Global Resource Scarcity Is Not a Serious Problem

Julian L. Simon

Julian L. Simon is a professor of business administration at the University of Maryland in College Park. His books include *The Ultimate Resource* and *Theory of Population and Economic Growth*. In the following viewpoint, Simon argues that global resources such as land, minerals, and oil will become more available for human use in the future. The author contends that more demand for resources spurs technological invention. Technological invention, Simon says, makes resources less scarce by increasing their availability.

As you read, consider the following questions:

1. How does Simon measure the scarcity of resources?
2. According to the author, what is wrong with the theory of increasing resource scarcity?
3. In Simon's opinion, what does the history of resource availability tell us about the future?

Will raw materials be more scarce, or less scarce, in future decades than at present? The actual outcome will have important consequences for our economic lives. And our *expectations* about the outcome will probably have even greater consequences than the outcome itself. Yet there are large and violent disagreements between two points of view, the "doomsdayers" who expect us to "run out" and who therefore forecast higher prices, and the "cornucopians" who expect prices to be progressively lower as raw materials come to be more available rather than less available. My own forecast is simply stated: I am quite sure that prices of all natural resources will go down indefinitely. . . .

Measuring Scarcity

Economists generally view the expenditures in physical or money terms necessary to obtain a good, relative to some other quantity of expenditures, as the appropriate measure of scarcity. This is in contrast to measuring scarcity with an actual or hypothetical estimate of physical quantities that are thought to "exist," as technologists are wont to do.

Two measures of cost are of particular interest here: The price of the raw material relative to consumer goods, and the price relative to wages. . . .

The price of natural resources *relative to wages* is, in my view, the best measure of scarcity with respect to human welfare. This measure tells us how much of our most valuable resource, our own lives, that we must give up in order to obtain the resources. . . .

We should note that it is not really the natural resource itself that is of interest to us, but rather the services that we get from the resource. Just as it is not a computer itself, but rather the computing services we get from it, and then the use of those computing services in the production of other goods, that affects us, it is not copper or land or oil that matters to us, but rather the services that they render in the creation of final products. Therefore the relevant measure of the available resource is the cost of the services that we get from the resource. . . .

Now that we have arrived at some operational measures of scarcity, let's look at the record. The historical cost record of raw materials is easy to summarize. Scarcity has been decreasing rather than increasing in the long run for all raw materials except lumber and oil, and even they have shown recent signs of becoming less exceptional. . . . And this trend of falling prices of copper has been going on a very long time. The price of copper in labor time in the year 1 A.D. was about 120 times as great as it is in the U.S. now. The price of iron was about 240 times as great then as now, and in 800 B.C. it was 360 times as great, while in 1800 B.C. it was 1620 times as great. Food is an especially important resource, and the evidence is especially strong that we are on a benign trend despite rising population.

The Doomsayer Theory

Let us consider contrary theories, because they cast light on the credibility of the theory I offer. The question that we wish to address theoretically must be kept firmly in mind: Must the cost of one or more important raw materials rise in the long run? The doomsayers assert that there is theoretical reason to answer the question in the affirmative, that there is no escaping a rise in raw material cost in some very long run. Their reasoning is as follows: The reservoir of some raw material X is fixed, meaning that the reservoir cannot be increased just as the reservoir of authentic Mona Lisa paintings cannot be increased. (They have in mind, however, generic materials such as, say, copper and land and energy rather than one-of-a-kinds such as the Mona Lisa; about those one-of-a-kinds there is no dispute.) Next they assume that the demand for the use of the material will either (a) increase due to population growth or income growth or both, or (b) the reservoir will decline due to some of it being lost or otherwise unavailable, or (c) there will be both increased demand and decreased reservoir. If humankind first exploits the richest lodes and ores, successive mining operations will be successively more expensive. Implicitly, those writers are also assuming that eventually there will be either stationarity of technology or a growth in technology slower than the rate of decrease in richness of lode. Under those assumed conditions, cost must indeed increase.

More Technology

I don't want to leave polluted rivers and putrid air for my children and grandchildren. But I think we will get there by more, not less technology, and more, not less development. The western world is far, far cleaner now than the Third World.

Mona Charen, *Conservative Chronicle*, May 2, 1990.

Certainly costs do increase during some periods, as reflected in real price rises at some times in history. And it is reasonable to suppose that during those periods the doomsday conditions hold (though price rises may sometimes be due to non-physical causes such as the formation of OPEC [Organization of Petroleum Exporting Countries]).

If the Malthusian [doomsayer] concept of diminishing returns is given content by specifying a period of the order of a human life expectation, give or take an expected length of life, that "theory" fails completely in its predictive record; as we have seen, the trends in scarcity have been downward throughout history despite forecasters having made dire predictions implicitly based on that concept since the beginning of recorded history and surely before.

If, instead of testing the Malthusian theory on the past, one looks to the future, but if one does not specify some observable (or even identifiable) time period during which prices will rise permanently to levels above what they are now, and, instead, one simply says increased scarcity will happen "sometime," then the Malthusian theory is meaningless scientifically, according to the standard canon of scientific meaning; a theory about "sometime" cannot be tested, not even in principle.

Predicting Plenty

A very different theoretical viewpoint sees the process by which resources have become progressively more available as part of the broader story of the creation and adoption of new technology largely in response to increased demand and/or increased prices for the resources due to population growth. The relationship between technology and demand assuredly is not that which is suggested by the vulgar idea of a "race" between them. More people certainly imply increased demand in the short run, and therefore higher costs than otherwise in the short run. But the long run is not just a sequence of short runs in this case, and hence it is fallacious to draw any conclusions from this short-run analysis. In the longer run, technology's advance comes from people, and technological advance is the sole factor responsible for the long-run declines in material cost.

The process by which increased demand due to more people and higher income causes advances in resource technology is only a special case of the general relationship between demand and technical advance. . . .

Increases in natural resource availability have accompanied (and in my view, have been caused by) increases in population and total demand. It seems reasonable to forecast continued increases for population and total demand in the future. Hence, this constitutes additional basis for forecasting continued increases in natural resource availability.

So, I believe that the first two steps of my forecasting method, examination of the experiential data, and analysis of theoretical arguments and, especially, inquiry into a theoretical mechanism that explains the observed data, lead solidly to the third-step conclusion that it is reasonable to forecast a continuation of the observed trend, continued decline in resource prices and increase in availability. . . .

If you find that there has indeed been a trend during the relevant past, then it is often reasonable to extend that trend as the basis of your prediction. But the pattern of the past is often not consistent, in which case you must decide which parts of the past to pay most attention to.

In my view, the most important element in making sound long-run predictions from trends is to examine the sweep of history as far back in the past as possible, to ensure that what one thinks is a trend is not just a blip in history.

The main reason for looking at a longer rather than a shorter period is because the longer period contains more information. But the relevance of the information from various periods in the past is, of course, a most difficult question. It is generally reasonable to weigh the recent past more heavily than the distant past, though never completely forgetting the distant past. The commonest source of error is extending an apparent trend during a short period of time—an uptrend in copper prices within the last three years, say—into a prediction for the long-run future—say, prices two decades from now. One of the many sad examples of fallacious short-trend extension was the conclusion by individuals and governments that the raw material scarcity that appeared in 1973-1974 would continue to get worse into the indefinite future. That conclusion was very costly in waste of social and personal resources.

"Technological advance [seems] to be a puny weapon to forestall climate change and loss of the ozone layer."

Using Advanced Technology Destroys Global Resources

Lester W. Milbrath

In the following viewpoint, sociologist Lester W. Milbrath argues that technology has allowed human beings to defeat and exploit all other species. But, he warns, this could lead to our future extinction unless we learn to control technology and abandon our focus on power and domination. Milbrath is the director of the research program in environment and society at the State University of New York at Buffalo.

As you read, consider the following questions:

1. What does Milbrath say is the danger in permitting more technology into our lives?
2. According to the author, what are the three main dangers posed by technological advancement?
3. What roles do values play in the future of the world, according to the author?

Lester W. Milbrath, "Learning to Control Human Exuberance." This article first appeared in *The Humanist* issue of November/December 1988 and is reprinted by permission.

The threatening problems faced by our species stem from our very success as a species. We are a "successful" species in that we have been able to defeat and bend to our will every other species. We are "successful" in that we have been able to appropriate for our own needs a great proportion of the planet's biological productivity—including dipping into Earth's crust to extract accrued productivity, such as fossil fuels, stored there long before we evolved as a species. We are "successful" in that we continue to reproduce at record rates while we reduce populations of other species or eliminate them altogether. Human population is now more than five billion and will double to ten billion in only fifty more years. We must, somehow, learn to control our extreme exuberance or our "success" will lead to our extinction. Why is this so?

Our ability to learn enabled us to do better and better those things that we have always tried to do. We wanted our children to survive and live long and good lives. Therefore, we reduced infant mortality, conquered disease, mended or replaced broken body parts, and we live longer and longer. We wanted sufficient food, so we appropriated much of Earth's bioproductivity for our own use. Now we are faced with a veritable explosion in human population.

We wanted to live more comfortable lives, so we isolated ourselves from extremes of weather. We wanted excitement, so we learned to travel swiftly to the far corners of the globe and to bring into our homes a vast array of entertainment. Our science and technology delivered into our hands ever greater power to manipulate the planet's resources for our own enjoyment. With this kind of success, why are so many of us worried?

Long-Term Consequences

We have failed to take into account the long term consequences of just doing what we have always done—but doing it better and better. Doubling the world's population in fifty years will more than double the burden we place on the environment, since most of those billions of people will strive to live at a higher and higher standard of living. We are using up the planet's resource at an unprecedented rate, especially fossil fuels, and we surely will encounter severe shortages of many of them as time passes. All of those consumed resources will eventually turn to waste and be cast into the environment. The biosphere is disrupted not only by the sheer volume of wastes but also by the fact that many wastes are unnatural compounds, or toxins, that biospheric systems do not know how to absorb and recycle.

In effect, we have built a society and an economic system that cannot sustain its trajectory.

How serious is the disruption we are inflicting on planetary systems? The damage will be far greater than we currently believe. The drought in the American midwest during the summer of 1988 signals that this damage may already have begun. The buildup of greenhouse-effect gases, due to burning fossil fuels and other production and consumption activities, has already initiated a global warming that will change climate patterns, perhaps more swiftly and drastically than we thought possible even a few years ago.

More Harm than Good

Improperly applied, ecologically appropriate technologies can do little good and sometimes do more harm than good. It is possible, for example, to design a process for producing ethanol from agricultural crops that interferes with food production and uses more energy than it produces. Such a design has been formulated by the Mobil Oil Company. Similarly, photovoltaic cells have been used in large, centralized power stations, a deployment that destroys their major economic advantage: the elimination of the cost and energy loss involved in transmitting electricity.

Barry Commoner, *The Nation,* April 30, 1990.

Think for a moment about the proportion of investment decisions that depend upon the premise of continuity, especially climatic continuity. Everything from choosing a place to live, building a house, starting a business, buying stock in a business, accepting collateral for a loan, or making contributions to a pension fund depends upon an assumption of continuity. My quick review of such decisions suggests that about 90 percent of investment decisions are premised upon continuity. If climate change forecloses continuity over large proportions of the globe—and scientists are now reasonably confident that it will—the socio-economic disruption will be horrendous. Savings will be wiped out, families will be forced to move, some communities will die out while others will be devastated by uncontrollable hordes of internal migrants. Some localities will be under water, and others will turn to desert; former deserts may be able to support plants again but must first build new plant and animal communities. It seems likely that many people will die because we depend for food upon plant and animal communities which are ill-adapted to a changing climate regime.

Devastation from climate change will be exacerbated by other global biospheric effects: loss of the ozone layer, acid rain, poisonous red tides of algae, toxic pollution of soil, water, and air, and species extinction. Nature may have many additional unpleasant surprises in store for us. When these effects are combined with resource shortages, we may well wonder how we can continue to support even the five billion people already living, much less the additional billions that are destined to arrive even if we strive vigorously to limit population growth. An additional population doubling from ten to twenty billion seems unthinkable.

Technology Offers Little

Many people believe that we can surmount these difficulties by developing more and better science and technology. The power of science and technology is the main reason our species is so successful, is it not? Perhaps this was true in the past, but it holds out little promise for the future. Not only does technological advance seem to be a puny weapon to forestall climate change and loss of the ozone layer but also it carries with it another great problem: the danger of losing our freedom. We sought development of science and technology to give us control over our lives, but now there is a very large prospect that the forces we have unleashed will control us. Science and technology are likely to become runaway forces that no human institution can control. . . . For example, three recently developed technologies have sufficient power to change nearly *everything* in our physical and social world.

First, we all know and are fearful of *nuclear power*. We all realize that we must avoid a global nuclear war—and its consequent nuclear winter—that could destroy most life on Earth. The power in nuclear fission—for peace or war—is generated in large physical installations that are visible and detectable and thus are, in principle, controllable. There have been and will be mistakes, but political institutions are developing some capability for control of nuclear power.

The second development, *recombinant DNA technology*, sometimes called bio-engineering, has the potential to be equally powerful and is, in principle, much more difficult to control. It gives to some humans the ability "to play God." It contains great potential to do good and equally great potential to do harm. Scientists and their supporters tell us only about the good and downplay the potential for evil. Scientists could develop and release new creatures with no natural enemies. Such creatures could reproduce epidemically and wreak havoc with delicately balanced ecosytems. Governments and scientific organizations are trying to develop effective controls, but this technology is inherently difficult to control. A new creature could be developed in any laboratory in any country. The potential of this technology to confer great wealth and power on its developers will motivate individuals and corporations to avoid controls. . . .

Finally, *nanotechnologies* are exceedingly small but have the potential for a greater impact than either nuclear power or recombinant DNA. Nanofabrication is analogous to nature's method of making things—molecule by molecule. It would revolutionize fabrication away from "bulk" methods toward the molecular, or nano, level. Imagine a computer that is one-hundred-thousand times more powerful than existing ones but is as small as a bacteria. The potential for good is enormous; the potential for evil is equally great. Whoever controls nano-technology will have the power to change everything in our world. Such power is also the power to subjugate. How could technologies so small and easily hidden ever be controlled? For the sake of our own survival, we had better learn how.

Needed: A New Worldview

In contrast to the worldviews of a majority of cultures around the world (especially those of indigenous people), the view that lies at the foundation of modern technological society encourages a mechanistic approach to life: to rational thinking, efficiency, utilitarianism, scientific detachment, and the belief that the human place in nature is one of ownership and supremacy. The kinds of technologies that result include nuclear power plants, laser beams, and satellites. This worldview has created and promoted the military-industrial-scientific-media complex, multinational corporations, and urban sprawl.

Stopping the destruction brought by such technologies requires not just regulating or eliminating individual items like pesticides or nuclear weapons. It requires new ways of thinking about humanity and new ways of relating to life. It requires the creation of a new worldview.

Chellis Glendinning, *Utne Reader*, March/April 1990.

These are only three recent scientific discoveries. What else will flow forth from the fertile brains of our scientists? Have we created a monster that will deprive us of our freedom or devastate our life-supporting ecosystems? Control of science and technology will likely become the dominant political concern of the twenty-first century. Meeting this challenge will require decisive change in the way we think and in the way we conduct politics. We will have to find ways to review the potential effects of a line of inquiry or the deployment of a technology before it has advanced so far that it is too late to curb its possible ill effects.

Already, we fail to recognize the impact of technology upon our social structure. We should perceive technology as a kind of legislation that structures our behavior. Consider the impact upon social structure and politics of such technologies as television, computers, automobiles, and nuclear power. We carefully consider and debate the expected impact of a proposed law, but we never do this for a proposed technology. . . .

In order to learn how to control technology, we will have to learn how to have an effective discourse about values. We cannot choose the kind of society in which we would like to live without coming to some agreement about values. Reasoning together about values is the essence of politics and will be essential to the preservation of our civilization and our species. . . .

Considering the Consequences

In our politics, we also must shift from a reactive to a pro-active mode. I call it a *learning mode* in which we utilize a holistic framework and think in a long-term perspective. We should learn how to be routinely anticipatory of the long run and cumulative consequences of simply doing what we do every day—and seem always to have done. Also, new technologies, new projects, and new programs should be reviewed for their long-term and cumulative consequences. . . .

At an even more fundamental level, politics must eventually abandon its central focus on power and domination. Our civilization is a dominator civilization; that means it is oriented toward allowing some people to subjugate others. We no longer condone outright slavery, but the many forces of domination have the effect of bending the will of weak creatures to serve the desires of the powerful. Power is so engrained in our thinking that most humans believe they have a right, even an obligation, to dominate nature. . . .

This emphasis upon domination is a central evil in our civilization. It leads us to injure each other. We are driven to acquire power in order to compete. We are led to believe we cannot decide *not* to compete, *not* to be strong, *not* to control and dominate. Such beliefs drive us to destroy our biosphere.

As we think about what we will do in the future, we need to be much more aware of and sensitive to biospheric systems. These systems are essential to life, and without life there is no meaning for other goals. Therefore, we must give *top priority* to maintaining the good functioning of biospheric systems. . . .

It seems obvious that we must turn our whole society around. We must curb our exuberance—our thrust for growth, power, domination, and thrills. I have no magic formula for doing this. I can only urge you to learn. Learn how to think in the long term. Learn how to think holistically. Learn how nature works. Learn how to think about values. Learn the need to learn from each other. Make a learning society.

4

"Technological innovations and the genius of the human spirit when pressed for solutions will keep America's lights on in the future, while respecting the laws and limits of nature."

Using Advanced Technology Conserves Global Resources

Philip C. Cruver

In the following viewpoint, Philip C. Cruver argues that the advent and use of advanced technology has produced a surplus of energy, food, and other usable goods for the world. Further advances in technology will ensure that the people of the world continue to meet their needs. Cruver is the president of a utilities firm, Titan Energy Ltd. He resides in Palm Springs, California.

As you read, consider the following questions:

1. What are America's main sources of electrical energy?
2. What does the author believe will "keep America's lights on" in the future?
3. What does the author believe technological innovations should also do?

Philip C. Cruver, "America Is Running Out of Power." Reprinted from *USA Today* magazine, July copyright 1989 by the Society for the Advancement of Education.

One of the most serious issues confronting our nation today is the lack of a long-term responsible energy policy that will stabilize prices and reduce imported supplies while respecting the environment. We haven't learned our lesson from the oil shocks in 1973 and 1979, and the day of reckoning inevitably will reappear when the U.S. is dependent upon imports for 50% of its oil. However, another more pressing problem—looming shortages of electricity supplies—is virtually unknown by most Americans and could pose an even greater threat to our nation's security and economic health.

Former Secretary of Energy James Schlesinger told the Senate Energy Subcommittee in May, 1988, that OPEC [Organization of Petroleum Exporting Countries] is currently or soon will be producing some 20,000,000 barrels per day, and that level of production traditionally has been considered a "magic point" at which the cartel will be able to increase prices unilaterally. The nation's first Energy Secretary also is concerned about another crisis and stated that U.S. energy security may face challenges from yet another sector—electric power production. In 1987, he said, electric demand in the U.S. increased by 4.5%, and, over the past six years, demand has risen by more than three percent annually. "Electric utilities are avoiding new commitments, embarking on a course of capital minimalization, and are avoiding new construction," he stated.

Future Shortages

Although there is a surplus of electric power in the U.S. today, this situation will reverse itself quickly in the 1990's. Schlesinger isn't the only Cassandra of near-term electricity shortages.

• The Department of Energy (DOE) produced a document in March, 1987, which revealed that serious problems confront all energy sectors in the U.S. Electric demand, the report predicted, will continue to grow at a two-three percent annual rate, with at least 100,000 megawatts of new capacity needed by the year 2000.

• The Electric Power Research Institute (EPRI), the utility-sponsored research organization, believes that, even if the growth rate in electric demand is as low as 1.4%, we will need as much as 250,000 megawatts of new capacity in place by the year 2010. That is equivalent to 250 large coal or nuclear plants which must be built in the next 21 years.

• A more realistic probability is that, as America becomes more competitive in world manufacturing markets, the economy will prosper and 1987's growth of 4.5% in electricity sales will continue. This actual growth rate is nearly double projections published by the government's Energy Information Administration and the North American Electric Reliability

Council, which conservatively have estimated electric growth rates ranging between 2.0 and 2.6% through the end of the century. If this growth continues as it did for the first six months of 1988, we are talking about major, serious shortages of electricity occurring soon, which could disrupt America's economy.

Electric utilities have reached a crossroad. Decisions now must be made by them about sources of additional electricity, since the lead time for the construction of conventional power plants exceeds 10 years. These decisions are not being made because regulatory, environmental, and legislative factors have clouded utilities' ability to forecast prudently. They no longer have any confidence that a conventional power plant can be placed into the rate base with an acceptable return on investment.

Energy Sources

The U.S. has approximately 700,000 megawatts of electric power capacity generated from the following sources: coal, 56.9%; nuclear, 17.7%; hydro, 9.7%; natural gas, 10.6%; oil, 4.6%; and other (geothermal, solar, wind, biomass, etc.) 0.5%. The need for a reliable supply of electricity for the future is a complex problem confronting utilities.

Dawn of Solar Age

Many technologies have been developed that allow us to harness the renewable energy of the sun effectively, but so far these devices are only in limited use. By 2030 they will be widespread and much improved.

Lester R. Brown et al., *World Watch*, March/April 1990.

Coal Combustion, the principal source of of baseload electric power in America, is evolving towards a new era. Smaller units having shorter construction schedules and utilizing more environmentally benign technologies are mandated to reduce capital risk and the belching of effluents that cause acid rain. Of the advanced technologies under development, the more promising are fluidized-bed combustion and coal gasification. These emerging technologies may be ready for widespread commercialization in the 1990s as a result of the successful demonstrations from pilot plants which already are in operation or under construction. However, utilities are slow to adopt new technologies and are particularly cautious in the wake of their experience with nuclear power. They may be a decade too late ordering these new plants if they impose rigorous economic and performance tests and wait for proven operating results.

Nuclear power, the other major source of electric power, is precluded as a viable future option using existing light-water reactor and pressurized water reactor technologies. In addition to moral and ethical issues concerning safety and permanent waste storage, today's reactors are proving uneconomical. A DOE study found that operating costs for nuclear plants in the U.S. are rising so fast that electric utilities may find it cheaper to close them before the end of their useful lives. According to the EPRI, capital costs for advanced reactors must be reduced by one-third from present levels, availability must improve 15-25%, and construction times must be cut about in half before nuclear power can be included as a viable future option.

Nuclear power also has lost its base of popular support fostered during the 1960s. Public confidence plummeted after Three Mile Island, and the Chernobyl accident frustrated any chance of near-term recovery. Although the potential environmental benefits of nuclear power are compelling, safety and economic issues must be resolved. New reactor designs that are smaller, modular, and safer are on the drawing boards, and proponents of nuclear power believe they will be ready for commercialization around the year 2010 or 2015.

Other Energy Sources

Hydropower is a mature technology that faces many problems, resulting in stagnant development activity. Small-scale systems, less than 30 megawatts, supplied 6,800 megawatts of power at the end of 1985. There are as much as 100,000 additional megawatts of small-scale hydropower to be developed in this country, but this technology is burdened with environmental issues, fear of reductions in water levels caused by the drought, and huge capital requirements. Although no major projects currently are being considered, a scarce 5,721 megawatts of additional small-scale hydropower capacity is being contemplated by 1995.

Natural gas as a fuel has only about half the carbon dioxide content of coal and 80% of oil. So, within the perspective of the recently ballyhooed greenhouse problem, natural gas is the fossil fuel of choice. The American Gas Association recognizes the new market for their product and predicts that, by 1995, natural gas production in the lower 48 states should be 50% greater than crude oil production. The 1987 repeal of the Fuel Use Act, which lifted restrictions on gas-burning power plants, significantly should increase gas sales to utilities. Combustion turbines will supply the bulk of the new generation capacity in the years ahead, according to the EPRI. This could mean a doubling of demand for natural gas supplies from utilities in the mid-1990s. . . .

Although gas turbines may be the panacea to mitigate power shortages for the short term, a longer-term energy policy should dictate less reliance on fossil fuel combustion. This will result in a greater contribution from renewable and nuclear energy to fill the void. The renewable path is clearly the choice of environmentalists, whose warnings are becoming increasingly more heeded by the public. The evolution of environmental protection from a symbolic gesture of the 1970's to a serious institutional commitment today may force utilities to wean themselves from the combustion of fossil fuels. Therefore, coal, oil, and natural gas could lose their century-old dominance as fuels for electricity production. Never before has the environmental cost of burning fossil fuels been considered in the power-generation cost equation. The impact of global warming may be so great that the burning of fossil fuels may prove uneconomical. The drought of 1988 focused public attention on this issue, and bottom-line economics could galvanize a renaissance for struggling renewable and nuclear power-generation options, which are really the only two alternatives capable of making the next century's transition from polluting and finite fossil fuel sources.

Technology Offers Increased Oil Production

The big story for the early '90s will be increasing oil production in the 48 contiguous states—the so-called Lower 48—and the major effort in that respect will be extracting more oil from existing wells.

It will be a story of technology, of using steam injections and chemical solvents and new techniques to get more from wells that originally yielded 35% of their oil. The gain could be sizable. . . And the secret of success for even small companies will be technology—supercomputers to read geological charts, angular drilling.

James Flanigan, *Los Angeles Times*, September 19, 1990.

As mentioned earlier, the economics of nuclear power are suspect and could become even more uncompetitive with other power generation sources when Federal subsidies are eliminated and the real costs of decommissioning and permanent storage are included. Moreover, uranium supplies are finite and, without the breeder reactor, our country soon will be relying on imports for the majority of its nuclear fuel. . . .

Renewably based electricity generating capacity represents approximately 14% of the nation's utility power output, of which large hydropower accounts for the bulk of nearly 100,000 megawatts. Unfortunately, tax incentives for most renewable technologies expired in 1988, and research and development funding, which peaked in 1980 at $900,000,000, has fallen 80% since then.

The principal obstacle to most technologies for mass-commercialization is their intermittent nature. Utilities claim they must have reliable power when they need it, particularly during periods of peak demand. Most renewable technologies have inherently low capacity factors and can not be relied on as baseload sources of electricity. Often, however, peak hours of sunlight and, in some locations, peak winds and water flows, coincide with daily and seasonal periods of maximum electrical demand. Accordingly, electricity produced from wind, solar, and small-scale hydropower plants is available during periods when the power is needed the most. Most utilities have a surplus of baseload power and are desperate in the near term only for peak power, for which they charge their customers a premium. EPRI studies indicate that U.S. utilities effectively could have six-12% of their total power supply capacity in some form of storage.

Energy Storage

Technical advances in energy storage systems rapidly are being developed which will encourage utilities and industrial users to take a more serious view of renewables and ultimately could classify these energy sources as baseload power. Compressed air energy storage (CAES) is a proven technology that virtually is unexploited. A 220-megawatt plant has been operating successfully in Germany since 1978, and the first U.S. utility, located in Alabama, has approved plans for a 100- megawatt plant pumping high-pressure air into a salt cavern overnight when demand is low and releasing it during the day to fire gas turbines. Above-ground storage tanks fabricated from steel and advanced fiberglass composites now are being designed to store compressed air, which will expand CAES applications with flexibility of size, location, and modularity.

Superconductivity also may have a dramatic effect on utilities' future choice between abundant renewable energy and selected conventional power options. As an example, peaking power now supplied by natural gas may be replaced in the future with superconduction magnetic energy sources (SMES). Thus, SMES may provide the means for the intermittent solar energies to displace natural gas, giving them the ability to provide firm and reliable electric power. . . .

Nearly two centuries ago, the Malthusians preached doom and gloom about the Earth's ability to feed its burgeoning population. Their prediction of food shortages proved apocryphal, and the Green Revolution today has produced a surplus of food for the world. Technological innovations and the genius of the human spirit when pressed for solutions will keep America's lights on in the future, while respecting the laws and limits of nature.

5

"World Bank policies have disastrous . . . ethical and ecological consequences."

World Bank Policies Cause Global Resource Scarcity

Rainforest Action Network

The World Bank, an international lending agency controlled by the governments of industrialized countries, provides many large loans to developing nations. In the following viewpoint, Rainforest Action Network, a nonprofit activist organization, accuses the World Bank of being an agent of environmental destruction in the Third World. The World Bank, the authors contend, bypasses environmental concerns in its support of large development projects and in its pursuit of profit.

As you read, consider the following questions:

1. Why does the World Bank prefer large development projects over smaller ones, according to Rainforest Action Network?
2. In the authors' opinion, what are some of the reasons behind the World Bank's poor environmental record?
3. What is "economic rate of return," and what is the problem with using it as the main criterion for assessing development projects, according to the authors?

Reprinted, with permission, from the *Rainforest Action Network Fact Sheet #5,* 1989.

The World Bank is a multilateral development bank (MDB), a multinational, international agency which lends money to help countries develop economically. Other MDBs include the Inter-American Development Bank, the African Development Bank and the Asian Development Bank. Due to the trend towards huge mega-projects and their emphasis on profitability over all other considerations, MDBs can be extremely dangerous for the environment.

Bank Organization

The World Bank funnelled close to $15 billion dollars into Third World nations in 1987 for projects aimed at development. It has been funding programs in the Third World since its founding shortly after World War II.

The Bank is an autonomous organization funded by money borrowed on international markets and by contributions from the 148 developed-nation member governments. A board of 21 Executive Directors from the member nations oversees World Bank activities. Bank policy is set by the member nations, who share voting power proportional to their financial contribution.

The United States is the most influential of the members with 20% of the vote. The president of the World Bank, Barber C. Conable, is a U.S. citizen. In deciding whether to vote for a particular project or policy, our World Bank representatives follow government directives from the Treasury Department and the Congress. The money which the U.S. supplies comes directly from American taxpayers.

The World Bank is composed of three separate institutions, each of which specializes in a specific type of loan: the International Bank for Reconstruction and Development (IBRD), the International Development Association (IDA) and the International Finance Corporation.

Contributing to the Problem

The Bank as a whole is a bureaucracy of roughly 6,200 people, dominated by economists. The business of the Bank is banking, and its primary interest is generating a return on its investments, not helping poor countries. Typically, project money may not even stay in the developing country: the money loaned for a dam goes to pay for materials and machinery bought from the United States. And tragically, many of the development plans do not sufficiently take into account the peoples and places they are intended to help. Especially lacking is concern for the ecological impact of projects.

The Third World suffers from underdevelopment and chronic poverty. It is also experiencing a crisis of damage to and destruction of the very environment that all development and ultimately all life depends upon. The development activities funded by the World Bank and other foreign aid institutions are causing much of the massive deforestation, erosion and desertification that is devastating large areas of the Third World. As a result, they contribute to the very cycle of underdevelopment and instability that they claim to be helping. One of the most grave threats posed by the World Bank in the Third World is deforestation, particularly of tropical rainforests.

The Harm of Big Institutions

There are limits to how environmentally or socially sensitive big institutions can be. They were set up to do large-scale development, which by its very nature causes ecological harm, dislocation, and social disorder.

Barbara Bramble, *Sierra*, September/October 1990.

The majority of projects funded by World Bank and other MDBs are in four ecologically sensitive areas: agriculture, rural development, power and road building. Giant mega-projects are preferred: hydroelectric dams in Latin American rainforests, mass government-sponsored migration into rainforests in Indonesia, or agricultural and industrial developments centering around roads built in previously inaccessible areas. Large projects are easier to administer than smaller projects, and they consolidate financial and political power and serve as showcases for "development". These mega-projects require millions or billions of dollars in loans and are one of the primary causes of the crushing international debt now crippling recipient nations and the international banking system.

Wide Influence

The World Bank is not only important because of the specific projects it funds but because of its key role in shaping development policy through its funding for research, training, technology transfer, planning and other forms of institutional support in host countries. Other aid institutions and private sources follow the World Bank's lead when making loans, further magnifying its influence.

The World Bank not only makes loans but also actively pursues and presents project ideas. Many factors contribute to the social and ecological irresponsibility of World Bank projects: shortstaffing of the World Bank environmental team, making it near impossible to review all the project proposals adequately; the Bank's obsession with confidentiality, which can make information on projects inaccessible to those they will affect; the apparent institutional incapability or unwillingness to follow environmental guidelines; and contradictions and flaws inherent in the projects themselves.

The Ji-Parana project on the Rio Machado in Rondonia, Brazil centered on a large hydro-electric dam. It was approved even though it risked inundating or seriously affecting two Indian reserves. It also threatened the Jari biological reserve, which the Bank had insisted on protecting as part of the conditions for another loan, The Polonoroeste project.

The Polonoroeste project is an example of a mega-project which has already proven itself to be an environmental disaster. The loan centered around paving a road through the Brazilian state of Rondonia to serve cattle ranching, mining and cash crop farming and other interests in an integrated effort to "develop" the area. The road, however, also paved the way for hundreds of thousands of land-starved colonists, who poured into the area and began destroying the forest through the only enterprise economically feasible to them, slash and burn agriculture. Another part of the mega-project provided loans for building hydroelectric dams such as the Balbina and Samuel dams. These dams inundate huge amounts of rainforest for a questionable return in electricity. On top of the direct destruction of rainforest for their construction, the electricity provided by the dams is designated to be used in mining operations which further damage the rainforest environment.

Not Accountable to Anyone

Because it is an independent organization, the World Bank is not accountable to anyone. The citizens of both donor and debtor countries have little say in how their money is being spent even though they will have to foot the bills, both now and in the future as the consequences of irresponsible projects manifest themselves. The people in the project areas are rarely consulted beforehand, and often are not informed of what is happening to them or the land they live on. In 1988, two Brazilian Kayapo Indians and an American anthropologist were charged by Brazil as foreigners for interfering in the internal affairs of Brazil. These outrageous charges stemmed from their attendance at a March 1988 World Bank meeting in Washington, D.C., where they voiced their concerns about the construction of a dam on their rainforest land and asked for information which had been denied them.

On May 5, 1987 the World Bank announced a number of reforms aimed at improving the environmental soundness of Bank projects. Included was the establishment of an environmental review committee and increased hiring of scientists and anthropologists for research into potential loan projects. In 1988 the U.S. Senate noted "with concern the delay of implementation of environmental World Bank reforms announced May 5, 1987." A House committee asked for studies akin to environmental impact statements from the Department of the Treasury for all MDB projects before voting on funding questions. This request was opposed and labeled "impractical" by the Secretary of the Treasury.

Benjamin Montag, 1990. Printed with permission.

During the 1987 World Bank/IMF [International Monetary Fund] Annual meeting, non-governmental and citizens' organizations issued a joint statement which proposed a number of reforms aimed at increasing the social, ethical and ecological responsibility of World Bank loans. Unfortunately, the World Bank still looks at "economic rate of return" (ECR) as the primary justification for projects. ECR is a calculation of profitability which ignores environmental and social costs. While massive infusions of capital by the World Bank into Third World countries have offered financial rewards for investors, they have led to the tragic acceleration of deforestation and wildlife extinction, destabilized local economies and destroyed native cultures. World Bank policies have disastrous political, social, ethical and ecological consequences.

6

"Task forces have. . . been organized within the World Bank to address desertification, deforestation. . . [and] protection of critical eco-systems."

World Bank Policies Help Conserve Global Resources

David R. Malpass

David R. Malpass is a representative of The United States Treasury Department, which administers World Bank affairs for the United States government. In the following viewpoint, Malpass defends the environmental policies of the World Bank and other development banks. The author argues that the World Bank has made significant progress in developing policies which both helps Third World countries economically and protects natural resources.

As you read, consider the following questions:

1. What are the objectives of the World Bank, according to the author?
2. In Malpass' opinion, what improvements has the World Bank made in its staff?
3. With whom does the World Bank cooperate in developing its policies, according to Malpass?

David R. Malpass, testimony before the U.S. Senate Subcommittee on International Economic Policy, Trade, Oceans and Environment, of the Committee on Foreign Relations, April 13 and April 27, 1988.

The adverse effects of unwise and unsustainable development programs and projects are only too evident in all parts of the developing world. Examples include desertification in Africa and South Asia and destruction of tropical forests in Latin America, in Central Africa and in Asia. There have also been serious problems with loss of wetlands as well as atmospheric pollution and pollution of waterways. In some cases, development is threatening the survival of indigenous peoples and their culture and causing extensive damage to wildlife, particularly to endangered species that can never be replaced.

The Congressional Mandate

There is very little disagreement on the urgent need to address these issues. We share the goals that have been outlined by Congress and members of the environmental community. Our policy in the multilateral development banks has been to seek to mitigate or eliminate such adverse effects in development projects and programs and to support national and regional programs to improve environmental management. This has meant the structuring of programs that encourage growth and reduce poverty while still protecting and preserving the natural resource base. . . .

Making Progress

Within the Treasury Department, we are working to improve our oversight of environmental issues in the multilateral development banks. During 1987, we abstained on six loans, citing concerns about adverse environmental effects. These loans included agricultural rehabilitation in the Sudan, electric power in Peru, a paper mill in Nepal, an abattoir in Botswana, livestock development in Benin, and agroforestry and livestock development in Mali. In February 1988, we abstained on a loan to Burkino Faso for a road and water project because of serious environmental issues.

We are continuing close coordination with the State Department and AID [Agency for International Development] and with environmental groups in a effort to improve the early warning system for problematic projects. We plan to take a more active role in international meetings on environmental issues, particularly those that involve projects and programs funded by the multilateral development banks.

We have had particularly strong support from a number of non-governmental organizations—the Sierra Club, Natural Resources Defense Council, Environmental Defense Fund and others—in gathering information and developing approaches to increase the effectiveness of our efforts. These organizations have assisted in the preparation of our position on loans for cattle production in open-range savannas of sub-Saharan Africa and on standards for evaluating projects that may adversely affect moist tropical forests. They have participated in the early warning system established by AID to identify projects that may adversely affect the environment. They have worked closely with us in analyzing problems associated with specific loan proposals or with projects that are being implemented. . . .

Training and Management Improvements

During 1987, the World Bank carried out a major reorganization of its management and staff. One of its primary aims was to strengthen the Bank's capacity for addressing environmental issues. A central environmental department was established in the Policy, Planning and Research complex. Twenty-three positions have been authorized for the three divisions in the department. In addition, environmental units have been created in the technical departments of the Bank's four regional offices. . . .

Significant progress has been made on training. In the World Bank, an environmental training program has been introduced for Bank staff. The program is designed to raise awareness of environmental issues in development, to convey new techniques, and to introduce the latest developments in the field. . . .

Participation of non-governmental organizations is also being encouraged in all of the banks. In the World Bank, the focal point for relations with non-governmental organizations has been shifted from Public Affairs to Policy, Planning and Research. This shift has facilitated the exchange of views and discussions on substantive issues. . . .

An Integral Part of Development

Since it is now recognized that sound environmental management is fundamental to the development process, the Bank's new policy emphasizes the need to make environmental issues an integral part of all its activities.

The World Bank, *The World Bank and the Environment*, 1990.

The multilateral development banks are providing funds for national and international agricultural research programs and for science and technology programs that support research into ecosystem management. The World Bank is working with Harvard University and the Institute for International Environment and Development to assess alternative approaches to natural resource management. Task forces have also been organized within the World Bank to address desertification, deforestation, industrial accident risk avoidance, protection of critical eco-systems and mitigation of natural disasters in urban areas. . . .

We have been holding regular meetings with representatives of other donor countries regarding improvements in the environmental performance of the multilateral development banks. These meetings have ranged from discussions in the Development Committee of the World Bank to more informal consultations and conversations about changes in policies and our positions on individual projects that may affect the environment. . . .

We have worked closely with our colleagues at AID in implementing the early warning system for identifying problematic projects. We believe we can continue to enhance this system and become more influential in shaping the environmental aspects of individual loan proposals in the banks. . . . We will collaborate with State and AID in analyzing more comprehensive strategies that can address natural resource problems through the multilateral development banks and in our bilateral aid program.

Attitudes Are Changing

To sum up, we have had a very extensive legislative mandate from Congress on environmental issues in the multilateral development banks. We have been fully engaged in implementing the provisions of that mandate. On some of the issues, particularly staffing, training and the involvement of non-governmental organizations, I believe we have been making substantial headway. In other areas, we will continue to press for further reforms. . . .

I am optimistic that attitudes are changing—both in the banks and in borrowing countries—and that we will have continuing progress to report.

Distinguishing Bias from Reason

When dealing with controversial issues, many people allow their feelings to dominate their powers of reason. Thus, one of the most important critical thinking skills is the ability to distinguish between statements based upon emotion or bias and conclusions based upon a rational consideration of the facts. For example, consider the following statement: "The liberal media exaggerate environmental problems because they have a vendetta against large corporations that use natural resources." This statement is biased. The author is basing her opinion on an emotional, unsubstantiated belief that the media have a vendetta against business. In contrast, the statement, "When the media latch on to a particular issue like the environment, they often exaggerate its importance" is a reasonable statement. Excessive media coverage of one issue can affect how the public perceives the issue. The author is using this fact to substantiate his opinion.

Another element the reader should take into account is whether an author has a personal or professional stake in advancing a particular opinion. For example, the president of an oil corporation may defend the use of oil as an energy resource. Since it is in the interest of oil corporations to sell more oil, the reader should ask whether this business interest influences the author's statement. A critical reader should always be alert to an author's background and credentials when attempting to identify bias. Note also that it is possible to have a strong interest in a subject and still present an objective case. A scientist who has spent fifteen years studying the effects of automobile emissions on the atmosphere is in an excellent position to estimate how additional emissions will affect the environment in the future.

The following statements are adapted from opinions expressed in the viewpoints in this chapter. Consider each statement carefully. *Mark R for any statement you believe is based on reason or a rational consideration of the facts. Mark B for any statement you believe is based on bias, prejudice, or emotion. Mark I for any statement you think is impossible to judge.*

If you are doing this activity as a member of a class or group, compare your answers with those of other class or group members. Be able to defend your answers. You may discover that others come to different conclusions than you do. Listening to the rationale others present for their answers may give you valuable insights in distinguishing between bias and reason.

R = *a statement based upon reason*
B = *a statement based upon bias*
I = *a statement impossible to judge*

1. Technology will solve all of our global resource problems.

2. The World Bank cares much more about money than protecting global resources.

3. The prices of natural resources have fallen over the past one hundred years and will continue to decline.

4. Since nonrenewable resources are, by definition, finite, it is possible for society to run out of such resources.

5. "The sustainability of economic development has recently become one of the topmost priorities of the World Bank." —R. Goodland, a staff member of the World Bank

6. Technology is the earth's worst enemy.

7. A scarcity of global resources could diminish our standard of living.

8. Global warming is a result of humanity's shortsightedness and greed.

9. Energy conservation is one possible way to lessen America's dependence on fossil fuels.

10. "Solar energy should be supported by the federal government."—Thomas Anderson, vice president of Solar International, a corporation that markets solar technologies

11. The world's population is expected to increase by close to 900 million people each year during the 1990s. This rate of population growth is the fastest ever experienced.

12. The World Bank's hiring of researchers devoted to environmental issues may be a sign that the organization is paying more attention to the environment.

13. Humans have been a cancer on the living world.

14. New fuel technologies give us hope that alternative energy sources may soon become practical.

15. "The partial regeneration of the rain forest is possible within a decade."—Samir Lone, an ecologist who has studied the rain forest for twenty years

Periodical Bibliography

The following articles have been selected to supplement the diverse views presented in this chapter.

William F. Allman	"Rediscovering Planet Earth," *U.S. News & World Report*, October 31, 1988.
Barber B. Conable	"Development and the Environment: A Global Balance," *International Environmental Affairs*, Winter 1990. Available from University Press of New England, $17^1/_2$ Lebanon St., Hanover, NH 03755.
Andrew Ferguson	"Apocalypse Whenever," *Reason*, April 1990.
Art Levine	"Bankrolling Debacles?" *U.S. News & World Report*, September 25, 1989.
Eugene Linden	"Now Wait Just a Minute," *Time*, December 18, 1989.
José Lutzenberger	"Roots of Environmental Problems Won't Be Found in Brazilian Rain Forests," *New Perspectives Quarterly*, Summer 1990.
Gretchen Morgenson and Gale Eisenstodt	"Profits Are for Rape and Pillage," *Forbes*, March 5, 1990.
National Geographic	"Can Man Save This Fragile Earth?" December 1988.
National Wildlife	"What on Earth Are We Doing?" February/March 1990.
Martin F. Price	"Global Change: Defining the Ill-defined," *Environment*, October 1989.
Peter H. Raven	"A World in Crisis," *USA Today*, May 1989.
Dixy Lee Ray	"Who Speaks for Science," *21st Century Science and Technology*, January/February 1989.
Robert Repetto	"The Need for National Resource Accounting," *Technology Review*, January 1990.
Jonathan Schell	"Our Fragile Earth," *Discover*, October 1989.
Vaclav Smil	"Our Changing Environment," *Current History*, January 1989.
Fred L. Smith and Kathy H. Kushner	"Good Fences Make Good Neighborhoods," *National Review*, April 1, 1990.
John Tierney	"Betting the Planet," *The New York Times Magazine*, December 2, 1990.

2 CHAPTER

Is the Greenhouse Effect a Serious Threat?

Chapter Preface

On any given day in America during rush hour, hundreds of thousands of cars flood the nation's roads and highways as people head for work. In the factories that churn out thousands of consumer products, huge engines generate power to keep the assembly lines moving. At the day's end, families cook their meals on electric or gas stoves, clean their clothes in washing machines, and are sheltered from the elements in centrally heated and air-conditioned homes.

These daily rituals have one thing in common—they may all contribute to the greenhouse effect. They all involve the burning of fossil fuels such as coal, gas, and oil. Burning these fuels produces carbon dioxide, a gas which accumulates in the earth's atmosphere. Carbon dioxide and other gases in the atmosphere warm the earth's surface by trapping heat that would otherwise escape into space.

Some scientists believe that the level of carbon dioxide in the atmosphere is becoming dangerously high. They predict that the average global temperature toward the end of the next century could be four degrees Celsius above the average in the pre-industrial age. This temperature rise could have a catastrophic effect on the world, melting ice caps and causing rising sea levels that would threaten coastal cities and ecosystems. Crop production could suffer in the transition to a new climate and the shifting of temperature zones. Species would also be jeopardized by the changes in climate.

But other scientists believe that the evidence for global warming is incomplete. Though they agree that greenhouse gases are rising, they insist the evidence that this will cause substantial warming is incomplete. These scientists argue that mitigating factors such as increased cloud cover could offset any potential warming. It is even possible that increased concentrations of carbon dioxide, a natural fertilizer, would enhance plant life and agricultural productivity. In any case, they conclude, the steps necessary to halt the progression of the supposed greenhouse trend, such as cutting the use of fossil fuels, would be impractically expensive.

Is the greenhouse effect a serious threat? The authors of the viewpoints in the following chapter debate this question.

"The greenhouse effect has been detected, and it is changing our climate."

The Greenhouse Effect Is Real

Irving Mintzer and James Hansen

Irving Mintzer, the author of Part I of the following viewpoint, and James Hansen, author of Part II of the following viewpoint, believe that the greenhouse effect will cause the surface temperature of the planet to rise. Mintzer, a senior associate at the World Resources Institute, a policy research center, describes the substantial warming which would result if human activity continues to contribute greenhouse gases to the atmosphere. Hansen, director of the National Aeronautics and Space Administration's Goddard Institute for Space Studies, argues that the greenhouse effect is already influencing the earth's climate.

As you read, consider the following questions:

1. What human activity bears the most responsibility for the increasing amounts of carbon dioxide in the atmosphere, according to the authors?
2. According to Mintzer, what would be the result of a doubling of carbon dioxide in the atmosphere?
3. What is the reasoning behind Hansen's assertion that the greenhouse effect has begun to cause global warming?

Irving Mintzer, "A Matter of Degrees: The Potential for Controlling the Greenhouse Effect," *Research Report #5* of the World Resources Institute, April 1987. Reprinted with permission. James Hansen, testimony before the U.S. Senate Committee on Energy and Natural Resources, June 23, 1988.

I

Many economically important human activities emit gaseous pollutants into the air. Some of these emissions, including carbon dioxide (CO_2) and certain other gases. . . alter the heating rates in the atmosphere, causing the lower atmosphere to warm and (in the case of CO_2) the stratosphere to cool. This phenomenon is commonly called "the Greenhouse Effect" because, like the glass roof of a greenhouse, these. . .gases temporarily trap heat that would otherwise rapidly escape into space.

Many different gases can induce. . .warming via the greenhouse effect. Some are highly stable and linger in the atmosphere for decades or even a century or more. The most important of these gases are water vapor, CO_2, methane (CH_4), nitrous oxide (N_2O), tropospheric ozone (O_3), and the chlorofluorocarbons (especially $CFCl_3$, commonly known as CFC-11, and CF_2Cl_2, commonly known as CFC-12). The atmospheric concentrations of each of these gases has been increasing since the beginning of the industrial era. Other atmospheric pollutants including certain aerosols and particulates may also affect future climate regimes. Most scientists agree that these factors may have significant effects on regional climates; none will have as large an effect on global climate as the build-up of greenhouse gases. Historically, CO_2 and water vapor have contributed most to the greenhouse effect. Indeed, the increasing concentration of CO_2 has added more to global warming since the Industrial Revolution than have changes in the concentration of any other trace gas.

Some of these other greenhouse gases, however, absorb infrared radiation up to 10,000 times more efficiently than CO_2 does on a per-molecule basis. In the last several decades, the balance between the effects of CO_2 build-up and the effects of other greenhouse gases has changed. Recent analyses indicate that together these other trace gases now contribute about as much annually to global warming as CO_2 does. In the future, greenhouse gases other than CO_2 are likely to contribute more than half of the total commitment to global warming.

Greenhouse History and Future

Over the last ten million years, the naturally occurring concentration of CO_2 has fluctuated substantially. Throughout this period, CO_2 and water vapor in the atmosphere have warmed the planet's surface. Together, clouds, water vapor, and pre-industrial concentrations of 275-285 ppmv [parts per million by volume] of CO_2 warmed Earth's surface by approximately 33° centigrade—from an estimated average temperature of -18° (in the absence of CO_2) to approximately +15°C. This background greenhouse effect figured centrally in the evolution of Earth's present climate, elevating the average surface temperature to a level between that of ice and steam. Save for this background effect, Earth would be a comparatively cold and lifeless planet.

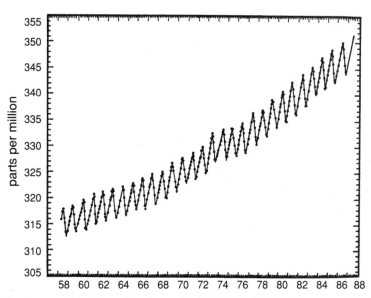

The inexorable rise of carbon dioxide. This is the 30-year plot of rising levels of carbon dioxide in the air at Mauna Loa in Hawaii. The seasonal wave is caused by plants releasing carbon dioxide in winter and taking it up in summer.

Fred Pearce, *Turning up the Heat: Our Perilous Future in the Global Greenhouse,* 1989.

Ironically, this same greenhouse effect now threatens to disrupt human societies and natural ecosystems. During the last century, emissions of carbon dioxide and other greenhouse gases have altered the atmosphere, which had been stable for thousands of years. Fossil fuel combustion (along with other industrial and agricultural activities) has caused the atmospheric concentration of carbon dioxide to increase approximately 25 percent since about 1860. The combined atmospheric build-up of carbon dioxide and the other greenhouse gases since 1860 are believed to have already committed Earth's surface to warm approximately 0.5° to 1.5°C above the average global temperature of the pre-industrial period. For perspective, a change in average global temperature of only 1°C separates the current climate regime of North America and Europe from that of the

Little Ice Age of the 13th to 17th Centuries.

Even small changes in average global temperatures can have large effects. At a 1985 meeting on the Greenhouse Effect sponsored by the WMO [World Meteorological Organization], United Nations Environment Programme (UNEP), and The International Council of Scientific Unions (ICSU), scientists from twenty-nine countries declared:

> Many important economic and social decisions are being made today on major irrigation, hydro-power and other water projects; on drought and agricultural land use, on structural designs and coastal engineering projects; and on energy planning, all based on assumptions about climate a number of decades into the future. Most such decisions assume that past climatic data, without modification, are a reliable guide to the future. This is no longer a good assumption since the increases of greenhouse gases are expected to cause a significant warming of the global climate. It is a matter of urgency to refine estimates of future climate conditions to improve these decisions.

Continuing emissions of CO_2 and other greenhouse gases will commit the atmosphere to significant future warming. Most atmospheric scientists agree that when the atmospheric concentration of CO_2 reaches approximately 550 ppmv, Earth will be committed to an average warming of 1.5°–4.5°C above pre-industrial temperatures. Recent experiments with the most advanced general circulation models of the atmosphere suggest that the planet's temperature sensitivity to doubled CO_2 is likely to be in the top half of this range, between 3.0° and 4.5°C. If current emission growth trends for all trace gases continue, the *combined* effects of the six most important greenhouse gases could, possibly as early as 2030, commit the globe to warm as much as a doubling of the pre-industrial concentration of CO_2. A global warming of even 1.5°C over pre-industrial levels could alter Earth's climate to an extent outside the range observed in the last 10,000 years.

II

I would like to draw three main conclusions. Number one, the earth is warmer than at any time in the history of instrumental measurements. Number two, the global warming is now large enough that we can ascribe with a high degree of confidence a cause and effect relationship to the greenhouse effect. And number three, our computer climate simulations indicate that the greenhouse effect is already large enough to begin to affect the probability of extreme events such as summer heat waves. . . .

The present temperature is the highest in the period of record. The rate of warming in the past 25 years is the highest on record. The four warmest years have all been in the 1980s. . . .

Now let me turn to my second point which is causal association of the greenhouse effect and the global warming. Causal association requires first that the warming be larger than natural climate variability and, second, that the magnitude and nature of the warming be consistent with the greenhouse mechanism. . . . The warming is almost 0.4 degrees Centigrade by 1987 relative to climatology, which is defined as the 30 year mean, 1950 to 1980 and, in fact, the warming is more than 0.4 degrees Centigrade in 1988. The probability of a chance warming of that magnitude is about 1 percent. So, with 99 percent confidence we can state that the warming during this time period is a real warming trend. . . .

Scientific Consensus

Evidence from a variety of sophisticated computer models points in the same direction—that some global warming is likely over the next several generations. Even the most vehement critics of the global warming theory admit that the earth may heat up. The most vocal such critic, MIT's Richard Lindzen, acknowledged that there was a one-in-four chance of significant warming over the next century. Virtually all other scientists working on the subject would place the odds much higher.

Union of Concerned Scientists, *The Global Warming Debate: Answers to Controversial Questions*, March, 1990.

We have considered several scenarios [of atmospheric trace gas growth] because there are uncertainties in the exact trace gas growth in the past and especially in the future. We have considered cases ranging from business as usual. . .to draconian emission cuts. . .which would totally eliminate net trace gas growth by year 2000.

The main point to be made here is that the expected global warming is of the same magnitude as the observed warming. Since there is only a 1 percent chance of an accidental warming of this magnitude, the agreement with the expected greenhouse effect is of considerable significance. Moreover, if you look at the next level of detail in the global temperature change, there are clear signs of the greenhouse effect. Observational data suggest a cooling in the stratosphere while the ground is warming. The data suggest somewhat more warming over land and sea ice regions than over open ocean, more warming at high latitudes than at low latitudes, and more warming in the winter than in the summer. In all of these cases, the signal is at best just beginning to emerge, and we need more data. Some of these details, such as the northern hemisphere high latitude temperature trends, do not look exactly like the greenhouse effect, but that is expected. There are certainly other climate change factors involved in addition to the greenhouse effect.

Altogether the evidence that the earth is warming by an amount which is too large to be a chance fluctuation and the similarity of the warming to that expected from the greenhouse effect represents a very strong case, in my opinion, that the greenhouse effect has been detected, and it is changing our climate now.

Extreme Events

Finally, I would like to address the question of whether the greenhouse effect is already large enough to affect the probability of extreme events, such as summer heat waves. . . . We have used the temperature changes computed in our global climate model to estimate the impact of the greenhouse effect on the frequency of hot summers in Washington, D.C. and Omaha, Nebraska. A hot summer is defined as the hottest one-third of the summers in the 1950 to 1980 period, which is the period the Weather Bureau uses for defining climatology. So, in that period the probability of having a hot summer was 33 percent, but by the 1990s, you can see that the greenhouse effect has increased the probability of a hot summer to somewhere between 55 and 70 percent in Washington according to our climate model simulations. In the late 1980s, the probability of a hot summer would be somewhat less than that. You can interpolate to a value of something like 40 to 60 percent.

I believe that this change in the frequency of hot summers is large enough to be noticeable to the average person. So, we have already reached a point that the greenhouse effect is important. It may also have important implications other than for creature comfort. . . .

The point that I would like to make is that in the late 1980s and in the 1990s we notice a clear tendency in our model for greater than average warming in the southeast United States and the midwest. In our model this result seems to arise because the Atlantic Ocean off the coast of the United States warms more slowly than the land. This leads to high pressure along the east coast and circulation of warm air north into the midwest or the southeast. There is only a tendency for this phenomenon. It is certainly not going to happen every year, and climate models are certainly an imperfect tool at this time. However, we conclude that there is evidence that the greenhouse effect increases the likelihood of heat wave drought situations in the southeast and midwest United States even though we cannot blame a specific drought on the greenhouse effect.

"The evidence of that alleged trend [global warming] is under increasingly sharp and solid scientific attack."

The Greenhouse Effect Is Exaggerated

Warren T. Brookes

In the following viewpoint, Warren T. Brookes examines scientific research that he believes calls into question the greenhouse theory of global warming. Some scientists have been too hasty in proclaiming the greenhouse effect a real threat, according to Brookes, and have ignored data which contradict the greenhouse theory. Brookes is an economics columnist who has written extensively on the greenhouse effect.

As you read, consider the following questions:

1. According to Brookes, what is the economic cost of halting the greenhouse effect?
2. According to the author, what are some of the problems with the models of the earth's climate?
3. How could politicians and bureaucrats benefit from concern over the greenhouse effect, according to Brookes?

Warren T. Brookes, "The Global Warming Panic," *Forbes,* December 25, 1989. Reprinted by permission of Warren T. Brookes and Creators Syndicate.

On Nov. 7, 1989 the U.S. and Japan shocked environmentalists around the world by refusing to sign a draft resolution at a Netherlands international conference on global climate change calling for the "stabilization" of emissions of carbon dioxide (CO_2) and other "greenhouse gases" by the year 2000. Instead, they made the conference drop all reference to a specific year, and to a specific CO_2 reduction target. The Bush Administration view was set forth by D. Allan Bromley, the presidential science adviser, in testimony to Senator Albert Gore's subcommittee on Science, Technology & Space: "My belief is that we should not move forward on major programs until we have a reasonable understanding of the scientific and economic consequences of those programs."

President Bush was immediately savaged by environmentalists, and by politicians like Senator Gore. The Bush viewpoint does not sit too well with most of the media, either. In January 1989, *Time* published a cover story on environmental catastrophes, declaring that greenhouse gases could create a climatic calamity. *The New York Times* weighed in with a story about how melting polar ice would flood the nations that can least afford to defend themselves, Third World countries like Bangladesh and India. . . .

Dire Predictions

Is the earth really on the verge of environmental collapse? Should wrenching changes be made in the world's industry to contain CO_2 buildup? Or could we be witnessing the 1990s version of earlier scares: nuclear winter, cancer-causing cranberries and $100 oil? The calamitarians always have something to worry us about. Consider this: In his 1976 book, *The Genesis Strategy*, Stephen Schneider lent support to the then popular view that we could be in for another ice age, "perhaps one akin to the Little Ice Age of 1500-1850. Climatic variability, which is the bane of reliable food production, can be expected to increase along with the cooling."

At the very moment Bromley was testifying to Gore's subcommittee, MIT's prestigious *Technology Review* was reporting on the publication of an exhaustive new study of worldwide ocean temperatures since 1850 by MIT [Massachusetts Institute of Technology] climatologists Reginald Newell, Jane Hsiung and Wu Zhongxiang. Its most striking conclusion: "There appears to have been little or no global warming over the past century." In fact, the average ocean temperature in the torrid 1980s was only an eighth of a centigrade degree (a quarter of a Fahrenheit degree) higher than the average of the 1860s. Ocean temperature is now virtually the same as it was in the 1940s. Since two-thirds of the buildup of CO_2 has taken place since 1940, the

MIT data blow all of the global warming forecasts into a cocked hat. President Bush wisely told reporters: "You can't take a policy and drive it to the extreme and say to every country around the world, 'You aren't going to grow at all.' "

Chuck Asay by permission of the *Colorado Springs Gazette-Telegraph*.

That is the central issue of the global warming debate, and it explains why the U.S. and Japanese position was supported by some 30 other developing nations which see that just as Marxism is giving way to markets, the political "greens" seem determined to put the world economy back into the red, using the greenhouse effect to stop unfettered market-based economic expansion.

Man and Nature

In simplest terms, the earth's atmosphere does operate as a greenhouse. In addition to oxygen, nitrogen and water vapor, the atmosphere contains several gases that trap radiated heat, including methane and CO_2. Carbon dioxide is essential not only to warmth but to vegetation. It is also essential to life in another way: Without its heat-containing effect the planet would freeze, like the atmospherically naked moon.

Throughout most of human history that atmospheric blanket has held global temperatures at an average of about 60 degrees

F., plus or minus 5 degrees F. During most of human history, the CO_2 concentration in that blanket has, until this century, hovered around 270 parts per million (ppm), although in earlier geologic epochs it reached as high as 20,000.

Over the last 100 years the CO_2 concentration has risen from 270 to today's level of 350. The culprit: man. Most of the greenhouse gas increase is the result of fossil fuel consumption. Add to that the rise in other man-generated trace gases—methane, nitrogen oxides and chlorofluorocarbons—and total greenhouse gases are now at 410 ppm. In other words, because of the combined effect of these gases, we have already gone over halfway to a doubling of CO_2. Even so, there has been less than half a degree of warming in the last 100 years.

Computer Models

What do the environmental pessimists make of all this? The earliest versions of their computer "general circulation models" predicted that the earth would warm up by anywhere from 3 to 5 degrees centigrade, or 5 to 9 degrees Fahrenheit, by the year 2050. The most extreme scenarios warn of coastal flooding (from melting ice caps) and rising inland droughts. However, as the level of sophistication of the models has risen, these forecast effects have been steadily reduced to a new range of 1.5 to 2.5 degrees centigrade.

One major exception to this declining rate of doom is the model run by James Hansen of the National Aeronautics & Space Administration, who shocked a congressional hearing in June 1988 during the middle of a scorching near-nationwide drought, by saying he was "99% confident" the greenhouse effect is now here.

Even though the vast majority of the climatological community was outraged by Hansen's unproven assertions, environmental advocate Stephen Schneider notes in *Global Warming*, "Journalists loved it. Environmentalists were ecstatic. Jim appeared on a dozen or more national television news programs. . . ."

By the end of 1988, with Hansen and Schneider's enthusiastic support, global warming was deeply embedded in the public consciousness. Now over 60% of the public is convinced it will worsen, even as the evidence of that alleged trend is under increasingly sharp and solid scientific attack. . . .

Here's another fact, noted by Hugh Ellsaesser of Lawrence Livermore Laboratories, that should trouble the calamity theorists: Most of the past century's warming trend took place by 1938, well before the rise in CO_2 concentration. From 1938 to 1970 temperatures plunged so sharply a new ice age was widely forecast. Furthermore, the warming trend since 1976 has been just the opposite of that forecast by the greenhouse model, with *cooling* in both the northern Pacific and North Atlantic.

In fact, the Northern Hemisphere shows no net change over the last 55 years, during which CO_2 concentration rose from approximately 300 to 350 ppm and other thermally active trace gases were in their steepest growth phases.

In spite of this clear lack of correlated warming evidence, one of the leading climate models now predicts that a 1% annual rise in CO_2 should, over 30 years, produce a 0.7-degree centigrade warming. But when Patrick Michaels of the University of Virginia applied that formula to the period from 1950 to 1988, when greenhouse gases rose 1.2% per year, he found a tiny 0.2-degree warming in land temperatures, where the model would have predicted 1.3 degrees. When a model cannot come within 500% of explaining the past, it is useless as a predictor of anything. . . .

The major weakness of the models is their assumption that the CO_2 buildup is the significant climate variable, and should *ceteris paribus* (all other things being equal) generate warming. But, as it turns out, the *ceteris* are decidedly not *paribus*.

Cloud Cover

One of those variables is cloud cover, which is at least 100 times more powerful in affecting temperatures than greenhouse gases and is infinitely variable. Yet, because cloud cover has been documented only for a decade or so (by weather satellites), the models have little to go on. Until recently, the modelers assumed that warmth gave rise to the kind of clouds that trap heat, contributing still further to warming, in a vicious cycle. But in June 1988, V. Ramanathan of the University of Chicago and a team of scientists at NASA [National Aeronautics and Space Administration] concluded from preliminary satellite data that "clouds appear to cool earth's climate," possibly offsetting the atmospheric greenhouse effect.

The supreme irony is that this "cooling effect," most pronounced in the Northern Hemisphere, coincides with the paths of coal-burning emission plumes with their high concentration of sulfur dioxide. That confirms a long-held thesis that sulfur dioxide creates "cool clouds." Of course, it is very upsetting to an environmentalist to discover that a pollutant has a beneficial side effect.

Sulfur dioxide emissions not only acidify rain, they combine with water vapor to form what are known as "aerosols," which have the effect of brightening clouds and making them reflect more heat away from the earth. Wisconsin's Reid Bryson described this effect as early as 20 years ago. Bryson's thesis was scorned at the time. But in June 1989, Thomas Wigley, one of England's top climatologists and a global warming enthusiast, conceded in a paper in *Nature* magazine that sulfur dioxide cooling "is sufficiently large that the effects may have significantly offset the temperature changes that resulted from the greenhouse effect.". . .

Ignoring Countervailing Effects

Hugh Ellsaesser says the main reason the models have been so completely wrong in "predicting" the past is that they completely ignore the countervailing, thermostatic effects of the hydrological cycle of evaporation and condensation. Two-thirds of the predicted global warming is due not directly to CO_2's radiative power but to an indirect effect: Carbon dioxide warming supposedly causes a threefold amplification of water vapor surface evaporation into the atmospheric blanket.

But Ellsaesser says in the warmer, tropical latitudes, where the temperature change from sea-level upward is most rapid, evaporation has the opposite effect. There, water vapor rises by deep convection in fast-rising towers. This in turn leads to more rapid condensation and precipitation, which then causes a drying and thinning of the upper atmosphere in a process called subsidence. "In the lower latitudes, a rise in CO_2 emissions will produce a 3-to-1 rise in greenhouse blanket *thinning* due to condensation. That's exactly the opposite of what the models predict," he says.

An eminent British scientist, Sir James Lovelock, says this hydrological process "is comparable in magnitude with that of the carbon dioxide greenhouse, but in opposition to it." National Oceanographic scientist Thomas Karl agrees: "We will eventually discover how naive we have been in not considering CO_2's effects on cloud cover and convection. As CO_2 speeds up the hydrological cycle, more convection creates more clouds and more cooling. So, the greenhouse effect could turn out to be minimal, or even benign."

MIT's Richard Lindzen thinks that correcting for deep convection alone could lower the global warming estimates by a factor of six. As a result, he says, "It is very unlikely that we will see more than a few tenths of a degree centigrade from this cause [CO_2] over the next century."

Opportunistic Politics

In the face of such mounting evidence, U.S. businesses may stop worrying about devastating legislative enactments. That could be a mistake. As Nobel economist James Buchanan argues, what drives Washington policymaking is not economic or scientific realities but "public choice," the pursuit of power and funding.

The public choice potential of global warming is immense. Under a global warming scenario, the EPA [Environmental Protection Agency] would become the most powerful government agency on earth, involved in massive levels of economic, social, scientific and political spending and interference. . . .

Senator Albert Gore is evidence of this public choice phenomenon. He seems determined to run his next presidential campaign at least in part on climate change, saving Mother Earth. Every year, at least one-sixth of the U.S. is classified by the government's Palmer Index as being in drought. Even though that index overstates the case, Gore could be looking at some very big political states—maybe California or Texas or Iowa—where his message will resonate with farmers and business. All he has to do is wait for a warm spell, and capitalize on what mathematicians call noise in the statistics.

Unreliable Computer Models

[One] way of making climate predictions is through computer models. These models are large systems of equations representing our understanding of climate processes. Because our understanding is limited, the models are of limited use. For example, these models have a hard time reproducing current climate from current data. They cannot be expected to predict future climate with any precision.

Andrew Solow, *The New York Times*, December 28, 1988.

Patrick Michaels explains: "We know that the Pacific Ocean current known as El Niño tends to warm and cool in two-year cycles. Just as its warming cycle produced the 1987-88 droughts, in 1989 it cooled sharply, making the U.S. much cooler and wetter than Hansen had forecast, and that is likely to happen in 1990, again. But that means that 1991 and 1992 should be warmer and drier than usual as the El Niño current warms. It won't matter that this has nothing to do with global warming, the media will perceive it that way, and people will tend to believe it."

Bernard Cohen, a physicist at the University of Pittsburgh, warns, in a 1984 book: "Our government's science and technology policy is now guided by uninformed and emotion-driven public opinion rather than by sound scientific advice. Unless solutions can be found to this problem, the U.S. will enter the 21st century declining in wealth, power and influence. . . . The coming debacle is not due to the problems the environmentalists describe, but to the policies they advocate."

"Global warming" may well prove Cohen right.

"Increasing the CO_2 [carbon dioxide] content of the air leads to many beneficial biological consequences."

The Greenhouse Effect Will Be Benign

Sherwood Idso

Sherwood Idso is a physicist with the United States Department of Agriculture. Idso believes that predictions of rising global temperatures are exaggerated. In the following viewpoint, he argues that increases in atmospheric carbon dioxide, the primary greenhouse gas, will actually result in greatly enhanced plant growth and agricultural productivity. Thus, he says, increased atmospheric carbon dioxide will actually have a beneficial effect.

As you read, consider the following questions:

1. What is the basic response of plants to increased levels of carbon dioxide, according to Idso?
2. What does the author mean by the term "water use efficiency"?
3. According to the author, what will be the overall effect of increased carbon dioxide on the earth's plant life?

Excerpted, with permission, from Sherwood Idso, *Carbon Dioxide and Global Change: Earth in Transition*. Tempe, Ariz.: IBR Press, 1989.

For about a century now, and as a result of well over a thousand laboratory and field experiments, scientists have known that increasing the CO_2 [carbon dioxide] content of the air around a plant's leaves nearly always leads to a significant increase in vegetative growth and development. Indeed, the plant science literature is replete with reviews and analyses of the subject; and fully fifty years ago, thousands of commercial nurseries were already enriching greenhouse air with extra CO_2 for the purpose of enhancing crop production, as they continue to do today.

The Basic Growth Response

The basis for this profound biological response to atmospheric CO_2 enrichment is to be found in the mechanics of the primary plant process of photosynthesis, whereby light energy is converted into chemical energy in the presence of certain plant pigments (chlorophyll, carotenoids, etc.) to produce carbohydrates from a. . . pool of carbon dioxide. . . .

All of the experimental evidence of the past hundred or so years suggests that with more CO_2 available for participation in the photosynthetic process, more carbohydrates will consequently be produced, which has, of course, been verified by direct experimental observation. In addition, it has also been demonstrated that less carbon will be lost to the process of photorespiration under such conditions. Hence, these observations would seem to suggest that the atmospheric CO_2 concentration on the Earth of today may well be far below what should be considered normal for optimal functioning of the planet's vast array of vegetation.

There are many consequences of this affinity of plant life for high levels of atmospheric CO_2. First, and most obvious, is the fact that plants grown in air enriched with CO_2 are generally larger than similar plants grown in ambient air. They are usually taller, have more branches or tillers, more and thicker leaves containing greater amounts of chlorophyll, more and larger flowers, more and larger fruit, and more extensive root systems. The bottom line, however, at least in terms of economic productivity, is the harvestable yield produced; and. . . comprehensive reviews of this subject indicate that for all of the many plant species which have been studied in this regard, the mean increase in harvestable yield produced by a 330 to 660 ppm [parts per million] doubling of the air's CO_2 content is approximately 33%.

Further increases in the CO_2 content of the air augment plant productivity even more, although generally at a somewhat diminishing rate. . . . Consequently, the response characteristics of Earth's plant life to atmospheric CO_2 enrichment would appear to allow the planet's blanket of vegetation to express its fullest growth potential under even the most "adverse" (highest) CO_2 concentrations which have been predicted to result from mankind's unrestricted burning of fossil fuels. Indeed, full use of all of the world's recoverable fuel reserves would likely return Earth's atmospheric CO_2 content to levels characteristic of the "optimal environments" of the early and mid-Cretaceous and the Permian and Carboniferous periods, when vegetation flourished from pole to pole and great coal beds were laid down on almost every continent producing a remarkable "greening of the Earth."

Chuck Asay by permission of the *Colorado Springs Gazette-Telegraph.*

In addition to enhancing vegetative productivity, atmospheric CO_2 enrichment tends to reduce the amount of water transpired by plants and thereby lost to the atmosphere. . . . Also well known for almost a century, this process too has been studied intently for the past several decades. . . . And like the stimulation of plant growth by atmospheric CO_2 enrichment, this phenomenon has also been found to continue far beyond a CO_2 concentration of 1,000 ppm, additionally indicating that plant water relations, like plant growth itself, should continue to improve as the CO_2 content of the Earth's atmosphere continues to rise, under even the "worst case" scenario of future fossil fuel utilization.

So just how good can things get? An illuminating answer to this question is provided by an analysis of the effects of atmospheric CO_2 enrichment on plant *water use efficiency,* defined as the ratio of plant photosynthesis or dry matter production to the amount of water transpired per unit area of leaf surface. Based upon the mean results of the preceding [discussion]. . .it is readily appreciated that such a doubling of the atmospheric CO_2 concentration fully *doubles* the water use efficiency of nearly all plants. . .as has been demonstrated in numerous experiments. . . .

What will be the result of this significant improvement in the ability of plants to utilize water? For one thing, it is almost self-evident that in the high CO_2 world of the future, many plants will be able to live in areas which are presently too dry for them. . . .

Soil and Water

Up to this point, we have dealt primarily with the direct effects of CO_2 on plants. Consider next what consequences some of these effects may have for the soil. . . .

Most obvious is the stabilizing effect of enhanced plant cover on the world's valuable topsoil. Each and every year, billions of tons of this most important resource are lost to the ravages of wind and water. However, as plants grow ever more vigorously with increasing concentrations of atmospheric CO_2 and as they subsequently expand their ranges to cover previously desolate and barren ground, both of these types of erosion should be significantly reduced, as has been demonstrated in numerous experiments with both natural and managed ecosystems. . . .

One of the major environmental problems currently confronting much of the world is the ominous threat of widespread contamination of the planet's dwindling supply of pristine groundwater, due primarily to the improper disposal of industrial waste products and the excessive agricultural use of fertilizers, herbicides, and pesticides. So serious has the problem become, in fact, that young children in many U.S. cities cannot drink the local water for fear of their developing methemoglobinemia (blue baby syndrome) as a result of the water's high nitrate content; while across the country literally thousands of wells have tested positive for harmful levels of noxious chemicals. And the worst is probably still to come, due to the slow rate of travel of the various pollutants down to the water table.

There are several ways in which higher atmospheric CO_2 concentrations may help to partially alleviate this regrettable situation. First, as plants respond to atmospheric CO_2 enrichment and grow more vigorously everywhere and more profusely in stressful environments, they should gradually increase the amount of organic matter in the soil; and as soil organic matter effectively adsorbs and immobilizes most water-born chemicals, its greater presence in the soil should slow the rate at which contaminants move downward to the groundwater. Second, as plant roots penetrate deeper into the soil profile with atmospheric CO_2 enrichment, the amount of time available for detainment and modification of potential groundwater contaminants should likewise be lengthened. And finally, associated with the augmented concentration and vertical extent of the enhanced soil organic matter should be correspondingly augmented populations of soil microorganisms which attack and detoxify would-be water pollutants. Considered in their totality, these several interrelated phenomena should play a major role in helping to reduce the amount of groundwater contamination likely to otherwise be experienced in the coming years. . . .

More Food

The higher temperatures combined with more carbon dioxide will favor crop and plant growth and could well provide more food for our burgeoning global population.

Robert Pease, *Human Events*, March 24, 1990.

Due to the fact that there may possibly be a greenhouse warming of the planet in the years to come (albeit a much less severe warming than that generally predicted), it is important to consider what effect such a warming may have on the basic growth response of plants to atmospheric CO_2 enrichment.

Over the past several years, a number of experiments have shed considerable light on this topic; and in reviews of the pertinent literature published in 1985 and 1986, there were indications that the stimulatory effects of atmospheric CO_2 enrichment may be significantly augmented as air temperature rises. Subsequent studies have clarified this point even more. . . .

In terms of the plant life of the planet, a 300 to 1,000 ppm increase in the CO_2 content of the atmosphere should produce about a tripling of the water use efficiency of almost all of the world's vegetation, as a result of the direct effects of atmospheric CO_2 enrichment upon the primary plant processes of photosynthesis and transpiration. And to this phenomenal response must be added the effects of a number of secondary amplifying processes and synergistic feedbacks.

First of all, if the planet does warm (which it may not. . .) the higher air temperatures should enhance plant growth still more. Secondly, many plants will greatly expand their ranges with augmented water use efficiencies, stabilizing the soil and protecting it from erosion. And with greater above-ground productivity, there will be greater below-ground productivity. Plant roots will grow deeper to utilize previously untapped nutrients. More organic matter will be returned to the soil. Microbial populations will rise. Earthworms will increase in number. Soil-forming processes will be enhanced. Water, salinity, nutrient, and air pollution stresses will be relieved. High and low temperature extremes should be better tolerated. Many plant diseases may be reduced. And there will be a greater supply of forage and habitat available for supporting a vastly increased animal population of all types.

Considered in their totality, these many interrelated phenomena could readily double, triple or even quadruple the primary direct effects of atmospheric CO_2 enrichment upon plant growth and development on a global basis, especially when one considers the potential for vegetative expansion over the large portions of the planet which are presently barren and the possibility for increases in oceanic productivity. Hence, it is by no means inconceivable that the vitality of the biosphere, or the totality of all life processes on planet Earth, could rise by a full order of magnitude or more over the next few centuries; for as Boyd Strain has noted, "we are moving from a carbon-starved to a carbon-fertilized world." Indeed, we seem destined to experience what no member of our species has ever before encountered, but something with which the earlier inhabitants of the planet were well acquainted. . . .

Beneficial Consequences

Hundreds of studies. . .conclusively demonstrate that increasing the CO_2 content of the air leads to many beneficial biological consequences. . . .

Consequently, it would be like cutting our own throats—or, more properly, the throats of "generations yet unborn"—to attempt to thwart the very phenomenon (the steadily rising atmospheric CO_2 concentration) which has the *proven ability* to dramatically boost crop yields, enhance plant water use efficiencies, and give us the edge we need in our fight against world hunger. Not even genetic engineering, for example, can presume to solve the problem of insufficient agricultural water supplies in many high-birthrate countries; for in spite of all that man might do for them, as *Time* quotes plant physiologist Anthony Hall, "you can't grow plants without water." Thus, the plus-600 ppm atmospheric CO_2 concentrations of the 2060s and beyond, which will enable plants to utilize water twice as efficiently as they did in the early 1900s, may well provide our only hope of properly feeding the peoples of the world at that future time without destroying what remains of the planet's natural ecosystems.

"There would be dramatic disruptions of agriculture, water resources, fisheries, coastal activity, and energy use."

The Greenhouse Effect Will Result in Disaster

Andrew C. Revkin

How would global warming affect the earth and its inhabitants? In the following viewpoint, Andrew C. Revkin gives his answer to this question. Revkin, a senior editor of the science magazine *Discover*, argues that the greenhouse effect will bring dire consequences. He contends that as a result of higher global temperatures sea level will rise, storms will become more dangerous, and wildlife and agriculture will be jeopardized.

As you read, consider the following questions:

1. Why, according to Revkin, is rapid climate change more serious than gradual change?
2. Why is the greenhouse effect particularly threatening to the Marshall Islands, in the author's opinion?
3. In the author's opinion, why shouldn't the Soviet Union look forward to the possibility of warmer temperatures resulting from the greenhouse effect?

Andrew C. Revkin, "Endless Summer: Living with the Greenhouse Effect," *Discover*, October 1988, © 1988 Discover Publications.

On June 23, 1988 the United States sizzled as thermometers topped 100 degrees in 45 cities from coast to coast: 102 in Sacramento; 103 in Lincoln, Nebraska; 101 in Richmond, Virginia. In the nation's heartland the searing heat was accompanied by a ruinous drought that ravaged crops and prompted talk of a dust bowl to rival that of the 1930s. Heat waves and droughts are nothing new, of course. But on that stifling June day a top atmospheric scientist testifying on Capitol Hill had a disturbing message for his senatorial audience: Get used to it.

This wasn't just a bad year, James Hansen of the NASA [National Aeronautics and Space Administration] Goddard Institute for Space Studies told the Senate committee, or even the start of a bad decade. Rather, he could state with "99 percent confidence" that a recent, persistent rise in global temperature was a climatic signal he and his colleagues had long been expecting. Others were still hedging their bets, arguing there was room for doubt. But Hansen was willing to say what no one had dared say before. "The greenhouse effect," he claimed, "has been detected and is changing our climate now."

Devastating Consequences

Even though most climatologists think Hansen's claims are premature, they agree that warming is on the way. Carbon dioxide levels are 25 percent higher now than they were in 1860, and the atmosphere's burden of greenhouse gases is expected to keep growing. By the middle of the next century the resulting warming could boost global mean temperatures from three to nine degrees Fahrenheit. That doesn't sound like much, but it equals the temperature rise since the end of the last ice age, and the consequences could be devastating. Weather patterns could shift, bringing drought to once fertile areas and heavy rains to fragile deserts that cannot handle them. As runoff from melting glaciers increases and warming seawater expands, sea level could rise as much as six feet, inundating low-lying coastal areas and islands. There would be dramatic disruptions of agriculture, water resources, fisheries, coastal activity, and energy use.

"Average climate will certainly get warmer," says Roger Revelle, an oceanographer and climatologist at the University of California at San Diego. "But what's more serious is how many more hurricanes we'll have, how many more droughts we'll have, how many days above one hundred degrees." By Hansen's reckoning, where Washington now averages one day a year over 100 degrees, it will average 12 such scorchers annually by the middle of the next century.

Comparable climate shifts have happened before, but over tens of centuries, not tens of years. The unprecedented rapid change could accelerate the already high rate of species extinction as plants and animals fail to adapt quickly enough. For the first time in history humans are affecting the ecological balance of not just a region but the entire world, all at once. "We're altering the environment far faster than we can possibly predict the consequences," says Stephen Schneider, a climate modeler at the National Center for Atmospheric Research in Boulder, Colorado. "This is bound to lead to some surprises.". . .

Matching the Rifle, Chainsaw, and Bulldozer

Realistically, if the greenhouse-affected future unfolds as anticipated, it will eliminate species in huge numbers. The impact of the rifle and harpoon, the chainsaw and plow, the bulldozer and pesticide pack could well be matched, if not exceeded, by the factory chimney, the auto exhaust and other sources of greenhouse gases.

Norman Meyers, *Greenpeace*, May/June 1989.

Some parts of the world could actually benefit from climate change, while others could suffer tremendously. But for the foreseeable future the effects will be uncertain. No nation can *plan* on benefiting. . . .

The big question is, given the inexorable buildup of these gases—a growth that even the most spirited optimists concede can only be slowed, not stopped—what will the specific effects be? It's hard to say, because the relationship between worldwide climate and local weather is such a complex phenomenon to begin with. The chaotic patterns of jet streams and vortices and ocean currents swirling around the globe and governing the weather still confound meteorologists; in fact, weather more than two weeks in the future is thought by some to be inherently unpredictable.

Computer Models

So far, the best answers have come from computer models that simulate the workings of the atmosphere. Most divide the atmosphere into hundreds of boxes, each of which is represented by mathematical equations for wind, temperature, moisture, incoming radiation, outgoing radiation, and the like. Each mathematical box is linked to its neighbors, so it can respond to changing conditions with appropriate changes of its own. Thus, the model behaves the way the world does—albeit at a very rough scale. A typical model divides the atmosphere vertically into nine layers and horizontally into boxes that are several hundred miles on a side.

Climate modelers can play with "what if" scenarios to see how the world would respond to an arbitrary set of conditions. . . . To study the greenhouse effect, climatologists first used models to simulate current conditions, then instantly doubled the amount of carbon dioxide in the atmosphere. The computer was allowed to run until conditions stabilized at a new equilibrium, and a map could be drawn showing changes in temperature, precipitation, and other factors. . . .

Even the best climate model, however, has to oversimplify the enormous complexity of the real atmosphere. One problem is the size of the boxes. The model used at the National Center for Atmospheric Research, for example, typically uses boxes 4.5 degrees of latitude by 7 degrees of longitude—about the size of the center's home state of Colorado—and treats them as uniform masses of air. While that's inherently inaccurate—the real Colorado contains such fundamentally different features as the Rocky Mountains and the Great Plains—using smaller boxes would take too much computing power.

Another problem is that modelers must estimate the influence of vegetation, ice and snow, soil moisture, terrain, and especially clouds, which reflect lots of sunlight back into space and also hold in surface heat. "Clouds are an important factor about which little is known," says Schneider. "When I first started looking at this in 1972, we didn't know much about the feedback from clouds. We don't know any more now than we did then."

So it is not surprising that while the more than a dozen major global climate models in use around the world tend to agree on the broadest phenomena, they differ wildly when it comes to regional effects. And, says Robert Cess, a climate modeler at the State University of New York at Stony Brook, "The smaller the scale, the bigger the disagreement.". . .

Sea Level Rise

There are, however, some consequences of a warming Earth that will be universal. Perhaps the most obvious is a rise in sea level. "If we went all out to slow the warming trend, we might stall sea level rise at three to six feet," says Robert Buddemeier of Lawrence Livermore National Laboratory, who is studying the impact of sea level rise on coral reefs. "But that's the very best you could hope for." And a six-foot rise, Buddemeier predicts, would be devastating.

It would, for one thing, render almost all low coral islands uninhabitable. "Eventually," Buddemeier says, "a lot of this real estate is going to go under water." For places like the Marshall Islands in the Pacific, the Maldives off the west coast of India, and some Caribbean nations, this could mean nothing less than national extinction. . . .

Coastal regions of continents or larger islands will also be in harm's way, particularly towns or cities built on barrier islands and the fertile flat plains that typically surround river deltas. Bangladesh, dominated by the Ganges-Brahmaputra-Meghna Delta, is the classic case, says Buddemeier. "It's massively populated, achingly poor, and something like a sixth of the country is going to go away.". . .

The Expanding Ocean

As temperatures rise the waters of the earth will expand. Glaciers and icecaps will melt. Still higher sea levels may occur if the warming breaks loose such large frozen ice masses as the West Antarctic sheet. If correct, the predicted temperature changes would escalate sea level by five to seven feet over the next century. Some climatologists now estimate that the rate of increase will accelerate after 2050, reaching about an inch per year.

Jodi L. Jacobson, *World Watch*, January/February 1989.

One mitigating factor for some coastal nations that are still developing, such as Belize and Indonesia, is that they generally have committed fewer resources to the coastline than their developed counterparts—Australia, for example, or the United States, with such vulnerable cities as Galveston and Miami. "Developed countries have billions invested in a very precarious, no-win situation," Buddemeier says. "The less developed countries will have an easier time adapting."

Indeed, the impact on coastal cities in developed countries may be enormous. The Urban Institute, a nonpartisan think tank, is completing a study for the Environmental Protection Agency on what a three-foot sea level rise would do to Miami. Miami is particularly vulnerable. Not only is it a coastal city, but it is nearly surrounded by water, with the Atlantic to the east, the Everglades to the west, and porous limestone beneath— "one of the most permeable aquifers in the world," says William Hyman, a senior research associate at the institute. "The aquifer in Miami is so porous that you'd actually have to build a dike down one hundred fifty feet beneath the surface to keep water from welling up." In an unusually severe storm nearby Miami Beach would be swept by a wall of water up to 16 feet above the current sea level.

Storms are an even greater danger to Galveston, which [Stephen] Leatherman has studied extensively. Given just a couple of feet in sea level rise, a moderately bad hurricane, of the type that occurs about once every ten years, would have the destructive impact of the type of storm that occurs once a century. And Galveston is typical of a whole range of resort areas on the eastern and Gulf coasts. . . .

Even as cities become more vulnerable to moderate storms, the intensity of hurricanes may increase dramatically, says Kerry Emanuel, a meteorologist at MIT [Massachusetts Institute of Technology]. Hurricane intensity is linked to the temperature of the sea surface, Emanuel explains. According to his models, if the sea warms to predicted levels, the most intense hurricanes will be 40 to 50 percent more severe than the most intense hurricanes of the past 50 years. . . .

Another worldwide consequence of global warming is increased precipitation: warmer air will mean more evaporation of ocean water, more clouds, and an overall rise in rain and snow of between 5 and 7 percent. But it won't be evenly distributed. One climate model at Princeton University's Geophysical Fluid Dynamics Laboratory predicts that central India will have doubled precipitation, while the centers of continents at middle latitudes—the midwestern United States, for example—will actually have much drier summers than they have now (the 1988 summer drought could, in other words, be a foretaste). Some arid areas, including southern California and Morocco, will have drier winters; and winters are when such areas get most of their precipitation. . . .

Agriculture and Shifting Climates

Food is another crucial resource that will be affected by the global greenhouse. Taken by itself, a rise in atmospheric carbon dioxide might not be so bad. For many crops more carbon dioxide means a rise in the rate of photosynthesis and, therefore, in growth; and with increased carbon dioxide some plants' use of water is more efficient, according to studies done in conventional glass greenhouses. Also, as the planet gets warmer, crops might be cultivated farther north. But as usual, things are not so simple. A temperature rise of only 3.5 degrees in the tropics could reduce rice production by more than 10 percent.

In temperate regions also, the picture is mixed. Cynthia Rosenzweig, a researcher based at Goddard, has been using crop-growth computer models to predict effects of carbon dioxide buildup and climate change on wheat, the most widely cultivated crop in the world. Plugging in temperature changes derived from the Goddard climate model, Rosenzweig tested a world with doubled carbon dioxide levels. Because the Goddard model is bad at predicting precipitation, she did separate runs for normal and dry conditions. She found that in normal years the wheat grew better, thanks to the extra carbon dioxide. But in dry years there was a marked increase in crop failures, because of excessive heat. Given the likelihood that heat waves and droughts are increasing, she says, no one should count on better yields in years to come.

The nations most likely to reap the benefits of warmer climate are Canada and the Soviet Union, much of whose vast land area is too cold for large-scale crop cultivation. . . .

But again, atmospheric scientists stress that no nation can count on benefits. "The models suggest that ecological zones will shift northward," says planetary scientist Michael McElroy of Harvard. "The southwestern desert to the Grain Belt; the Grain Belt to Canada. There might be winners and losers if this shift occurs slowly. But suppose it shifts so fast that ecosystems are unable to keep up?" For example, he says, there is a limit to the distance that a forest can propagate in a year. "If it is unable to propagate fast enough, then either we have to come in and plant trees, or else we'll see total devastation and the collapse of the ecosystem."

According to Irving Mintzer, a senior associate with the Energy and Climate Project of the World Resources Institute in Washington, there is another reason to be leery of projections for regional agricultural benefits. Just because climatic conditions conducive to grain cultivation move north, that doesn't mean that other conditions necessary for agricultural superpowerdom will be present. Much of Canada, for example, does not have the optimum type of soil for growing wheat and corn.

Fragile Ecosystems

Wildlife will suffer, too. In much of the world, wilderness areas are increasingly hemmed in by development, and when climate shifts, these fragile ecosystems won't be able to shift with it. Plants will suddenly be unable to propagate their seeds, and animals will have no place to go. Species in the Arctic, such as caribou, may lose vital migratory routes as ice bridges between islands melt.

In the United States the greatest impact will likely be on coastal wetlands: the salt marshes, swamps, and bayous that are among the world's most diverse and productive natural habitats. James Titus of the Environmental Protection Agency estimates that a five-foot rise in sea level—not even the worst-case scenario—would destroy between 50 and 90 percent of America's wetlands. Under natural conditions marshes would slowly shift inland. But with levees, condominiums, and other man-made structures in the way, they can't. The situation is worst in Louisiana, says Titus, which has 40 percent of U.S. wetlands (excluding those in Alaska); much of the verdant Mississippi River delta may well vanish.

"If we begin to act today, we might achieve everything that needs to be done to hold the global average temperature."

The Greenhouse Effect Requires Immediate Action

Michael Oppenheimer and Robert H. Boyle

Michael Oppenheimer is a senior scientist with the Environmental Defense Fund, a public interest group. Robert H. Boyle has written on the environment for over thirty years, and has authored several books on environmental issues. The following viewpoint is excerpted from their coauthored book *Dead Heat: The Race Against the Greenhouse Effect.* Oppenheimer and Boyle argue that immediate measures to counter the greenhouse effect are needed in order to avoid disastrous consequences for the earth's climate.

As you read, consider the following questions:

1. What do the authors mean by the "lag time" and "irreversibility" of the greenhouse effect?
2. Why, according to the authors, does the greenhouse effect present a dilemma to politicians?
3. What do Oppenheimer and Boyle believe would be the result of a "wait and see" approach to the greenhouse effect?

During the long, hot summer of 1988, Ted Koppel opened an ABC "Nightline" program on the greenhouse effect by asking one of us, "I'd love to be able to say to you that I think the American public can get energized over some perceived threat forty years down the road, but I don't believe it. Do you?"

Koppel obviously didn't think the American public had absorbed the lesson that Wile E. Coyote, the "Roadrunner" cartoon character, learns the hard way when he races along a road that, unbeknownst to him, is about to end at the edge of a cliff. Wile E. Coyote moves so fast that he's ten feet past the sheer dropoff when he freezes, looks down, and, in shock, comprehends his situation. For a split second, while suspended in midair, he flails his arms in a futile attempt to reach the cliff. Then gravity takes over, and he plummets out of sight. It is worth bearing this image in mind as we explore the reasons for applying the brakes to global warming sooner rather than later.

A Top Priority

The 1980s seem to have thrown up one obstacle after another to focusing on distant threats. . . . The Iran-Iraq War and the Soviet invasion of Afghanistan lasted throughout most of the decade. The contras fought the Sandinistas in Nicaragua, death squads roamed El Salvador, Lebanon was torn to pieces, Palestinians in the West Bank erupted against Israel, and South Africa threatened to explode. . . . The AIDS [Acquired Immune Deficiency Syndrome] epidemic ran unchecked in central Africa and parts of the West, China erupted briefly with an insurrection of democracy, and the political landscape of eastern Europe changed overnight. With so many immediate life-and-death decisions to be made, why should political leaders take time to ponder the seemingly remote hazards posed by the greenhouse effect? . . .

In a logical sense, the arguments for immediate action are compelling, and they arise from both the physical nature of the problem and the customarily protracted pace of government, even once it has decided to move. . . .

Let us consider the . . . need for immediate action on the greenhouse effect. It is the result of two menacing features, demons if you will, of global warming: irreversibility and the lag time between emissions and effects. These characteristics distinguish global warming from other environmental issues, and they have the vicious consequence of increasing the need for an urgent response while at the same time making it politically difficult to implement one.

As long as greenhouse gases are emitted in quantities close to current amounts, Earth will become warmer and warmer for an indefinite period lasting at least hundreds of years. If emissions increase continuously as they have in the past, warming will accelerate. Should emissions be reduced, greenhouse-gas levels still would remain elevated for centuries, making their consequences irreversible in any human time-frame.

By permission of Mike Luckovich and Creators Syndicate.

To understand why, consider a bathroom sink. With the drain partly shut and the water running fast, the level will rise and the sink will overflow. Conversely, with the drain wide open and the faucet almost shut, the sink won't fill at all. But if both the faucet and the drain are wide open, or both are almost shut, or both are somewhere in between, the sink will fill to a certain depth and that level will hold. This level is called the steady state, and it remains constant because the inflow from the faucet is exactly matched by the outflow from the drain. There is a balance.

Another property goes hand in hand with the steady-state behavior: reversibility. For example, if the faucet is opened a little bit more, the water level will begin to increase but the pressure of the extra water will also force an increase in the flow into the drain. The depth of the water will increase until the higher outflow exactly matches the increased inflow, and a new steady state is reached. If the faucet is then tightened to its original position, the water level will begin to drop; but the pressure will also drop, so the flow out the drain will begin to slow down. The water again reaches the old steady-state level. The change was reversible. . . .

Now consider what happens when the drain is tightened until it is only open a crack. If the faucet is left in the same position, the water level will begin to rise. Even if the faucet is turned down somewhat, the level will climb. How fast it rises depends on how much the faucet is opened, but in any event the climb will continue until a new and much higher steady water level is reached. If the drain is shut completely, the water level will rise forever, onto the floor, out the door, no matter how slowly the water runs.

Unfortunately, greenhouse gases resemble water in a sink with a nearly closed drain and a wide-open faucet. Much more of these gases is emitted into the atmosphere by human activities than the drain can accommodate. Thus, the level of greenhouse gases in the atmosphere keeps rising. In the case of carbon dioxide, the drain is the ocean and the forests, which can absorb only half of each year's emissions from the atmosphere. The process of removing the remainder is so gradual that if all human carbon-dioxide sources were eliminated today, the extra gas already accumulated would remain airborne for more than 300 years. Compared to the faucet, the drain is nearly shut tight, so the carbon-dioxide buildup is effectively irreversible. . . .

Continuously higher greenhouse-gas levels must translate into an ever-warmer Earth unless negative climate feedbacks eventually come to dominate the positive ones. But there is no compelling evidence to suggest that they will. As emissions grow, the buildup of greenhouse gases, and Earth's consequent warming, could continue without limit until the sources, like fossil fuels, simply run out. . . .

Lag Time

The full extent of the warming that will accompany any particular level of greenhouse gases will be realized about forty years after their release into the atmosphere. To understand why this is so, consider two Thanksgiving turkeys, one stuffed, the other not. Put the birds in separate ovens and turn the dials to the same setting. The stuffed turkey will take far longer to cook than the empty bird because the stuffing is slow to warm, and it keeps the rest of the bird relatively cool. Still, if the turkey were left in the oven long enough, its temperature would eventually reach the level of the oven setting and stop rising.

Think of the atmosphere as the turkey, the ocean as the stuffing, and the level of greenhouse gases in the atmosphere as the oven thermostat. Without the ocean, the atmosphere would heat quickly, like the empty bird. Add the ocean and the warming rate slows, because heating the great mass of water in the ocean takes a very long time. . . . If atmospheric levels of greenhouse gases are allowed to increase continuously as they are now, it is as though the cook kept turning the thermostat up higher and higher: the stuffed turkey would always lag behind the oven setting. Conversely, if emissions of greenhouse gases were reduced so much that a steady state of the gases' levels was achieved at today's levels, it still would take the Earth's temperature decades to level off after the gases were stabilized.

Arresting Climate Change

The worst effects of a greenhouse-induced climate cataclysm can be averted. And the sooner action is taken, the more effective it will be. Conversely, the longer a policy response is delayed, the greater the warming that will have accumulated "in the bank" and the more radical the measures that will be required to prevent further climatic upheaval.

David Wirth, *Foreign Policy*, Spring 1989.

Unfortunately, the Earth's thermostat is already set rather high. If by some miracle we could stabilize the amount of greenhouse gases in the atmosphere immediately, the global mean temperature would likely climb at least another degree or two. Surely it will take decades to implement a response fully, during which time the thermostat will move higher and higher.

Lag time and irreversibility cut the legs out from under the politicians' responses of "Let's see how bad things get before we spend any money" or "We need more research." Any time our leaders decide to control emissions, there will always be more warming in the pipeline; and they will never fully be able to anticipate its consequences. . . .

Politics as Usual

These two characteristics put policy makers in an unaccustomed position. Take one who has been told for years that the Earth is warming but that the risks can never be completely assessed. He or she knows that without action, the greenhouse effect will build indefinitely and irreversibly. Yet even if he presses for emission reductions, the climate will continue to warm due to the two demons, and the public will see no immediate benefit. This is a patently different situation from others he has faced in the past, when the consequences of a decision were obvious within a relatively short time. . . .

Earth's temperature hasn't quite reached the point that people notice the warming. Without a happenstance string of hot summers, it could be decades before the dire consequences are made absolutely clear. In the meantime, a politician will be inclined to do little or nothing.

But if politicians respond to global warming in this way. . . wait-

ing a decade for dramatic discoveries and then taking another fifteen years to eliminate the cause, the planet could be in big trouble. . . .

The Three-Degree Cliff

Warming beyond three degrees, the boundary of experience
for the modern human species, is like going over a cliff with little notion of how far we will fall. Circumstances are changing
so rapidly that, even without knowing it, we may approach the
edge in a few short years. The faster we emit greenhouse gases,
the further we will be committed to an overshoot before much
can done, and the harder the fall will be when the effects are
manifest. . . .

Early in the next century, global temperature could be surging
at the substantial clip of one-half to one degree per decade, far
beyond what civilization has ever experienced on a sustained
basis. By then, the world will be about a degree warmer than it
is now, and the scientific community will presumably have settled the argument over whether the warming is due to the
greenhouse effect; but if nothing has been done in the meantime, the lag factor will guarantee that an additional two-degree
warming is already in the pipeline.

If the standard, leisurely posture toward environmental problems is assumed at that point, it could take thirty or forty years
to make political decisions, to utilize the existing technologies
fully, and to develop and implement new ones, which would allow a big reduction in fossil-fuel use. So one might figure that
another three or four degrees of warming could be built in before the greenhouse-gas levels are stabilized.

Record Warming

Thus, if we treat global climate change like any other political
problem, the mean temperature of the planet can be expected to
reach six or seven degrees above the current level. We will be
committed to record rates of warming and unprecedented dislocation. . . . A seven-degree rise is probably enough to guarantee
the disintegration of the West Antarctic ice sheet and an eventual
eighteen-foot rise in sea level. A seven-degree warming is barely
within the range of reliability of the climate models, so we have
no idea what other shocks might loom in that new world.

By comparison, another degree or two of warming is inevitable as the temperature of the oceans catches up to the present greenhouse-gas level. If we begin to act today, we might
achieve everything that needs to be done to hold the global average temperature to a mere three degrees above what it is now.
The difference between three degrees and seven degrees is the
difference between the edge of the cliff and the bottom of the
abyss, from which there is no return.

VIEWPOINT

"Scientific knowledge about global warming is seriously incomplete."

Immediate Action on the Greenhouse Effect Is Unwarranted

Jane S. Shaw and Richard L. Stroup

In the following viewpoint, Jane S. Shaw and Richard L. Stroup, senior associates of the Political Economy Research Center, a non-profit think tank, argue that calls for government regulations to counter the greenhouse effect are premature. Not only are these regulations unnecessary, but they would be costly and potentially dangerous, the authors contend. The solution for the near future, the authors conclude, is to build scientific knowledge on the subject.

As you read, consider the following questions:

1. What are some of the authors' criticisms of the greenhouse theory?
2. According to the authors, how does political decisionmaking on the environment get distorted?
3. What is the relationship, according to Shaw and Stroup, between economic and scientific progress and the ability to cope with potential disaster?

Jane S. Shaw and Richard L. Stroup, "Getting Warmer?" *National Review*, July 14, 1989, © 1989 by National Review, Inc., 150 E. 35th St., New York, NY 10016. Reprinted by permission.

Self-appointed guardians of the environment are urging immediate steps to reduce emissions of "greenhouse gases"—especially CO_2 [carbon dioxide], but also methane, nitrous oxides, and CFCs (chlorofluorocarbons), which are believed to trap heat radiating from the earth. They urge cutting back on fossil-fuel use by such measures as special taxes on carbon-dioxide emissions, increased funding for alternative energy sources, incentives for solar and nuclear power, an end to deforestation, and a doubling of the current fuel-efficiency standards.

Evidence Incomplete

Cutting back significantly on the use of fossil fuels would require great sacrifices. Is global warming a sufficiently pressing issue to justify such steps?

The case for a greenhouse effect is based on the fact that the amount of CO_2 in the atmosphere is indeed increasing. Studying gas trapped in glacial ice, scientists estimate that in the 1850s, at the start of the industrial revolution, the atmosphere had less than 290 parts of CO_2 per million parts of air; that has risen to over 340 ppm, an increase of about 20 per cent over some 135 years.

There is also evidence that global temperatures have been going up during the past century. [James] Hansen and his colleagues at NASA [National Aeronautics and Space Administration] believe that the average global temperature has increased by between 0.5° and 0.7° C. since 1860. And the six warmest years globally during the past century appear to have been in the 1980s, with 1988 the warmest.

But whether there is a connection between the two factors is highly debatable. Scientists aren't even sure the warming has occurred. Andrew R. Solow, a statistician at Woods Hole, points out that measured global temperatures are "not really global at all." Monitoring stations tend to be located on land rather than on oceans, where trends may be quite different, and more are in the Northern Hemisphere than in the Southern Hemisphere. Furthermore, some regions, including the contiguous United States, have not shown any observable warming during the past century. The Northern Hemisphere actually experienced a cooling period between the 1940s and the 1970s, which led to predictions in the 1970s that we might be headed for a new Ice Age. Some scientists are convinced that the recent warm years can be explained by a periodic weather perturbation known as El Niño.

Assuming, however, that the global warming trend is real, could CO_2 be the cause? If so, says Solow, we should be seeing much warmer temperatures than we have seen so far. "For example, for the planet to warm by 2°C. in the next hundred years, the average rate of warming would have to be four times greater than that in the historic record." Greenhouse warming is expected to be greatest at high latitudes and more rapid in the north than in the south, but this pattern hasn't appeared either, he says. . . .

Irrational Public Policy

Even so, most people probably believe the greenhouse effect has arrived. In January 1989, *The New York Times* airily dismissed a recent report that there was no warming in the U.S. during the last century. Any sign of the trend would be "hard to spot," explained *The Times*, and the uncertainty should not stand in the way of immediate action. ("The Greenhouse Effect Is for Real," read the editorial's headline.) In the U.S. and other Western democracies, public perceptions are critical to political outcomes. These perceptions are strongly influenced by the media, and they frequently differ from those of experts. The process has been substantiated by Stanley Rothman and S. Robert Lichter in a study published in *American Political Science Review*. They found that journalists are far more opposed to nuclear power than scientists who actually study nuclear issues, and that journalists more often quote the smaller group of scientists who are opposed to nuclear power. So, as *Science* editor Daniel Koshland put it, the government is "tilted to overreaction."

The Costs of Greenhouse Policies

In light of the uncertainty concerning the degree of global warming. . . it is very premature to propose policies that would restrict severely the burning of fossil fuels. Such policies, after all, would impose huge costs on all Americans and on American living standards and competitiveness. They would shut many American factories, throw great numbers out of work, and raise the cost of production and of fuel for every factory and household.

Kent Jeffreys, *The Heritage Foundation Executive Memorandum,* February 7, 1990.

Thus the stage is set for very strong measures to reduce emissions of greenhouse gases. These measures would give governments greater power, would force people to make large sacrifices, and would probably limit innovation. Yet such measures will be introduced as moderate, even conservative, steps—in the words of *The New York Times*, as "cheap insurance against risks of such magnitude."

Costly Measures

Yet any measures to remove CO_2 and other gases from the atmosphere will divert resources—land, labor, and capital—from other productive uses. The unintended consequences of mandatory action can be severe.

Take *The Times*'s recommendation to force Detroit to double the fuel efficiency of its cars. Such a requirement would result in many deaths. A study by Robert W. Crandall of the Brookings Institution and John D. Graham of the Harvard School of Public Health indicates that current fuel-efficiency standards are already causing deaths because automakers have had to lighten their cars, giving less protection in crashes. Crandall and Graham estimated that the congressionally established standards for 1989 models would have caused between 2,200 and 3,900 deaths. (The executive branch softened the standards a bit, so not quite that many people are dying.). . .

Then there was the multi-billion-dollar Synthetic Fuels Corporation that the U.S. Government set up in response to the energy crisis of the late 1970s to spur production from new energy sources such as gasified coal. With no assistance from the Corporation, the oil shortage turned into a worldwide glut; the Synfuels effort was simply wasted.

Playing Environmental Politics

In general, government policies in the environmental arena shift with the political winds and nurture special interests. For example, after World War II the Federal Government wished to encourage nuclear power; the Price-Anderson Act was passed, limiting owners' liability for nuclear accidents, which reduced the incentives for effective safety measures. Then, in the Sixties, anti-nuclear groups became politically powerful. This led to extensive regulation of nuclear utilities; costs became prohibitive and safety regulations became so complex that some analysts contend that they actually reduce safety.

Environmental policy often becomes a political tool of regional interests. The 1977 amendments to the Clean Air Act required that all electric utilities use scrubbers to eliminate sulphur-dioxide emissions—even if they could reduce emissions more effectively by just using low-sulphur coal. As Bruce Ackerman and W. T. Hassler show in *Clean Coal, Dirty Air*, the scrubber requirement saved the Appalachian coal-mine owners and unions from serious competition from low-sulphur Western coal.

If things are this bad on a national scale, what can we expect on a global scale? Negotiations over the past decade to establish a Law of the Sea Treaty illustrate the problem. Nations couldn't agree on how to develop seabed minerals; Third World governments demanded that an international authority be formed to collect fees that would be distributed to Third World nations. The U.S. opposed this demand and refused to sign the treaty. Similar conflicts are emerging with the effort to control CFCs. China has indicated it plans to increase its use of CFCs ten-fold by the year 2000.

Even modest familiarity with history adds to one's skepticism about taking immediate and drastic action to combat global warming. Over the centuries, competent, highly respected people have predicted timber shortages, worldwide famines, permanent energy crises, and critical mineral depletion. None of these predictions has materialized.

In 1865, the noted British economist William Jevons argued that industrial growth could not be continued for long because the world was running out of coal. He concluded that it was "inevitable that our present happy progressive condition is a thing of limited duration.". . .

In 1968 Paul Ehrlich wrote: "In the 1970s the world will undergo famines—hundreds of millions of people are going to starve to death." Fortunately, this did not prove correct, and increasing privatization of agriculture in the Third World has significantly increased food production.

Finally, what confidence can we have in the global-warming predictions when we note that less than 15 years ago the idea that another Ice Age was pending was popular enough for a book, *The Cooling*, to be written and to receive respectful scientific comment?

Don't Stop Progress

Nevertheless, the doomsayers could be right. The good news is that we probably have time to find out. Scientists are constantly accumulating information that brings them closer to understanding climatic sensitivity to greenhouse gases. As this knowledge emerges, a true consensus may develop that something should be done about the greenhouse effect.

But, since massive government solutions tend to be counterproductive, what should we do? As we learn more about the potential for global warming (or cooling), individuals will adapt their plans to defend their property, and to take advantage of the new conditions. If they are allowed to do this each in his own way, the results will be illuminating—whereas if individuals believe instead that the government will prevent the problem, then less will be tried and less will be learned. If the governments actually try and fail, then more serious dangers are likely.

The most effective thing that we can do to cope with global warming is to allow progress to continue. This is just the opposite of what Lester Brown, president of Worldwatch Institute, would like. He and two colleagues, Christopher Flavin and Sandra Postel, wrote that climate change "calls the whole notion of human progress into question" and urge that we take action "before it is too late." Yet Brown is flat wrong. Human progress is exactly what enabled people to cope with catastrophes in the past and it can continue to do so.

What countries can best handle the epidemic of AIDS?

Clearly, countries that have sophisticated medicine, extensive hospital facilities, and a population in generally good health will cope better than countries lacking even basic sanitation for much of their population. Similarly, political scientist Aaron Wildavsky points out that an earthquake in California in 1971 caused 62 deaths. The next year a slightly less powerful earthquake in Nicaragua killed tens of thousands. Why the difference? The wealthier country had better-built houses, better transportation and communication, better health facilities. Shouldn't we encourage such progress, rather than stop it in its tracks?

Chuck Asay by permission of the *Colorado Springs Gazette-Telegraph*.

In sum, mandatory steps to avert this potential disaster are the wrong way to go—especially in the near future, while scientific knowledge about global warming is seriously incomplete. As scientific understanding of the global atmosphere improves, our ability to make well-informed policy decisions should improve, too. Let's hope that those decisions take into account the resilience that comes from freedom and material progress.

Distinguishing Between Fact and Opinion

This activity is designed to help develop the basic thinking skill of distinguishing between fact and opinion. Consider the following statement: "Carbon dioxide levels are 15 percent higher now than they were in 1950." This statement is a fact which could be verified by checking scientific studies. But the statement, "It is very premature to severely restrict the burning of fossil fuels" is clearly an opinion. There is a debate whether the current understanding of global warming justifies a cutback in the use of fossil fuels.

When investigating controversial issues it is important to distinguish between statements of fact and statements of opinion. It is also important to recognize that not all statements of fact are true. They may appear to be true, but some are based on inaccurate or false information. For this activity, however, we are concerned with understanding the difference between those statements which appear to be factual and those which appear to be based primarily on opinion.

Most of the following statements are taken from the viewpoints in this chapter. Consider each statement carefully. *Mark O for any statement you believe is an opinion or interpretation of facts. Mark F for any statement you believe is a fact. Mark I for any statement you believe is impossible to judge.*

If you are doing this activity as a member of a class or group, compare your answers with those of other class or group members. Be able to defend your answers. You may discover that the reasons others present for their answers may give you valuable insights in distinguishing between fact and opinion.

O = opinion
F = fact
I = impossible to judge

1. Government policies on the environment shift with the political winds and nurture special interests.
2. A one-degree change in average global temperature would create another Little Ice Age in North America.
3. Humans affect the ecological balance of the world.
4. Plants grow better when the carbon dioxide content of the air around them is increased.
5. Most of the increase in greenhouse gases over the last one hundred years is the result of fossil fuel combustion.
6. Environmentalists are using the greenhouse effect to stop economic growth.
7. Some regions have not shown any observable warming during the past century.
8. Without the natural greenhouse effect, earth would be much colder than it is now.
9. It would be like cutting our own throats to halt the buildup of carbon dioxide in the atmosphere.
10. Individuals should be allowed to adapt to global warming as they see fit, without government intervention.
11. Mandatory steps to avert this potential disaster would be ineffective.
12. Our government's science and technology policy is guided by emotion-driven public opinion.
13. The increase in atmospheric carbon dioxide may well provide our only hope of feeding the peoples of the world without destroying the planet's ecosystems.
14. Major climate shifts have happened before, but over tens of centuries.
15. If politicians do not take action on the greenhouse effect immediately, the planet could suffer disastrous consequences.
16. Carbon dioxide traps heat in the lower atmosphere.
17. Continuing emissions of greenhouse gases will bring significant future warming.
18. If the greenhouse effect causes the sea level to rise, the impact on coastal cities would be enormous.
19. Every year, at least one-sixth of the U.S. experiences drought.
20. Energy conservation reduces emissions of greenhouse gases.

Periodical Bibliography

The following articles have been selected to supplement the diverse views presented in this chapter.

John A. Ahladas	"Global Warming—Fact or Science Fiction?" *Vital Speeches of the Day*, April 1, 1989.
Robert James Bidinotto	"What Is the Truth About Global Warming?" *Reader's Digest*, February 1990.
Betsy Carpenter	"A Faulty Greenhouse?" *U.S. News & World Report*, December 25, 1989/January 1, 1990.
Martin and Kathleen Feldstein	"Reduce Global Warming at Lowest Economic Cost," *Los Angeles Times*, July 8, 1990.
Al Gore Jr.	"To Skeptics on Global Warming. . .," *The New York Times*, April 22, 1990.
Jill Jager	"Priorities for Action," *Environment*, September 1988.
William Lanouette	"Global Warming: How Much and Why?" *The Bulletin of the Atomic Scientists*, April 1990.
Samuel W. Matthews	"Under the Sun," *National Geographic*, October 1990.
Michael E. Murphy	"What the Greenhouse Effect Portends," *America*, December 30, 1989.
Peter Nulty	"Global Warming: What We Know," *Fortune*, April 9, 1990.
Oliver S. Owen	"The Heat Is On," *The Futurist*, September/October 1989.
Ari Patrinos	"Greenhouse Effect: Should We *Really* Be Concerned?" *USA Today*, September 1990.
Dixy Lee Ray	"The Greenhouse Blues," *Policy Review*, Summer 1989. Available from The Heritage Foundation, 214 Massachusetts Ave. NE, Washington, DC 20002.
Elliot L. Richardson	"How to Fight Global Warming," *The New York Times*, February 7, 1990.
Stephen H. Schneider	"Cooling It," *World Monitor*, July 1990.
Andrew R. Solow	"Pseudo-Scientific Hot Air," *The New York Times*, December 28, 1988.
David A. Wirth	"Climate Chaos," *Foreign Policy*, Spring 1989.

Are Population Control Measures Needed to Protect Global Resources?

Chapter Preface

According to the Population Reference Bureau, an educational organization concerned with population issues, the earth's population in A.D. 1000 was probably no more than 345 million people. By 1989, there were fifteen times that number. The most startling growth has occurred in the twentieth century, with the population expanding rapidly from about 1.5 billion in 1900 to 5.2 billion in 1989.

This unprecedented population growth leads many experts to conclude that more and more people will continue to compete for fewer finite resources. They conclude that this competition will ultimately result in lower living standards for the world's population. As an example, these experts point to countries like Brazil, where significant population growth has resulted in the destruction of vast tracts of rain forest. People, seeking more land on which to live and cultivate food, began to slash and burn the forests. But when these forests are gone, some people predict, Brazil's poor will have few other resources to exploit. Thus Brazil's growing population will be left with meager resources to sustain it.

On the other hand, experts such as writer Karl Zinsmeister argue that the Brazil example is irrelevant. Zinsmeister blames resource depletion not on population, but on Third World countries' inefficient political systems and economies. Countries with strong, free-market economies and efficient governments can compensate for large populations, he maintains. As examples, economists point to countries such as Japan and the Netherlands, which are densely populated yet maintain high standards of living.

The viewpoints in the following chapter address the issues of population growth and what, if anything, should be done about it.

"If humanity fails to act, nature may end the
population explosion for us—*in very unpleasant
ways—well before 10 billion is reached."*

Population Growth Threatens Global Resources

Paul R. Ehrlich and Anne H. Ehrlich

Paul R. Ehrlich is Bing Professor of Population Studies at
Stanford University in Palo Alto, California, and a member of
the National Academy of Sciences. Anne H. Ehrlich is a senior
biology researcher at Stanford.
In the following viewpoint, the
authors predict that the world's population will reach ten billion
or more. Unless the world acts immediately to curb population
growth, the Ehrlichs contend, nature will curb population
through famine, disease, and the depletion of natural resources.

As you read, consider the following questions:

1. What do the authors see as being some of the negative effects
   of the population explosion on the earth and its inhabitants?
2. How do the authors respond to the theory that "there is no
   population problem, only a problem of distribution"?
3. Why do the Ehrlichs believe there are taboos against the
   discussion of the population crisis?

Excerpted, with permission, from "The Population Explosion: Why Isn't Everyone as Scared
as We Are?" by Paul R. Ehrlich and Anne H. Ehrlich, *The Amicus Journal,* Winter 1990.
Reprinted with permission.

In the early 1930s, when we were born, the world population was just 2 billion; now it is more than two and a half times as large and still growing rapidly. The population of the United States is increasing much more slowly than the world average, but it has more than doubled in only six decades—from 120 million in 1928 to 250 million in 1990. Such a huge population expansion within two or three generations can by itself account for a great many changes in the social and economic institutions of a society. It also is very frightening to those of us who spend our lives trying to keep track of the implications of the population explosion.

One of the toughest things for a population biologist to reconcile is the contrast between his or her recognition that civilization is in imminent serious jeopardy and the modest level of concern that population issues generate among the public and even among elected officials.

Much of the reason for this discrepancy lies in the slow development of the problem. People are not scared because they evolved biologically and culturally to respond to short-term "fires" and to tune out long-term "trends" over which they had no control. Only if we do what does not come naturally—if we determinedly focus on what seem to be gradual or nearly imperceptible changes—can the outlines of our predicament be perceived clearly enough to be frightening. . . .

Twentieth Century Trends

After an unhurried pace of growth over most of our history, expansion of the population accelerated during the Industrial Revolution and really shot up after 1950. Since mid-century, the human population has been growing at annual rates ranging from about 1.7 to 2.1 percent per year, doubling in forty years or less. Some groups have grown significantly faster; the population of the African nation of Kenya is estimated to be increasing by over 4 percent annually today—a rate that if continued would double the nation's population in only seventeen years. That rate *has* continued for over a decade now, and only recently has shown slight signs of slowing. Meanwhile, other nations, such as those of northern Europe, have grown much more slowly in recent decades.

But even the highest growth rates are still *slow-motion changes compared to events we easily notice and react to*. A car swerving at us on the highway is avoided by actions taking a few seconds. The Alaskan oil spill caused great public indignation, but faded from the media and the consciousness of most people in a few months. America's participation in World War II spanned less than four years. During the last four years, even Kenya's population grew by only about 16 percent—a change hardly perceptible locally, let alone from a distance. In four years, the world population expands only a little more than 7 percent. Who could notice that? Precipitous as the population explosion has been in historical terms, it is occurring at a snail's pace in an individual's perception. It is not an event, it is a trend that must be analyzed in order for its significance to be appreciated.

Bob Englehart/Copley News Series. Reprinted with permission.

The time it takes a population to double in size is a dramatic way to picture rates of population growth, one that most of us can understand more readily than percentage growth rates. Human populations have often grown in a pattern described as "exponential." Exponential growth occurs in bank accounts when interest is left to accumulate and itself earns interest. Exponential growth occurs in populations because children, the analogue of interest, remain in the population and themselves have children.

A key feature of exponential growth is that it often seems to start slowly and finish fast. A classic example used to illustrate this is the pond weed that doubles each day the amount of pond surface covered and is projected to cover the entire pond in thirty days. The question is, how much of the pond will be covered in twenty-nine days? The answer, of course, is that just half of the pond will be covered in twenty-nine days. The weed will then double once more and cover the entire pond the next day. As this example indicates, exponential growth contains the potential for big surprises.

The limits to human population growth are more difficult to perceive than those restricting the pond weed's growth. Nonetheless, like the pond weed, human populations grow in a pattern that is essentially exponential, so we must be alert to the treacherous properties of that sort of growth. The key point to remember is that *a long history of exponential growth in no way implies a long future of exponential growth.* What begins in slow motion may eventually overwhelm us in a flash.

The last decade or two has seen a slight slackening in the human population growth rate—a slackening that has been prematurely heralded as an "end to the population explosion." The slowdown has been only from a peak annual growth rate of perhaps 2.1 percent in the early 1960s to about 1.8 percent in 1990. To put this change in perspective, the population's doubling time has been extended from thirty-three years to thirty-nine. Indeed, the world population did double in the thirty-seven years from 1950 to 1987. But even if birth rates continue to fall, the world population will continue to expand (assuming that death rates don't rise), although at a slowly slackening rate, for about another century. Demographers think that growth will not end before the population has reached 10 billion or more.

So, even though birth rates have declined somewhat, *Homo sapiens* is a long way from ending its population explosion or avoiding its consequences. In fact, the biggest jump from 5 to 10 billion in well under a century, is still ahead. But this does not mean that growth couldn't be ended sooner, with a much smaller population size, if we—all of the world's nations—made up our minds to do it. The trouble is, many of the world's leaders and perhaps most of the world's people still do not believe that there are compelling reasons to do so. They are even less aware that if humanity fails to act, *nature may end the population explosion for us*—in very unpleasant ways—well before 10 billion is reached. . . .

Effects of Overpopulation

Global warming, acid rain, depletion of the ozone layer, vulnerability to epidemics, and exhaustion of soils and groundwater are all related to population size. They are also clear and present dangers to the persistence of civilization. Crop failures due to global warming alone might result in the premature deaths of a billion or more people in the next few decades, and the AIDS epidemic could slaughter hundreds of millions. Together these would constitute a harsh "population control" program provided by nature in the face of humanity's refusal to put into place a gentler program of its own.

We should not delude ourselves: the population explosion will come to an end before very long. The only remaining question is whether it will be halted through the humane method of birth control, or by nature wiping out the surplus. We realize that religious and cultural opposition to birth control exists throughout the world; but we believe that people simply do not understand the choice that such opposition implies. Today, anyone opposing birth control is unknowingly voting to have the human population size controlled by a massive increase in early deaths.

Of course, the environmental crisis is not caused just by expanding human numbers. Burgeoning consumption among the rich and increasing dependence on ecologically unsound technologies to supply that consumption also play major parts. This allows some environmentalists to dodge the population issue by emphasizing the problem of malign technologies. And social commentators can avoid commenting on the problem of too many people by focusing on the serious maldistribution of affluence.

Population a Major Factor

But scientists studying humanity's deepening predicament recognize that a major factor contributing to it is rapidly worsening overpopulation. The Club of Earth, a group whose members all belong to both the U.S. National Academy of Sciences and the American Academy of Arts and Sciences, released a statement in September 1988 that said in part:

> Arresting global population growth should be second in importance only to avoiding nuclear war on humanity's agenda. Overpopulation and rapid population growth are intimately connected with most aspects of the current human predicament, including rapid depletion of nonrenewable resources, deterioration of the environment (including rapid climate change), and increasing international tensions.

When three prestigious scientific organizations cosponsored an international scientific forum, "Global Change," in Washington in 1989, there was general agreement among the speakers that population growth was a substantial contributor toward prospective catastrophe. Newspaper coverage was limited, and while the population component was mentioned in *The New York Times*'s article, the point that population limitation will be essential to resolving the predicament was lost. The coverage of environmental issues in the media has been generally excellent in the last few years, but there is still a long way to go to get adequate coverage of the immediately connected population problem. . . .

Some environmentalists are taken in by the frequent assertion that "there is no population problem, only a problem of distribution." The statement is usually made in a context of a plan for conquering hunger, as if food shortage were the only consequence of overpopulation.

Food Shortages

But even in that narrow context, the assertion is wrong. Suppose food *were* distributed equally. If everyone in the world ate as Americans do, less than half the *present* world population could be fed on the record harvests of 1985 and 1986. Of course, everyone does not have to eat like Americans. About a third of the world grain harvest—the staples of the human feeding base—is fed to animals to produce eggs, milk, and meat for American-style diets. Would not feeding that grain directly to people solve the problem? If everyone were willing to eat an essentially vegetarian diet, that additional grain would allow perhaps a billion more people to be fed with 1986 production.

Would such radical changes solve the world food problem? Only in the *very* short term. The additional billion people are slated to be with us by the end of the century. Moreover, by the late 1980s, humanity already seemed to be encountering trouble maintaining the production levels of the mid-1980s, let alone keeping up with population growth. The world grain harvest in 1988 was some 10 percent *below* that of 1986. And there is little sign that the rich are about to give up eating animal products.

Prospects for the Future

While the causes of hunger are multiple—including poverty, imperfect distribution, and food shortages—most experts agree that unless population pressures ease, a lasting victory over food and hunger will not be seen. . . .

More people will be added to the world's population in the 1990s than in any previous decade. Avoiding a life-threatening food situation may depend on quickly slowing world population growth to bring it in line with food output. The only reasonable goal will be to try and cut population growth rates in half by the end of the century.

Zero Population Growth Fact Sheet, October 1989.

So there is no reasonable way that the hunger problem can be called "only" one of distribution, even though redistribution of food resources would greatly alleviate hunger today. Unfotunately, an important truth, that maldistribution is a cause of hunger now, has been as a way to avoid a more important truth—that overpopulation is critical today and may well make

103

the distribution question moot tomorrow. . . .

There is no more time to waste. Human inaction has already condemned hundreds of millions more people to premature deaths from hunger and disease. The population connection must be made in the public mind. Action to end the population explosion *humanely* and start a gradual population *decline* must become a top item on the human agenda: the human birthrate must be lowered to slightly below the human death rate as soon as possible. There still may be time to limit the scope of the impending catastrophe, but not *much* time.

A Clear Choice

Of course, if we do wake up and succeed in controlling population, that will still leave us with all the other thorny problems to solve. Limiting human numbers will not alone end warfare, environmental deterioration, poverty, racism, religious prejudice, or sexism; it will just buy us the opportunity to do so. As the old saying goes, whatever your cause, it is a lost cause without population control.

America and other rich nations have a clear choice today. They can continue to ignore the population problem and their own massive contributions to it. Then they will be trapped in a downward spiral that may well lead to the end of civilization in a few decades. More frequent droughts, more damaged crops and famines, more dying forests, more smog, more international conflicts, more epidemics, more gridlock, more drugs, more crime, will mark our course. It is a route already traveled by too many of our less fortunate fellow human beings.

Or we can change our collective minds and take the measures necessary to lower global birth rates dramatically. People can learn to treat growth as the cancer like disease it is and move toward a sustainable society. The rich can make helping the poor an urgent goal, instead of seeking more wealth and useless military advantage over one another. Then humanity might have a chance to manage all those other seemingly intractable problems. It is a challenging prospect, but at least it will give our species a shot at creating a decent future for itself. More immediately and concretely, taking action now will give our children and their children the possibility of decent lives.

"Research. . .has shown that much of the alleged harm from population growth has turned out to be nonexistent."

Population Growth Does Not Threaten Global Resources

Karl Zinsmeister

Karl Zinsmeister is a Washington-based writer and an adjunct fellow at the American Enterprise Institute, a research organization in Washington, D.C. In the following viewpoint, the author states that the population explosion theory is incorrect and that efforts to reduce global population have resulted in violence and the collapse of Third World governments. He maintains that well-organized societies view their people as valuable resources rather than "ecological nuisances."

As you read, consider the following questions:

1. What does the author believe are the reasons for the shift in the population debate during the 1980s?
2. What does Zinsmeister cite as some false claims regarding the negative impact of population growth?
3. Why does the author believe people are a valuable resource?

Karl Zinsmeister, "Supply-Side Demography." Reprinted with the permission of *The National Interest,* © Spring 1990, no. 19, *The National Interest,* Washington, D.C.

For more than two decades, population control groups have waged a powerful political and philosophical campaign to advance the proposition that a continued rise in human numbers is one of the world's gravest problems. Popular concern took root in 1968, when Professor Paul Ehrlich wrote a best-selling book in which he described population growth as a "bomb," and claimed that during the 1970s it would "explode," causing hundreds of millions of deaths, leading to war and violence, and destroying the planet's ability to support life.

An equally apocalyptic view was expressed five years later by Robert McNamara, then president of the World Bank:

> The greatest single obstacle to the economic and social advancement of the majority of the peoples in the underdeveloped world is rampant population growth. . . . The threat of unmanageable population pressures is very much like the threat of nuclear war. . . . Both threats can and will have catastrophic consequences unless they are dealt with rapidly.

A large international apparatus of population control groups has promoted the idea that we are in the midst of a runaway crisis. Population growth, these groups maintain, is a major cause of poverty, starvation, pollution, unemployment, and political tension today; extreme measures are called for. The United Nations and the World Bank have made population control a central part of their work. Public opinion has also been strongly influenced. Polls show that much of the public in the Western world believes mankind is darkly threatened by current population growth. Indeed, this view has become so strong that until very recently it was considered intellectual heresy to question it publicly.

But in the last few years that has begun to change as an expanding revisionist school of population studies has taken root. Research by economists, demographers, and social historians has shown that much of the alleged harm from population growth has turned out to be nonexistent and that population change has often been used as a scapegoat for problems that actually have other sources. Revisionists point out that it is not slowed population growth that brings social prosperity, but rather social prosperity that brings slower population rise. The result: A great, new population debate is now underway.

Three Reasons for Change in Thought

What brought about this turnaround? Why is it that the last decade's conventional wisdom has suddenly been called into question? Three reasons stand out.

First, there was the shock of reality itself. As new data on population growth and its effects came in over the last decade or so, it was clear that the dire predictions of the "population explosionists" had failed, and failed utterly, to come true. There were no population wars in the 1970s. There were famines but they were not population famines. The exponential growth and predicted calamities just didn't take place. On the contrary, there were many pleasant surprises.

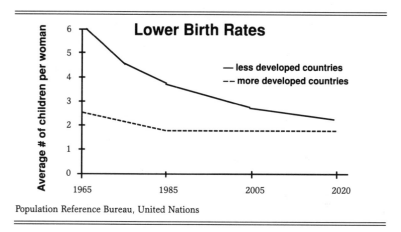

Lower Birth Rates

— less developed countries
-- more developed countries

Population Reference Bureau, United Nations

For instance, Paul Ehrlich wrote in 1968 that it was a "fantasy" to think that India—which he cites as a paradigm of overpopulation—could feed itself anytime in the near future, "if ever." One participant at the Second International Conference on the War on Hunger in 1968 argued that India's 1967-68 grain production of approximately 95 million tons represented the maximum possible level. Yet today India's annual grain production is over 150 million tons, and the country has become a net *exporter* of food. The fact that the quality of life has improved so markedly and so rapidly even in India—which, until recently, was referred to as an international "basket case"—suggests that those who argue that production can never keep up with growing numbers of people do not appreciate how quickly new technology and improved economic structures can convert formerly "redundant" people into productive resources.

Another fact the traditional population theorists did not fathom was how fast the world was changing demographically when they made their dire predictions. As recently as 1970, women of the less developed world were bearing an average of 6 children each. Today, that average is down to 3.7 children. When you consider that about 2.2 children would produce *stable* populations in the less developed countries (that is, each generation merely replacing its parents, with a small factor for childhood mortality, etc.) then this remarkable fact can be seen: *In just the last fifteen years or so, the less developed world moved three-fifths of the way toward a fertility rate that yields "zero population growth."*

107

So great was the change, it now appears, that the official United Nations' estimates of world population in the year 2000, put together at the end of the 1960s, will be more than 20 percent too high.

To be sure, it should be noted that the less developed countries did not all share equally in the fertility fall. Fertility in Asia dropped very rapidly, while in parts of Africa it has remained high. But, after all, it was in Asia (with 2.8 billion people, almost 60 percent of the world's total) that the population problem was supposed to be the worst. Africa, the partial exception to the worldwide downward fertility trend, is still a relatively sparsely inhabited continent with a total of 550 million residents and low overall population density, even excluding desert areas.

Standard of Living Improving

Another factual development often overlooked by population alarmists is that, contrary to popular claims, the standard of living in most of the Third World has been rapidly improving, not declining, during the last few decades—the very decades when population was growing fastest. The Third World infant mortality rate has fallen from 125 deaths per 1,000 births in 1960, to 69 in 1986; life expectancy at birth has risen incredibly—from 42 years to 61 years; adult literacy rates in the Third World doubled in 20 years; the number of physicians per 100,000 people went up 2.5 times; and the calorie supply per capita rose from just 87 percent of healthy daily requirements to 102 percent. The claim that rapid population growth vetoes social progress runs head-on into strong countervailing evidence from the last 25 years.

Human Rights Violations

The second major factor that led many to question the prevailing orthodoxy was the serious human rights violations that followed in the wake of the population control alarms of the 1960s and 1970s

In 1976 the Indian government declared, "Where a state legislature. . .decides that the time is ripe and it is necessary to pass legislation for compulsory sterilization, it may do so." In the six months following that ruling, over six million Indians were sterilized, many thousands forcibly. That episode inspired such fierce resistance among Indians that the government of Indira Gandhi was eventually brought down. . . .

An even more massive campaign of intimidation and violence in the name of population control has been, and to a considerable extent continues to be, conducted in China. In the early 1980s reports began to reach the West that the Chinese government was exerting enormous and often brutal pressure on couples to limit their family size to one child. . . .

In addition to the problem of making such fundamental decisions for people without their consent, there is a deeper philosophical issue. The argument is often made by advocates of state-dictated population control that the life of certain Asian or African or Latin American peasants is miserable, and that we who understand cannot allow them to perpetuate their misery. Population revisionists, on the other hand, start with the belief that there is dignity and potential in every human life, that even an existence considered deprived by modern standards can carry great meaning and pleasure. Population revisionists believe it is very dangerous to construct a generalized, systematic argument the bottom line of which is that humans are economic, social, and ecological nuisances—in short that people are a kind of pollution.

So, sharp changes in demographic conditions as well as worrisome human rights trends helped spark some of the new thinking on population. But probably even more important in reshaping the debate has been a third factor: the influence of new research and empirical analysis on the actual results of population growth. Over the last decade the prevailing shibboleths about alleged economic and social ill effects have been examined, one by one. Most of them have been found wanting.

For instance, it was claimed in the 1960s that the presence of children in a society would depress savings and investment. It was also argued that population growth would have major negative effects—slowing income growth, increasing unemployment, and deterring technological innovation. None of these assertions has proven true.

False Claims

When the population scare was in full bloom, it was claimed that population growth reduced educational attainment—which turned out to be absolutely false. Population rise was said to be responsible for the growth of Third World mega-cities. In truth, the rural to urban shift has been shown to spring primarily from other sources. It was asserted that population was the major cause of world hunger. But population level has had almost nothing to do with the famines of recent decades. Experts agree that those famines have been, almost without exception, the result of civil strife, of political and economic disruptions.

Through most of the 1970s those who saw population as a problem insisted that less was always better. After all, more people meant more mouths to feed, more feet to shoe, more schools to build. More people, in short, meant more trouble.

Plenty of activists still think that way. But many scientists have changed their minds, believing it is a mistake to talk of population as an undifferentiated global problem. What matters is not some abstract total number of people in existence, but where they are and how they are living. There are certain countries with ample population and others with too few people.

It does not matter to the people of Zaire—which suffers underdevelopment partly because in many parts of the country there are not enough people to support an efficient infrastructure —that there are 97 million people in Nigeria. Zaire has certain needs and Nigeria has certain needs, and it is nonsense to lump them together under the simple heading of "overpopulated Africa."

Related to this is another insight of the new demographic thinking: The number of people which a given area can "support" is subject to constant change, and is related to the way those people are economically and socially organized. There are 120 million people jammed onto the rocky islands of Japan. Yet, because of their well-structured and highly-productive society, they are among the richest and longest-lived people in the world. If you had asked the Algonquian Indians who inhabited the island of Manhattan in the 1700s how many people they thought it could support, they might have told you it was already full. Holland—which few people would describe as being unable to support its population—has a population density of 354 people per square kilometer; India, which we are told is one of the most overpopulated nations in the world today, contains 228 people per square kilometer.

There are many other such interesting contrasts. The United States is the richest nation in the world, and is sparsely populated with 25 people per square kilometer. West Germany is the second richest nation, and is densely populated—246 people per square kilometer. South Korea is even more densely populated— 409 citizens per square kilometer—yet it is also one of the fastest-growing countries on earth. A very slow growing and very poor nation is Bolivia—thinly populated with just 6 persons per square kilometer. The poorest nation in the world is Ethiopia. It is also one of the more sparsely populated—35 Ethiopians per square kilometer.

In other words, there are dozens of lightly populated countries that are poor, dirty, and hungry. And there are plenty of countries with large, dense populations that are prosperous and attractive. This is not to argue that density is an advantage, but rather that the number of people is not the critical variable in determining these things.

People Are a Valuable Resource

There is no such thing as a "proper" number of people—economic success can be achieved in both sparsely and densely populated countries. Revisionist demographers like to point out that each baby comes equipped not only with a mouth, but also with two hands and a brain. People not only consume, they produce—food, capital, even resources. The trick is to organize society so that each person will be an asset and not a burden. In a country whose economy is a mess even one additional baby can be an economic liability. But if the country is structured in such a way as to allow that child to labor and think creatively, he becomes an asset.

In short, people are a valuable resource. The fundamental insight of a diverse group of revisionist scholars—including Simon Kuznets, Colin Clark, P.T. Bauer, Ester Boserup, Albert Hirschman, Julian Simon, Richard Easterlin, and others—was in building up a body of thought that emphasizes the creative potential of individual humans and demonstrates their productive capacities when living in well-organized societies. Because these thinkers have emphasized production more than consumption, human supply more than human demand, their school might rightly be called "supply-side demography.". . .

Increased Population Benefits the World

It is time to abandon the Malthusian theorizing of the Ehrlichs for a theory that fits the facts: Growth of population and of income in capitalist states creates shortages, which make prices rise. A price increase represents an opportunity for entrepreneurs to seek new ways to satisfy the shortages, which in a free economy the entrepreneurs can pursue. Some fail, at cost to themselves. A few succeed. The final amazing result is that we end up *better off* than if the shortages had never arisen.

Julian L. Simon, *Fortune,* May 21, 1990.

It is now possible to leave behind the erroneous belief that population growth is a catastrophic, uncontrollable horror. The obvious, long-neglected truth is that in addition to consuming and making demands on society, people also produce. It is not governments, corporations, banks, or even natural resources that produce wealth, but people availed of efficient and open economic systems—witness the Japanese, the Swiss, the Taiwanese.

What prevents most developing countries from providing for their growing populations is not a lack of family planning programs or a paucity of physical resources or a shortage of Western aid. Rather it is a defective economy and government. Individuals concerned for the welfare of people in poor countries around the globe ought to focus not on raw numbers, but on the institutions that prevent citizens from exercising their creative and productive potential.

"Universal access to contraceptives and family planning services would have a dramatic impact on population growth."

Family Planning Programs Are Needed to Protect Global Resources

Zero Population Growth

Zero Population Growth (ZPG) is a national organization that works to achieve a sustainable balance between population, resources, and the environment throughout the world. In the following viewpoint, ZPG argues that overpopulation is largely responsible for the depletion of resources and pollution. An aggressive, worldwide family planning campaign would decrease the world's population and help conserve global resources.

As you read, consider the following questions:

1. Which nations do the authors believe are responsible for deforestation and land degradation?
2. How do the authors propose we achieve the limit of eight billion people in the world?
3. Why do the authors believe family planning efforts should not focus only on married females?

The ZPG Reporter, "Setting a Limit: The Higher the Population, the Fewer the Options," August 1990, © 1990 by Zero Population Growth, 1400 16th St. NW, Washington, DC, (202) 332-2200. Reprinted with permission.

Worrld population, currently at 5.3 billion, could stabilize at 8 billion by the year 2050. Or, if current trends continue, global numbers will continue to grow, and population could nearly triple to 14 billion. *That difference of 6 billion people is more than the total world population today!*

These alternative population scenarios imply vastly different prospects for the Earth. The impact of our present numbers has already been enough to threaten rainforests, hasten wildlife extinction, erode millions of acres of farmland, deplete the ozone layer, initiate water and food shortages, and begin a global warming whose full consequences cannot yet be determined.

Global Problem

At present, the populations of industrialized countries are responsible for the largest proportion of resources consumed and waste produced. These are the nations overwhelmingly responsible for damage to the ozone layer and acidification, as well as for about two-thirds of global warming.

At the same time, in developing countries the combination of poverty and population growth is resulting in massive deforestation and land degradation. Furthermore, as developing nations increase their share of industrial production and consumption, their share of pollution is also rising, and will continue to rise.

"The world's ability to control its numbers will determine whether the pace of environmental degradation speeds up or slows down" says Susan Weber, executive director of ZPG. "Ultimately, our success or failure will determine the quality of lives of present and future generations."

For example, in terms of per capita greenhouse gas emissions 35 years from now, the low projection of 8 billion would yield about 25 percent less total emissions than the high projection. *This would hove as much impact on carbon dioxide emissions as eliminating deforestation entirely.*

Similarly, less land would be required to provide housing, roads, food and so on.

And in Africa—where the difference between the U.N. [United Nations] high and low projections is equal to the size of its current population—increased impact on the continent's fragile environment and stressed wildlife could spell the difference between survival and extinction.

Even where technological improvements are possible, population growth will still have an enormous impact. The Chinese government, for instance, has declared its ambition that there should be a refrigerator in every home by the turn of the century. But most of those fridges are likely to be produced using old, CFC [chlorofluorocarbon]-reliant technology—a major contributor to global warming and ozone depletion.

ZPG has launched an aggressive public information and advocacy campaign that urges adoption of a national and international goal to stop world population growth before it reaches 8 billion. If the countries of the world are willing to provide the leadership and commit the right resources, it can be done.

A Lack of Resources

The biggest frustration for [family planning] advocates is that, after years of resistance to such planning, a majority of third-world governments now welcome it—but resources are not there.

AID [Agency for International Development], for example, will have more than 100 million fewer condoms than it needs to meet demand. . . . If current demand for family planning of all types were met, there would be 35 percent fewer births in Latin America, 33 percent fewer in Asia, and 27 percent fewer in Africa.

If $2 billion more were dedicated each year to family planning, birth control use would rise from 465 million couples today to 730 million in the year 2000 to 1.2 billion by the year 2025. Currently, 45 percent of all fertile couples use birth control.

Linda Feldmann, *The Christian Science Monitor*, May 17, 1989.

For instance, the U.N. estimates that to achieve its low population projection for the world, the total fertility rate in developing countries would have to drop by 2.2 children per woman in the next 35 years.

Yet, several nations such as China, Cuba and the Republic of Korea, have achieved such declines in less than half that time.

According to Family Health International, family size in many developing countries has decreased faster than it has in the United States. While it took 58 years for the average American family size to shrink from 6 to 3.5 children (1842-1900), it took only 23 years to accomplish the same transition in Indonesia (1961-1984) and only eight years in Thailand (1969-1977).

East Asia's advances have been most spectacular. Contraceptive usage rose from 13 percent in 1960-65 to around 74 percent today—higher than the developed country average. A corresponding reduction in birth rates also took place.

The future success or failure of population programs in certain areas will have a sizeable impact on global numbers. The most explosive growth is expected to occur in Africa and south Asia, for instance. And about one-third of the difference between the U.N.'s high and low projections for the entire world is contributed by the world's two largest countries—China and India.

Universal access to contraceptives and family planning services would have a dramatic impact on population growth. If this could be achieved by the turn of the century, it is estimated that the number of contraceptive users in developing countries would rise from 45 percent today to about 75 percent.

As soon as possible, nations need to meet *existing demand*, that is to make sure that everyone who at present wants effective contraception can get it easily. The World Fertility Survey, carried out between 1974 and 1984, revealed a striking need for contraception and family planning programs. In Africa, for example, 77 percent of married women who want no more children are not using contraception.

The U.N. has calculated that if all women who said they wanted no more children were able to stop childbearing, the number of births would be reduced by 27 percent in Africa, 33 percent in Asia, and 35 percent in Latin America.

Nations also need to work to increase the *level of demand*. Most family planning programs have focused on married women. But demand for family planning can be increased by reaching new and neglected groups, especially teenagers. Not reaching these young people could have tragic consequences not only for efforts to slow population growth, but also for the future quality of life for millions of young women. It has been estimated that 40 percent of all 14-year-old girls alive today will have been pregnant at least once by the time they are 20.

Increasing contraception options is another important aspect of improving access and choice in family planning programs. According to the U.N., adding one extra method to the mix available can increase contraceptive use by 6 percent.

Currently, the most popular method worldwide is sterilization, followed in popularity by the IUD and then the pill. Existing methods are very diverse in their effectiveness, risks and side-effects. Methods also differ in convenience and cultural acceptability.

Options Decreasing

Unfortunately, contraceptive options are diminishing. In the 1970s, some 13 companies—eight of them American—were researching and developing new contraceptives. But the threat of lawsuits, tighter controls on testing, and pressure from anti-abortion extremists took their toll. Now only one major U.S. drug-manufacturing company, Ortho Pharmaceutical Corp., and two European companies remain active in the field. The leading role has been assumed by the World Health Organization and by non-profit organizations such as the Population Council and Family Health International.

At the same time that family planning services are expanded, improving women's health, education and status can help secure population goals. Reducing infant mortality has the effect of stimulating interest in reducing family size. And education opens up new horizons for women, beyond the traditional roles of childbearers. The more educated a woman, the higher the level of contraceptive use, and the smaller the chosen family size.

The greatest effect occurs when women have seven years or more of education. These women have, on average, 2.2 less children each than those who have had no education at all. There is a great deal to be done in female education. Women make up almost two-thirds of the illiterate adults in developing countries.

Making the Commitment

As the number of reproductive age couples in developing countries will grow by about 18 million a year over the next decade, just to maintain the present level of contraceptive use will demand greater funding.

In order to achieve 75 percent contraceptive use worldwide by the next decade, annual expenditures on family planning for couples in developing countries will need to more than triple to about $10.5 billion.

Overpopulation Affects Everyone

The demand for family planning services has grown dramatically. For example, several sub-Saharan countries, where birth rates are the highest in the world, are trying to limit population increase. Unfortunately, they don't have the resources to do the job. . . .

The United States can't isolate itself from the world population crisis. Pollution respects no national borders. The misery caused by too many mouths to feed challenges our moral principles. The political and economic problems brought by resource depletion and the need of governments to control unruly citizens threaten international stability and prosperity.

Mary Morain, *The Humanist,* March/April 1989.

Funding increases in health and education would help maximize the success of family planning programs. The Worldwatch Institute reports that to provide elementary education for the estimated 120 million school-age children not now in school would cost about $6 billion per year. And to immunize the 55 percent of the world's children not now protected from diphtheria, polio, tuberculosis and measles would cost roughly $2 billion a year.

Where will the money come from? With few exceptions family planning has never commanded more than a small proportion of government budgets in developing countries. In the 1980s it accounted for shares ranging from 0.04 percent in

Singapore to 3.1 percent in Bangladesh. Still, 80 percent of the $3.2 billion spent on family planning comes from developing countries themselves.

Like all sound investments, it shows benefits over time. Countries like the Republic of Korea, Malaysia and Thailand, which have invested heavily in health and education since the 1960s, have attracted foreign investment and experienced faster economic growth. Improvements in health, education and family planning reduce population growth and reduce the future cost of schooling and health services.

Foreign Donors

While developing countries (governments and consumers) can and should spend more on family planning, the largest increases are needed in assistance from foreign donors. In recent years, with the exception of Japan, industrialized nations have decreased their level of financial assistance for family planning programs in developing nations. Currently, the United States and other industrialized nations combined spend less money annually to help deliver family planning services to the developing world than U.S. consumers spend each year on Halloween costumes!

The United States and other industrialized nations can do much to help. In an era of decreasing superpower tension, military expenditure is a potential source of funds. The U.S. annual military budget totals about $300 billion. A 10 percent cut in the U.S. arms budget alone would yield $30 billion.

But money alone will not be enough to meet the challenges of the 1990s. "Political leadership and individual commitment, particularly from the United States, is imperative," says Weber. Noting preliminary reports that show the U.S. total fertility rate is the highest it has been in two decades, she adds: "How can we ask the developing nations to support aggressive population programs when our own numbers continue to rise?"

117

"Family planning programs in and of themselves have not had a dramatic impact on reducing fertility."

Family Planning Programs Alone Are Ineffective

Frances Moore Lappé and Rachel Schurman

Frances Moore Lappé is the author of the book *Diet for a Small Planet*, and one of the founders of The Institute for Food and Development Policy (also known as Food First), a research and education center that investigates the root causes of hunger. Rachel Schurman, a former research assistant at Food First, is a graduate student at the University of Wisconsin in Madison. Lappé and Schurman have coauthored other works including *Betraying the National Interest*. The following viewpoint has been taken from their book, *The Missing Piece in the Population Puzzle*. In it, the authors reject the notion that widespread hunger is caused by population growth and emphasize the need to combine family planning programs with economic and political reform.

As you read, consider the following questions:

1. What do the authors believe is the problem with programs that promote family planning as an alternative to social change?
2. Under what circumstances do the authors think family planning programs are effective in Third World countries?
3. What social changes do Lappé and Schurman say need to occur before overpopulation and poverty can be relieved?

Frances Moore Lappé and Rachel Schurman, "Taking Population Seriously," *Food First Development Report No. 4*, September 1988. Copyright © 1988 The Institute for Food and Development Policy. Reprinted with permission.

The promotion of family planning programs in the third world sounds beneficent. Indeed, we have stressed all along that access to birth control is essential both to the empowerment of women and reducing birth rates. But we observe a critical difference between those family planning programs developed as part of an overall attack on the social forces keeping birth rates high and, by contrast, programs that promote family planning as an *alternative* to *social change*.

It is this later approach that we find both ethically questionable and self-defeating. Once the social roots of high fertility are deemed impossible to address and fewer births becomes *the* goal, noble ends get sacrificed to dubious means. Many women are hurt in the process, and ultimately even the end itself—halting population growth—is unattainable. . . .

The argument that it is not possible to address the social conditions leading to high birth rates, but that it is possible to reduce growth rates anyway, starts with evidence of unmet demand for contraception. Those focusing on family planning cite data showing that in many third world countries almost half of all women of child-bearing age want no more children but lack access to birth control. Fertility rates would drop by a third if we could just meet this unmet need, they claim.

This argument entails a big assumption: without altering social conditions—especially the powerlessness of women vis-à-vis men and the meager access of the poor to security resources—women will in fact be able to *act* on their stated desire for fewer children. But might many women indeed declare their preference for fewer children yet lack the power to act on their preference—*even if* the technical means of birth control were available? In other words, to believe that the mere provision of contraception will suddenly allow women to step out of their subordinate role in the family, or alter the fact that children still represent a source of security for many third world parents, is to ignore the findings of decades of fertility-oriented research.

Moreover, if unmet demand were truly as great as it is assumed, why, we ask, have population planners had to resort to incentives and disincentives? In some cases, downright coercion has been deemed necessary to get people to accept birth control, suggesting that people must be made to override their own judgments about their need for children. . . .

How Far Can Birth Control Alone Take Us?

Even if population control advocates are willing to ignore the wealth of evidence showing why fertility rates remain high and plunge ahead with ever more intrusive and coercive methods of family planning, we ask, what will this buy the third world country or the world community? Are birth rates likely to fall to replacement levels, and if so, what is the price—the ethical and human costs—we must pay?

First, how much are birth rates likely to drop in the absence of other changes leading to more democratic power structures?

A number of demographers have sought to isolate the impact of family planning programs on fertility, independent of what we would consider key indicators of poor peoples' relative power, i.e., literacy and educational levels, life expectancy, and infant mortality rates. But virtually all have run into a similar snag: family planning programs and these social realities are almost nowhere independent. . . .

Family Planning Alone Is Not the Answer

Are family-planning programs the answer to halting population growth before world-population size reaches projected levels? Clearly, they are not. Family planning means only that couples have the right freely to choose the number and spacing of their children. While easy access to contraceptive services is important as a means of complementing other measures designed to lower fertility, recent studies have shown that family-planning programs alone have only a marginal effect on reducing fertility.

Donald Mann, *The New York Times,* May 9, 1985.

In fact, the main conclusion of most of these studies is that while family planning programs do have some effect on fertility over and above improvements in social and economic conditions, the two work best together. "Countries that rank well on socioeconomic variables and also make substantial [family planning] program effort," write the authors of a widely respected study on this issue, "have on average much more fertility decline than do countries that have one or the other, and far more than those with neither." They also note that for countries at the bottom of the socioeconomic scale, the probable impact on contraceptive use of simply adopting a family planning program would be slight. . . .

While a number of poor countries have achieved major reductions in fertility without significantly improving the security of the majority of citizens—Thailand, Indonesia, and Mexico being three examples—none has come close to halting population growth. Nor is there much likelihood, given current trends, that they can do so in the near future. In fact, among low-income countries, aside from some small island populations, only China and Cuba have reached or nearly reached an annual increase as low as 1 percent. China has had a government-sponsored family program for some time; Cuba has not. The Cuban government provides contraceptives, including abortion, through its free health care system, but has never undertaken an organized family planning campaign. However, both countries have addressed the structural roots of insecurity and opened opportunities to women outside the home.

Highlighting the fact that family planning programs *in and of themselves* have not had a dramatic impact on reducing fertility does not mean that we belittle their value. Making contraceptives widely available and helping to reduce inhibitions against their use are critical to the goal of greater human freedom—especially the freedom of women—as well as essential to halting population growth.

Can Reducing Population Growth Alleviate Hunger?

The power-structures analysis poses one additional question to those advocating family planning as a means of enhancing human well-being and alleviating stress on the environment: Can reducing births reduce poverty, hunger, and environmental degradation? Since rapid population growth is not the cause of these closely intertwined problems, we doubt that simply slowing growth can alleviate them.

Consider a few of the countries that have managed to reduce birth rates without significantly redistributing access to survival resources—land, jobs, and health care.

In Mexico, for example, despite a 37 percent decline in fertility rates since 1960, there is little evidence that the people are any less hungry. Data on malnutrition indicate that fully a fifth of all Mexicans are malnourished, with the estimates ranging as high as 40 to 60 percent for children under four in Mexico's rural areas.

The estimates refer to the late 1970s—well *after* Mexico's fertility decline was underway and at a time when the country was still experiencing an economic boom from oil exports. The economic crisis of the 1980s has made life harder for many Mexicans and falling fertility has provided no measurable relief for Mexico's poor.

Thailand's experience is similar. In part because of an effective family planning program, Thailand's fertility rates have been cut in half since 1960. But according to a 1984 survey conducted by the Thai Ministry of Health, over half of all children under five suffer from malnutrition—equivalent to 3.3 million children. Malnutrition has been increasing despite both lowered birth rates and improved agricultural production. Thailand is not only a major net exporter of rice, the country's main staple food, but of meat, corn, cassava, beans, sugar cane, and many fruits and vegetables, all of which could be used for domestic consumption. Most of Thailand's hunger results from highly skewed farmland ownership, especially in the central plain, where land is most productive.

India is yet another example. India's fertility rates—while still comparatively high—have declined 32 percent in twenty-five years. Yet is the Indian population any better fed? Despite the country's dramatic economic and industrial development of the last several decades, the majority of the population has not benefited economically. Nearly half the population lacks the income necessary to buy a nutritious diet. Its own people's widespread hunger notwithstanding, India actually exports food; in 1984, its net agricultural exports were worth almost $1 billion. It could be argued, of course, that without a slowdown in population growth in such countries, the poor majorities would be still worse off. Even more people would be going hungry, and more families would be without jobs or land.

Not Just a Matter of Biology

"Overpopulation" is as much a technological and political question as it is a matter of biology. Social inequality, for example, is an insidious factor deserving of more attention by serious ecologists and animal defenders. Around the world today, fast population growth, coupled with much animal killing, poaching, and wanton habitat destruction occurs as a result of desperate poverty and chronic unemployment afflicting most of the population—a phenomenon liberation theologians have dubbed the "marginalization of peoples." In the affluent world, on the other hand, a measure of population stability has been achieved, but there the prevailing mode of consumption, production, and waste disposal can't be indulged much longer without irreversible damage to the biosphere.

Patrice Greanville, *The Animals' Agenda*, December 1988.

Stepping back for a minute to consider the deeper implications of this argument—that all we can do is to reduce the rate of population growth today so things won't be worse for even more people tomorrow—we see that it leads to an untenable moral stance. Can we ethically claim success if we hold the number of hungry people in the world to 700 million? Obviously not. The moral imperative is clear. We cannot let ourselves get sidetracked from addressing the undemocratic power structures that give rise to the problems of poverty, environmental destruction, and population growth by "solutions" which *at best* can only limit the numbers hurt. . . .

An alternative approach to solutions flows from what we have called the power-structures perspective on the population problem.

In this perspective, rapid population growth is a *moral* crisis because it reflects the widespread denial of essential human rights to survival resources—land, food, jobs—and the means to prevent pregnancy. A power-structures perspective therefore holds that far-reaching economic and political change is necessary to reduce birth rates to replacement levels. Such change must enhance the power of the poorest members of society, removing their need to cope with economic insecurity by giving birth to many children. Social arrangements beyond the family—jobs, health care, old-age security, and education (especially for women)—must offer both security and opportunity.

The Need for Education

In this process, education is key to opportunity. As the opportunity for primary and secondary education becomes more widespread, taking children away from family support activities, the immediate economic value of children to the family will diminish.

Second, the power of women must be augmented through expanded opportunities for both men and women.

Third, limiting births must become a viable option by making *safe and acceptable* birth control devices universally available.

Family planning cannot by itself reduce population growth, though it can speed a decline; it best contributes to a demographic transition when integrated into village- and neighborhood-based health systems that offer birth control to expand human freedom rather than to control behavior.

"United Nations officials believe [population control programs and goals] are absolutely essential to maintain the habitability of the planet."

International Population Control Programs Are Necessary

Don Hinrichsen

Don Hinrichsen is a contributing editor of *The Amicus Journal* which is published quarterly by the New York City-based Natural Resources Defense Council, an organization concerned with national and international environmental policies. In the following viewpoint, Hinrichsen argues that global resources are being depleted by population growth. He believes that the earth's limited resources necessitate ambitious international population control programs to curb this growth.

As you read, consider the following questions:
1. According to the author, how has urban crowding affected Third World cities?
2. What does Hinrichsen cite as some examples of land overuse and mismanagement?
3. Why does the author believe large families are a common occurrence in Africa and the Middle East?

Don Hinrichsen, "The Decisive Decade: What We Can Do About Population," *The Amicus Journal*, Winter 1990.

Former West German Chancellor Willy Brandt, in a keynote address to the International Forum on Population in the Twenty-first Century held in Amsterdam in November 1989, referred to the decade of the 1980s as, "a lost decade for development cooperation." In assessing the failures of the past, Brandt suggested that the role played by the multilateral agencies of the United Nations and other international organizations be strengthened by joining forces to address the critical developmental, population, and environmental issues facing Africa, Latin America, and Asia. "We need capable international and regional organizations for a broad surveillance of the performance of national governments, regardless of their power status," Brandt told the assembled delegates from over eighty countries. "We probably need something like a security council for the global environment and population matters."

A few years ago, talk like this would have drawn yawns from policy makers from north and south alike. No longer. If the indecisive 1980s were the "lost decade," the 1990s promises to be the decade for decision and action.

"What we do over the course of the next decade will determine the future of our planet," insists Nafis Sadik, executive director of the United Nations Population Fund (UNFPA) in New York. "Governments have started to recognize this. They have started to see that these great increases in population are reducing their ability to respond effectively to the crisis of resources."

Brandt and Sadik, amongst a chorus of others, consider the next ten years to be absolutely critical—a decade during which the global community must confront the challenges of population growth and distribution, urbanization, resource use, and environmental deterioration on a broad scale. Decisions postponed and actions not taken during this period will have devastating consequences for the generations of the twenty-first century.

The Need for Planning

Sadik, a former medical doctor from Pakistan, who has been with UNFPA for nearly twenty years, is convinced that nothing short of integrated planning on both a national and international level will get effective results in time to make a difference. "We (the UN) need to begin strategic, integrated planning of our own programs, but governments must be encouraged to do the same," she affirms.

Numbers may be numbing, but the arithmetic of population growth and the urban explosion can no longer be ignored. There is no doubt that the human ark is bulging at the seams. Every day we share the earth and its resources with 250,000 more people than the day before. Every year there are another 90 million mouths to feed. That is the equivalent of adding a city the size of Philadelphia to the world population every week; a Los Angeles every two weeks; a Mexico every year; and a United States and Canada every three years.

Urban Growth

Along with population growth has come urban crowding. The doyens of demographics at the UN estimates that by the year 2000, 75 percent of Latin America's population will be urbanized, along with 42 percent of Africa's, and 37 percent of Asia's. Unlike cities in the industrialized North, Third World cities are experiencing explosive growth. Mexico City, crammed with close to 19 million people, is expected to have 25 million by the turn of the century. Already its air is so polluted that breathing it is the equivalent of smoking two packs of cigarettes a day!

Though fertility rates are dropping, the sheer momentum of population growth ensures that at least another 3 billion people will be crowded onto the planet between now and the year 2025. At current growth rates, 1 billion people are added to the ark every eleven years.

If these trends are not reversed or at least slowed down, we could be facing a global population of close to 14 billion by the year 2100. But the problem is not population growth *per se.* "The problem is that over 90 percent of the people being born now live in the developing world, those countries least able to cope with the resource and environmental consequences of burgeoning populations," points out Alex Marshall, deputy director of information at the United Nations Population Fund. A simple comparison shows the dichotomy. Between now and the turn of the century, the population of industrialized countries will grow by only 56 million, or 5.2 percent, while that of the Third World will [grow] to over 900 million, a staggering 25 percent increase.

Unfortunately, many of the people born over the course of the next few decades in the Third World will find themselves at the bottom of the heap, locked into grinding poverty with little hope of escape. The number of households living in what writer Erik Eckholm calls the "global underclass" is expected to reach nearly 1 billion by the year 2000, more than double the number of absolute poor recorded in 1975.

Much of the damage inflicted on the developing world's environment comes from the bottom billion poorest people, forced by poverty and sheer weight of numbers to over-exploit limited resources. But the top billion richest also contribute their share to the destruction through "indirect" consumer preferences. The Japanese wood chip industry in Indonesia, for example, clears more mangrove trees than poor fisherfolk who cut them down to build fish and shrimp ponds. Much of the wood hauled out of tropical forests ends up as furniture, paneling, and veneer in rich world homes.

Land Abuse

Globally, we are losing a minimum of 15 million acres of prime agricultural land to overuse and mismanagement every year. Desertification is threatening about one-third of the world's land surface, or 16 million square miles. Tropical rain forests, repositories of immense biological wealth, are being destroyed at the rate of 25 million acres a year, an area roughly the size of Austria. Through a combination of ignorance, greed, and neglect, we may be condemning several million species of plants and animals to the awful finality of extinction by the turn of the century. To complicate matters, there are holes in our ozone shield, and climate change on a global scale threatens to alter rainfall patterns and raise sea levels.

Although resource and environmental issues affect every country, runaway population growth is almost exclusively a developing world problem. The "population transition" has been made in the highly developed countries of Europe, Asia, and

North America. Populations in Europe and North America, for example, have stabilized and are growing on average by only 1 to 2 percent a year.

Much of the Third World, however, has yet to make this critical transition—from rapid population growth rates to sustainable ones. In many developing countries, particularly in Africa and the Middle East, growth rates hover around 3 percent a year, doubling their populations every twenty-three years.

Large Families

One of the reasons for continued high population growth rates is that the average woman in Africa and the Middle East bears between six and eight children during her reproductive years. Children are seen as assets, not liabilities. Large families are culturally acceptable and socially desirable. In some countries, like Senegal, nine children per woman is the norm. Compare this against a global average of slightly more than four children per woman; in industrialized countries it is only two. High population growth rates aggravate poverty and impede economic development. As human numbers continue to outpace needs, Third World countries cannot cope with the consequences. The results are only too evident: mounting unemployment; spreading slums and squatter settlements; lack of access to clean water and sanitation facilities; not enough school rooms; too few doctors, nurses, teachers, and other skilled professionals; and no (or very limited) access to family planning services. Poverty deepens. More people are pushed to the edge of survival.

Examples

Take Kenya as an example. Population growth in this East African country is running at 4 percent a year, enough to double its population every seventeen years. One of the results of such explosive growth is increasing pressure on land. The best land in Kenya has already been subdivided again and again, as rural families have expanded. The average amount of land per person has fallen from about one acre in 1969 to less than half an acre today. Increasingly, poor farmers are forced to till marginal land, which swiftly deteriorates without expensive doses of fertilizers and pesticides.

In drought-prone and water-short sub-Saharan Africa, poor soils wear out quickly. Collapsing rural economies coupled to population pressures continue to push millions of poor, subsistence farmers off the land and into urban squatter settlements and slums. Kenya's capital, Nairobi, grew 600 percent between 1950 and 1979. Most of the new arrivals end their days in squalid shanty towns and squatter settlements, like Kibera, which ring the city in a widening belt of misery.

Although growth rates in Asia and Latin America are beginning to slow down as population programs and family planning services take root, the crisis is far from over. In the crowded countries of China, India, Bangladesh, Indonesia, and the Philippines, human numbers are already bumping into resources limitations. Consider the Philippines. Most poor Filipinos were better off a decade ago than they are today. Nearly half of the entire population—about 29 million—live at or below the poverty line. Pressure on the country's coastlines is so intense that fish stocks have plummeted in many areas. In the drive for economic development and export income, tropical forests and mangrove swamps have been reduced to a pathetic remnant of their former acreage.

Youthfulness of the Population

Getting out of poverty and indebtedness is made more difficult by the youthfulness of Third World populations. According to the United Nations Population Fund, in 1985 around 37 percent of the total population in the developing world—1.3 billion—were children below the age of fifteen. In Africa, where fertility has remained markedly high, children make up nearly 50 percent of the population. This many dependents puts added strain on creaky economies.

But in the final analysis, it is lack of access to family planning and health services that really makes a big difference in individual family size. The World Fertility Survey, carried out in forty-one developing countries between 1972 and 1984, revealed a striking unmet need for contraception and family planning. If all women who said they wanted no more children were able to stop childbearing, the number of births would be reduced by 27 percent in Africa, 33 percent in Asia, and 35 percent in Latin America. These figures imply a cruelly inadequate supply of contraception to women who want it, and that there is a growing need for family planning services.

Given the severity of the population crisis and all its environmental ramifications, the United Nations Population Fund, along with international non-governmental organizations, such as the International Union for Conservation of Nature and Natural Resources (IUCN), are spearheading a renewed effort to put population and resource issues squarely on national and international development agendas during the "decisive decade" of the 1990s.

The UNFPA-sponsored International Forum on Population in the Twenty-first Century, hosted by the Netherlands' ministry of foreign affairs, was an attempt to bring these interrelated problems to the attention of policy makers and politicians in both the developed and developing worlds.

"This conference differed from all previous international meetings on population by setting specific targets to be met within a specific period of time," observed Dr. Sadik. There was an unusual sense of accord as the forum ended; a stark contrast to many such gatherings which are often remembered more for what they don't accomplish than for what they do.

Multilateral Approach

Foremost in the restoration of U.S. leadership must be the refunding of the United Nations Population Fund, the largest multilateral provider of family planning services. Multilateralism is the way to resolve many of the world's problems. It is now incontrovertible that the multilateral approach has become an indispensable way of running the affairs of the planet.

Werner Fornos, *The Humanist*, May/June 1990.

In order to keep population growth to 6.2 billion by the year 2000 and to no more than 10.5 billion by the end of next century—rates considered sustainable given the earth's finite resources—the forum urged the following specific targets be met by the end of this decade:
• Adopt integrated population, environment, and natural resource management policies;
• Increase the number of couples using contraception from the current 326 million to 535 million;
• Make every effort to increase current spending on population programs from $3.5 billion to $9 billion;
• Strive to improve the status of women throughout all spheres of life;
• Ensure that couples and individuals are guaranteed their basic human right to decide freely and responsibly the number and spacing of children;
• Increase the quality, effectiveness and outreach of national population programs. . . .
Ambitious as those goals seem, UN officials believe they are absolutely essential to maintain the habitability of the planet. The nine billion dollars needed may sound like a vast amount, but says Sadik, "we consider it a modest sum. It would still be only 3 to 4 percent of total development assistance, as opposed to 1.2 percent today." Increasingly, developing countries, especially those with rapid population growth rates, are beginning to get the message—that investments in population programs, linked to resource development plans, contribute to the safety and security of the nation itself and reinforce development efforts in other related areas.

"The World Bank and the International Monetary Fund are engaged in a full-scale attack on the Third World's poor people."

International Population Control Programs Are Harmful

Betsy Hartmann

Betsy Hartmann is director of the Population and Development Program at Hampshire College in Amherst, Massachusetts. She is the author of *Reproductive Rights and Wrongs: The Global Politics of Population Control and Contraceptive Choice,* as well as other works. In the following viewpoint, Hartmann asserts that international population control programs have done great harm to the world's poor because such programs use high-pressure, coercive techniques that undermine basic health services. Hartmann states that population control programs do not address the unequal distribution and scarcity of resources which are the cause of much of the world's poverty.

As you read, consider the following questions:

1. What does the author believe are the two main problems with forcing down birth rates in the Third World through population control programs?
2. Why does Hartmann think the payment of referral fees to health and family planning workers has undermined freedom of choice for the poor of Bangladesh?
3. Why does the author believe the international women's health and reproductive rights movement has challenged the population control efforts of the World Bank?

Betsy Hartmann, "Bankers, Babies, and Bangladesh," *The Progressive,* September 1990. Reproduced by permission from *The Progressive,* 409 E. Main St., Madison, WI 53703.

For more than twenty years, the World Bank has played a strategic role in pressuring Third World governments to implement population-control programs. It can do this by virtue of its leverage over other forms of development aid.

Although there is a divergence of opinion within the institution, the dominant Bank view of population is neo-Malthusian. By procreating too often, the logic goes, the poor help to create and perpetuate their own poverty. Their numbers spread scarce agricultural and environmental resources too thin, keep wages low, and cost governments too much money in social services. Forcing down birth rates through population-control programs will thus help the poor help themselves.

There are two main problems with this analysis. First, it obscures the real cause of poverty in the Third World: the unequal distribution of resources and power within individual countries and between the developed and underdeveloped worlds. The Bank has always turned a blind eye to inequality; moreover, it actively allies itself with the same Third World elites who monopolize resources within their countries and thus prevent real development.

Second, the emphasis on population control distorts social policy and undermines the delivery of safe, voluntary family-planning services. In many countries, the World Bank has urged governments to make population control a higher priority than basic health care. It has also pressured them to relax prescription guidelines for contraceptives and aggressively push those considered most "effective"—intrauterine devices, pills, injectables, and now the implants—in the absence of adequate screening and treatment for side effects, which can be serious and even life-threatening. As a result, many women have become disillusioned with these methods and dropped out of family-planning programs altogether.

In Bangladesh, the World Bank has gone one step further to support a coercive sterilization-incentive scheme. . . .

Quality of Life Ignored

Bangladesh is a country of gross inequalities. Ten percent of rural households own more than 50 per cent of the land; almost half the rural population is landless and chronically underemployed. Political power is concentrated in the hands of a military government, which annually receives more than $1.5 billion in foreign aid. The World Bank is among the largest donors.

Foreign aid flows primarily to the rich. As big landowners, businessmen, and corrupt politicians line their pockets, the situation of the poor deteriorates. Today three-quarters of Bangladesh's population is malnourished. Less than a third is literate or has access to basic health care. In the government budget, military spending has a much higher priority than either health or education.

In the face of grinding poverty, poor people in Bangladesh, as in many other Third World countries, are forced to rely on children as their only form of economic security. Children are a vital source of agricultural labor, and adult sons are the only source of financial support in old age. In a situation where only one-fifth of the children born in a year grow up healthy and fit, parents need to have many children to ensure that a few survive to adulthood. Even when women want to control their fertility, family-planning services of good quality are few and far between.

Foreign Population Control Is Unjustified

Even if the overpopulation notion were correct, while it might on pragmatic grounds justify a program of domestic population control, it would not justify a United States program of foreign population control because of the effects on foreign goodwill toward the United States. State Department population ideologues have acted as if procuring the cooperation of a few key people like the Shah of Iran and Ferdinand Marcos were enough to counterbalance any amount of pushing around that might go on among the ordinary people; but any television viewer of the furious multitudes in Teheran and Manila should have serious reservations about that. The crusade to control world population growth began during a decade when American power was at its peak. It involves risks that the United States can no longer afford in the interests of its own survival as a free world power.

Jacqueline R. Kasun, *Society,* July/August 1988.

Ignoring these realities, the Bangladesh government has tried to force down birth rates in the absence of any real improvement in people's lives. It has acted under direct pressure from the World Bank and other international agencies.

In the spring of 1983, the World Bank, the U.S. Agency for International Development, and the United Nations Fund for Population Activities circulated a position paper in Dhaka [the capital city], calling for a "drastic" reduction in population growth, the creation of an autonomous National Population Control Board with emergency powers, and an increase in sterilization incentives. Pressure intensified several months later when World Bank Vice President W. David Hopper sent a letter to a senior government minister instructing him to "outline necessary measures to strengthen the program so that agreed national population objectives could be met on time."

The Bangladesh government responded quickly, instituting a

crash program to reduce the birth rate, including enhanced incentives and punitive measures against family-planning personnel who fail to meet monthly sterilization quotas. The stage was set for abuse.

Under the government's revised incentive system, each person—man or woman—who agrees to be sterilized receives 175 taka and a free sari or sarong. Until recently, doctors and clinic staff received a special payment for each sterilization they performed, and government health and family-planning workers, as well as village midwives and members of the public, received a referral fee for each sterilization client they brought to the clinic. Smaller incentives were also offered to women who agreed to use IUDs.

Incentives for Sterilization

Until 1988, the U.S. Agency for International Development financed 85 percent of these incentive and referral fees, despite the fact that Congress explicitly prohibits the use of U.S. funds to "provide any financial incentive to any person to undergo sterilization." According to AID, the incentives were really "compensation payments" designed to cover transportation, food costs, and wages lost due to the sterilization operation. The free clothing was justified as "surgical apparel."

In rural Bangladesh, where chronic hunger and unemployment are realities for much of the population, the distinction between compensation and incentives is dubious. A hungry person can buy many meals for 175 taka and a piece of clothing is a powerful inducement for a person who owns only one worn-out garment.

As a result, incentives, coupled with pressure from health and family-planning workers, are instrumental in persuading many poor people to be sterilized. Numerous studies have shown that sterilization clients in Bangladesh come disproportionately from the poorest sections of the rural population. More prosperous couples tend to choose such reversible methods of birth control as the IUD and the pill. Moreover, government statistics show that the number of sterilizations tends to increase dramatically during the lean autumn months before the rice harvest, when many landless peasants are unemployed and destitute.

Freedom of Choice Threatened

The payment of referral fees to health and family-planning workers has also undermined freedom of choice. Not only have workers tended to promote sterilization at the expense of other contraceptive methods, but many also failed to give adequate information on the possible side effects of sterilization, for fear of losing clients. Members of the public acting as sterilization agents have been even more unscrupulous. . . . The agent system, which was only recently abolished, accounted for almost half of the male sterilizations in Bangladesh.

The emphasis on sterilization distorts the health-care needs of the people of Bangladesh. In financial terms alone, population control now absorbs a full third of the government's health budget. Mother and Child Health, supposedly a cornerstone of Bangladesh's population policy, has consistently taken a back seat to sterilization, with tragic consequences.

According to World Bank figures, only 2 percent of children in Bangladesh had been immunized by 1987 against the common infectious diseases. Almost half of infant deaths and one-third of childhood deaths are caused by illnesses which could be prevented or readily cured. More than half of the appallingly high number of maternal deaths could also be prevented by basic care—yet most health facilities are inaccessible to poor, pregnant women (unless they come for sterilization) and traditional midwives have been encouraged to spend most of their time recruiting sterilization candidates and women who will accept IUDs.

Ironically, this emphasis on family planning over health is counterproductive even in narrow population-control terms, since one of the chief causes of high birth rates in Bangladesh is the high level of infant and child mortality.

Once an incentive system is in place, it also opens the way to other, even more coercive methods of population control. In 1984, for example, large parts of Bangladesh suffered serious summer flooding which made the lean season even leaner than usual for the poor. While monitoring food relief, field workers from British voluntary agencies discovered that local government officials had withheld U.N. emergency food aid from destitute women unless they agreed to be sterilized. . . .

Other Countries Affected

The harmful effects of World Bank population policies are not limited to Bangladesh. In Indonesia, the Bank has supported the government's program of aggressively pushing the IUD, pill, and injectables through "acceptor clubs," in which women who agree to use contraception (usually without adequate health backup) receive preferential access to credit and training.

In Indonesian-occupied East Timor, where human-rights activists charge the Indonesian army has killed almost one-third of the population, the Bank has financed the highly controversial construction of family-planning facilities. Answering charges that the East Timor population program has used coercion, a Bank official stated, in language reminiscent of Bangladesh, that there may have been "isolated cases of overzealousness on the part of family-planning workers."

Regarding Nepal, one of the poorest countries in the world, a

1989 confidential Bank report says that nation's population problem calls for a Chinese-type solution "although something less than this is probably the best that can be expected." As in Bangladesh, this policy is likely to have disastrous human consequences.

The report downplays socioeconomic inequalities and asserts that fertility reduction "must be the single most important objective of Nepal's health and population sectors."

Structural Adjustment

Today, the World Bank and the International Monetary Fund are engaged in a full-scale attack on the Third World's poor people through "structural adjustment," applying the screws to Third World economies already burdened by massive foreign debt. No more foreign exchange, the agencies insist, unless the government devalues its currency, denationalizes its industries, opens its doors to foreign imports and investment, freezes wages, raises food prices, and slashes its budget for social services. The result, according to the United Nations Children's Fund, has been increasing malnutrition, decreasing school enrollment, and a tragic rise in child deaths in many Third World countries.

A Local Problem

We will make no progress with population problems, which are a root cause of both hunger and poverty, until we deglobalize them. Populations, like potholes, are produced locally, and, unlike atmospheric pollution, remain local. . . .

We are not faced with a *single* global population problem but, rather, with about 180 separate national population problems. All population controls must be applied locally; local governments are the agents best prepared to choose local means. Means must fit local traditions. For one nation to attempt to impose its ethical principles on another is to violate national sovereignty and endanger international peace.

Garrett Hardin, *The Humanist,* July/August 1989.

Structural adjustment gives the Bank even greater leverage to promote population control in countries starved for foreign exchange. This is especially true in sub-Saharan Africa, the region hardest hit by economic reversal. In 1986, the Bank announced that population assistance was its "highest priority" in Africa and called for massive increases in foreign population aid. It blames many of Africa's problems on rapid population growth, ignoring its own role in setting back development through structural adjustment.

The Bank's population strategy for Africa looks distressingly similar to its programs elsewhere. It encourages governments to set population-control targets, to promote the pill, injectable contraceptives, and IUD in the absence of adequate health backup, and if necessary use incentives and disincentives.

World Bank Challenged

Pursuit of population control by the World Bank has not gone unchallenged. The international women's health and reproductive-rights movement is gaining momentum, as activists in both Western and Third World countries share information and organize campaigns. They are not opposed to family planning—on the contrary, they are fighting to make safe birth control, including abortion, accessible to women as a part of a more comprehensive health-care system and larger social reforms.

Solidarity work has been made more difficult by the anti-abortion movement, which would like to capture the population-control issue for its own narrow purposes. Another dilemma faced by reproductive-rights activists is the extent to which they should ally with reformers in the population field, who would like to see improvements in the "quality of care" provided by family-planning programs. While quality of care is a noble goal, too often its advocates fail to recognize the basic contradiction between population control and the reforms they would like to see.

Population control has done much to harm the quality of life for millions of poor people—by, for example, undermining basic health services. Improving care in family-planning programs is a step forward, but it is not enough.

Recognizing Deceptive Arguments

People who feel strongly about an issue use many techniques to persuade others to agree with them. Some of these techniques appeal to the intellect, some to the emotions. Many of them distract the reader or listener from the real issues.

A few common examples of argumentation tactics are listed below. Most of them can be used either to advance an argument in an honest, reasonable way or to deceive or distract from the real issues. It is important for a critical reader to recognize these tactics in order to rationally evaluate an author's ideas.

a. *bandwagon*—the idea that "everybody" does this or believes this

b. *categorical statements*—stating something in a way that implies there can be no argument or disagreement on the issue

c. *deductive reasoning*—the idea that since *a* and *b* are true, *c* is also true, although there may be no connection between *a* and *c*

d. *personal attack*—criticizing an opponent *personally* instead of rationally debating his or her ideas

e. *slanter*—to persuade through inflammatory and exaggerated language instead of through reason

f. *testimonial*—quoting or paraphrasing an authority or celebrity to support one's own viewpoint

The following activity can help you sharpen your skills in recognizing deceptive reasoning. The statements below are derived from the viewpoints in this chapter. *Beside each one, mark the letter of the type of deceptive appeal being used. More than one type of tactic may be applicable. If you believe the statement is not any of the listed appeals, write N.*

1. Governments throughout the Third World recognize the vital importance of family planning.

2. Since modern birth control methods decreased population growth in industrialized countries, they will also decrease Third World population growth.

3. Advocates of family planning are heartless bureaucrats representing impersonal, uncaring international organizations.

4. The planet is overpopulated.

5. It is clear: the population explosion will end shortly.

6. Esteemed thinkers like Julian Simon refute the theories that blame stagnant economies on population growth.

7. Continued population growth will produce widespread starvation, serious illness, and grinding poverty.

8. Every scholar of Third World issues understands that family planning will not work without social reforms.

9. Reputable social scientists know that Third World inequality causes as many problems as overpopulation.

10. Critics of family planning are mindless slaves to their reproductive urges.

11. People are an asset, not a liability.

12. Paul Ehrlich, a member of the National Academy of Sciences, has shown that overpopulation causes environmental destruction.

13. Family planning critics are arrogant religious zealots who let their morality interfere with common sense.

14. Coercive family planning is both morally degenerative and hopelessly impractical.

15. Just as Mexico's family planning program failed to achieve population stability, so will similar programs by other nations fail.

16. In the Third World family planning is conducted without regard for human rights and is the worst example of inhumanity imaginable.

Periodical Bibliography

The following articles have been selected to supplement the diverse views presented in this chapter.

David Berreby	"The Numbers Game," *Discover*, April 1990.
James K. Boyce	"The Bomb Is a Dud," *The Progressive*, September 1990.
Jon Christensen	"In Brazil, Sterilizing Women Is the Method of Choice," *The Progressive*, September 1990.
Paul Demeny	"World Population Trends," *Current History*, January 1989.
Werner Fornos	"Gaining People, Losing Ground," *The Humanist*, May/June 1990.
Garrett Hardin	"There Is No Population Problem," *The Humanist*, July/August 1989.
Jodi L. Jacobson	"The Population Picture Worldwide," *Utne Reader*, May/June 1988.
Jacqueline R. Kasun	"Gnats and Camels: Congressional Oversight of Population Programs," *Society*, July/August 1988.
Nathan Keyfitz	"The Growing Human Population," *Scientific American*, September 1989.
Kim A. Lawton	"Is There Room for Prolife Environmentalists?" *Christianity Today*, September 24, 1990.
Jessica Tuchman Mathews	"Redefining Security," *Foreign Affairs*, Spring 1989.
Heather L. McCulloch	"Abortion Cutoff," *The Nation*, April 9, 1990.
Ray Percival	"Malthus and His Ghost," *National Review*, August 18, 1989.
William Petersen	"Staying Alive," *The American Scholar*, Winter 1988.
Nafis Sadik	"How to Handle Population Growth," *The New York Times*, May 16, 1987.
Julian L. Simon	"The Unreported Revolution in Population Economics," *The Public Interest*, Fall 1990.
Anastasia Toufexis	"Too Many Mouths," *Time*, January 2, 1989.
Ben J. Wattenberg	"World's Population Bomb May Be a Dud," *Los Angeles Times*, June 3, 1987.

How Can Rain Forests Be Saved?

Chapter Preface

The world's tropical rain forests are disappearing at the rate of one-and-a-half acres per second every hour of every day of the year. Places of great beauty and biological diversity, these arboreal pockets are located in a broad band around the equator—in Southeast Asia, Latin America, and Africa. Their destruction is both tragic and perilous. At least half of the earth's species of flora and fauna, many of which have not yet been scientifically catalogued, live in the rain forest. Some rain forest plants are vital sources of medicine and others are used to create hybrid species of disease-resistant plants that greatly increase the world's farm production. Rain forest destruction not only threatens the loss of many vital and rare species of plants and animals but the destruction of several indigenous human cultures as well.

Yet the value of the rain forest has not protected it from destruction. At the current rate of deforestation, most of the world's rain forests will disappear within fifty years. The causes are complex. Logging, cattle ranching, development projects, and the migration of small farmers have all contributed to the problem. However, there is cause for hope that the rain forests might yet be saved. Environmental groups and concerned citizens have worked toward this end in both industrialized and developing nations. In response, the growing realization that something has to be done has been translated into action by governments, corporations, international agencies, and nongovernmental organizations.

The authors in the following chapter share a deep concern for the rain forests and propose several solutions for saving them.

"This battle will be won through understanding and meeting the needs of the world's rural peoples."

Changing Farmers' Lifestyles Can Save Rain Forests

New Forests Project

The New Forests Project is a branch of the International Center for Development Policy, a public interest group. In the following viewpoint, the New Forests Project argues that innovative agriculture and forestry policies are needed to aid small farmers in the tropics. Only when policies that preserve the forests benefit these people, the New Forest Project reasons, will the policies have a chance of success.

As you read, consider the following questions:

1. What are the consequences of tropical deforestation, according to the New Forests Project?
2. In the authors' opinion, why is "slash-and-burn" agriculture becoming increasingly outdated?
3. What kinds of agricultural systems does the New Forests Project promote?

New Forests Project, "Forests of the Future: The New Forests' Role in Achieving Biological Diversity," *New Forests Project Newsletter,* April 1989. Reprinted with permission.

Biological Diversity—it's the favorite rallying cry of environmental groups. But what does it mean and how can you help? The New Forests Project stands firmly in favor of encouraging the restoration and preservation of biological diversity and leads the way with new, appropriate, effective solutions to recovering our lost diversity. Let's examine the problem:

There's an old saw about not being able to see the forest for the trees and perhaps it applies here. Some environmentalists, in their quest for biological diversity, fail to appreciate that the root problem lies with PEOPLE at whose hands this diversity either thrives or disappears. People do their best to survive and sometimes, in doing so, destroy the forests. Usually because nobody has shown them a better way.

Invaluable Forests

The needs and concerns are real: we must restore and protect the fantastic diversity of plant and animal life which abounds in the world's natural forests. Tropical forests deserve special attention because they house and comprise $1/2$ to $3/4$ of all living species. And because they are being destroyed at an alarming rate . . . an area the size of Ohio is lost every year and that rate is increasing.

As these forests are lost, so also are the many species of rare plants and animals. Some of these have never been seen, and never will be, before they are lost forever. Think about it . . . it's entirely possible that a plant which holds the key to curing the common cold, or cancer, or even AIDS, may be about to perish under the logger's jackboot or the farmer's machete blade.

More important, these same tropical forests are crucial to maintaining the Earth's weather systems. These are the locomotives which drive the complex patterns of rainfall, wind currents and differential heating that are the world's weather. They drink in much of the excess carbon dioxide in the air and exhale life-giving oxygen into the atmosphere. That's a valuable exchange, which we cannot afford to lose. . . .

Underlying Roots of the Problem

It is too simple to point the finger of blame only at the multinational corporations who buy the logs and cheap beef that is produced without regard for the environmental consequences. Agreed, they have little conscience about how they make their short-term profits. But the deeper underlying roots of the problem must be traced to the expanding populations of tropical countries.

There are millions of families who, without the benefit of education about innovative agricultural/forestry methods, continue their fight to survive, often in degrading poverty, using the only methods they have ever known.

In most tropical areas, traditional agriculture uses the so-called "slash-and-burn" system. As its name suggests, the land is first cleared of trees and brush, which are sold for firewood and charcoal, and the remaining weeds are burned. A food or cash crop is then planted, perhaps for one or two seasons, until the thin soil is depleted. The farmer then moves on to a new area, allowing a new growth of trees and brush to restore the soil and protect the land. In perhaps eight years, he returns and repeats the cycle. It is marginal, inefficient farming in light of a rapidly growing population.

Wicks/Rothco. Reprinted by permission.

Villages where we work may have grown from 50 families 20 years ago to 100 families today, and will reach 200 families in another 20 years! As these new families build needed housing, as the tillable land area shrinks, the need for better, more efficient, farming systems becomes more and more necessary. And yet, in the development programs, these are the people receiving the least technical assistance.

The New Forests Project offers new, environmentally-sustainable land management systems to the farmers of these areas to permit more productivity, on less land and which improve environmental conditions so that biological diversity can be restored.

Rain Forests and Livestock

Livestock farmers of these upland areas face a similar dilemma: how to manage their herds in the face of reduced land areas and deteriorating forage quality. They burn the grazing lands annually to get rid of dead grass and weeds, encouraging new grass growth to feed their animals during the dry season. In the process, fire destroys the new tree seedlings which are essential to restore the forest diversity we must achieve.

It has often been suggested that the first step toward restoration of biological diversity should be the elimination of these herds of cattle, sheep, goats and buffalo. This is simply not possible nor is it reasonable. Farmers of developing rural communities must employ an integrated farming system which depends heavily on livestock to till the fields, produce manure to maintain soil fertility, act as collateral for production credit and, in many cases, represent the only product for cash sale to meet emergencies. These people cannot give up their livestock. It would be financial and cultural suicide.

These traditional agricultural systems have served the peoples of tropical countries for hundreds, often thousands, of years. These farmers seldom know of any other methods. Until recently, these systems served them well. The situation today is very different. There are more people on less land and little firewood. Mudslides destroy entire villages and floods become more catastrophic and common every year.

The cries of need for new forests are being heard from all corners of the Earth, especially from the people who must live on land that was, itself, once a forest. The New Forests Project is listening . . . and acting.

Forgetting the Uplands

What about the big dollar, international "rural development" programs you ask? While spending billions of your tax dollars over the past three decades, they have done little to demonstrate low-input, sustainably productive farming systems, especially for the peoples of these uplands. On the contrary, these costly programs have concentrated their efforts on the more productive lowland agricultural areas where spectacular production increases—for the short term—are possible.

These "Green Revolution" gains depend heavily on chemical fertilizers, pesticides, growth hormones and genetically manipulated seed varieties which bring huge profits to the commercial partners of the "development" programs. It's fair to say they widen the gap between the rich and poor. One must wonder who the real beneficiaries of these programs are. The planners of these programs have forgotten that the upland regions, once heavily forested, are the source of life—or death—to the more fertile lowlands.

It is critically important that the upland areas be again covered with trees, and the sooner the better, for the sake of the entire agricultural system. Yet improvements are less spectacular in such areas and "development" planners, intent on realizing immediate targets, are slow to assist people living such a marginal existence, even though, in the long run, this must be the first priority.

Trees for People

The New Forests Project takes this priority seriously and directs its efforts toward renewing the life-giving tropical forests of the world. Now with more than eight years experience in over two thousand rural villages, we have demonstrated repeatedly that trees must be for people—if we expect to have trees.

If there is to be a restoration of the biological diversity of a watershed area, we must show people better methods so that these people are the ones who benefit from their labors.

Great successes are possible: we work with the most receptive audience imaginable. These marginal hillside farmers know they're already in real trouble. They see the land every day and can tell you, more accurately than any forester, how rapidly it's being degraded. They are ready to try something new because, for them, there is no future without the land.

This is where the New Forests Project works. We introduce trees such as Leucaena for villagers to plant as village woodlots and they are so enthusiastically planted that they become major components of new, more productive, agricultural systems. Let's examine some of these systems:

• Contour Farming/Alley-Cropping—where slash-and-burn farming permitted one or two harvests every eight years, contour planting of "Alley-Crops" between hedgerows of trees permits continuous farming of the land, with much higher annual yields. The farmer gets this productivity sustainably, without additional expenses for commercial fertilizer or other chemicals. One acre produces eight times as much per year as before.

• Confinement Rearing—where open grazing supported one cow on eight acres of fragile hillsides, confinement rearing that includes forage trees allows one acre to support as many as twenty cattle, increasing the growth rates of the animals three times! The animals themselves are kept off the land so that desertification is avoided.

• Family Woodlots—where "lopping" of trees for firewood and forage required an average of fifty working hours per household per week and rapidly destroyed the forests, fast-growing fuelwood trees allow a continuous harvest of firewood sufficient for family needs, on a small area of untillable land right at the family homesite.

• Watershed Improvement—where upland springs failed as the forests were cleared, planting woodlots above the springs permits a return of wildlife and native tree species and, within two years, can bring a spring back to life.

Slash and Burn

To survive on poor tropical soils, forest farmers for millennia have practiced "shifting cultivation" by slash and burn. Burning adds ash which raises soil pH and minerals, providing for two or three years' harvests before the farmers are forced to cut more forest and begin the process again. This type of agriculture, although hard work, was sustainable when plots were small and the forest had decades to regenerate. Today, it not only permanently destroys the forest, but its inefficient productivity is too low to meet the demands of growing populations.

Dorothy Calhoun Zbicz, *Ripon Forum*, September 1990.

How do these systems accomplish our goal of restoring biological diversity? By reducing pressures on the land caused by human need. Natural forces can then take over. Nature can plant trees far better and faster than we can—with a little help from her friends. When people see they can produce all they need on less land by changing their methods in understandable ways, they leave marginal land areas alone. In the tropics three or four years is sufficient time to achieve a return of indigenous species to such areas.

Forests of the Future

The next step is, logically, the concept Forests of the Future. Marginal lands can support the increased populations of the future, at acceptable living standards, with the technology we have today—if it is implemented. On such lands, we are now planting useful and fast-growing trees. People plant these trees because they can realize important, and continuous, income.

These trees are tough and they protect the land. They virtually fireproof it against natural or man-made brushfires. They shade out coganal grasses that hinder the growth of more valuable species. They make the area an attractive habitat for deer, wild pigs, birds, monkeys and other far-ranging wildlife species. These in turn deposit more seeds from near and far and forest diversity takes another giant step forward.

Such regenerated areas are the Forests of the Future. They

will never again recapture the glorious diversity of the primeval tropical forests but they are a highly diverse, achievable alternative to what is presently there. They can restore life to vast watershed areas—and well support growing populations at the same time.

Man can live in harmony with Nature. These future forests will be harvested, continually and with an always expanding diversity of products. Not with the clear-cutting, burning-over process the international pirates now employ to gain a harvest of one, or a few, species from the immense diversity of a forest. But with an understanding of all that such a restored area can offer to us.

And all of this within a period of time these families, now living on the brink of extinction, can understand. In the first year, such a forest produces its first harvests of wood, charcoal and food crops. In the second year, there is more. By the third year, fruit trees begin to produce. Flowers, mushrooms, the list goes on and on. Every year, the land supports more people, supports them better, and increases its own diversity. . . .

Biological diversity is a goal worth fighting for. But unlike other wars, this battle will be won through understanding and meeting the needs of the world's rural peoples.

2 VIEWPOINT

"Eliminating government subsidies would make the current destruction of the Amazon rain forest (and Alaska's Tongass rain forest) unprofitable."

Eliminating Government Support for Deforestation Can Save Rain Forests

Gregory F. Rehmke

In the following viewpoint, Gregory F. Rehmke argues that government support for projects, companies, and individuals to develop rain forests is causing deforestation both in the United States and Brazil. Without subsidies, tax breaks, and other incentives, Rehmke says, current deforestation by ranchers, farmers, and developers would not be undertaken because it would not be profitable. Gregory F. Rehmke leads the Economics in Argumentation program for the Reason Foundation, a nonprofit public policy research organization.

As you read, consider the following questions:

1. According to Rehmke, how does Brazilian tax policy encourage deforestation?
2. Who benefits from deforestation in Brazil, according to Rehmke?
3. What is the ultimate solution to deforestation, in the author's opinion?

Gregory F. Rehmke, "Who Is Destroying the World's Forests?" *The Freeman*, November 1989.

Time began its January 2, 1989, "Planet of the Year" issue with a two-page photo of a burning Brazilian forest, and declared: "Man is recklessly wiping out life on earth." A February 23, 1989 *Rolling Stone* article, "The Scorched Earth," shows cattle in the state of Rondonia in western Brazil nibbling at still-smoldering shrubs.

Government-sponsored television advertisements, says *Rolling Stone*, encourage impoverished Brazilians "to seek their fortune in the farming, ranching, mining, lumber and hydroelectric projects under way in Rondonia." The article explains that the 900-mile Highway BR-364, financed by the World Bank, cheaply transports settlers to Rondonia from urban areas.

The "National Security" Excuse

Nearby, in the western state of Acre, residents depend on the Brazilian government for 85 percent of their income. But these subsidies are only the latest in a long series of uneconomic policies subsidizing rain-forest development.

The Brazilian military has insisted that building roads and settling the Amazon basin is necessary for national security. "The Amazon is ours," declared Brazilian President Jose Sarney, in a speech announcing a new internationally financed program he said would "permit the rational siting of economic activities" in the Amazon basin.

The speech was reported to be strongly nationalistic, and many Brazilian officials see pressure to limit Amazon development as part of a "campaign for the internationalization of the Amazon." General Leonidas Pires Goncalves, Brazil's Army Minister, complained of "that tiresome grinding on and on" about forest destruction. Meanwhile, Fernando Cesar Mesquita, head of the new Brazilian environmental agency, believes "There is a true danger of foreign occupation of the Amazon."

Citing "national security" to justify uneconomic programs is a popular ploy for special interest groups around the world and is certainly not unique to Brazil.

Subsidizing Rain Forest Destruction

The cattle-ranching and road-building projects that first drew Brazilians into the Amazon were heavily subsidized with funds from the World Bank, the Inter-American Development Bank, and the International Monetary Fund. By 1983, the Brazilian government had spent $2.5 billion to subsidize deforestation for large-scale cattle ranching that, according to the World Resources Institute, "would not be economically viable in the absence of the subsidies."

After decades of subsidizing cattle ranching in the Amazon, the Brazilian government apparently decided it needed to subsidize farming communities to balance the concentrated wealth of cattle ranchers. The Polonoroesta plan, a project in northern Brazil funded by the International Monetary Fund, foreign lenders, and the government, was to develop 100,000 square miles of tropical forest for small farmers. Seventeen percent of the land has been deforested so far.

Ambitious Plans

When the military took power in 1964, the generals placed Amazônia—with an ideological overlay of manifest destiny, national security and national integration—at the center of their efforts to transform the Brazilian economy. The Amazon was viewed as a place for sending "surplus population" released by structural changes in agriculture, and, given the buoyant international beef market of the 1960s, as a potential site for the cattle industry. It was thought that by expanding long-term lending and providing juicy incentives, Brazil's highly successful agroindustrial elite might be enticed into the region to transform it from a provincial backwater into a thriving agricultural zone.

Susanna B. Hecht, *NACLA Report on the Americas,* May 1989.

Yet the program, in addition to being environmentally destructive, has apparently led to an even greater concentration of land in the hands of ranchers. After a section of forest is burned, nutrients left in the ashes support only a couple years of crops. With the nutrients exhausted, the soil will support only grasses —making the land suitable for raising cattle.

Local cattle ranchers then purchase the land cheaply, and settlers move on to raze new acreage. The burning program continues to redistribute income from taxpayers (both domestic and foreign) in order to provide subsidized labor and land for cattle interests.

In "How Brazil Subsidises the Destruction of the Amazon," *The Economist* (March 18,1989) cites a new World Bank study outlining a variety of misguided policies: "Brazil's laws and tax system have made deforestation and ranching in the Amazon artificially profitable." High inflation encourages people to invest in land, since money savings are wiped out. Agriculture is exempted from taxation, so legitimate farmers are bought out by those looking for tax havens, and farmers then move deeper into the forests to clear new land.

Land taxes on unimproved land are reduced 90 percent when cleared for crops or pasture, thus punishing private preservationists. Tax credits subsidize money-losing development schemes, generally benefiting rich cattle ranchers at the expense of poorer Brazilian taxpayers. Finally, government regulations give "squatters' rights" to those who wander onto private land and begin using it "more effectively," i.e., clearing the forests and planting crops. However, this last policy seems to work both ways: *The New York Times* reported that the squatters' rights policy has allowed rubber-tappers in some areas to delay landowners' plans to clear forests.

The Brazilian government, however, isn't alone in subsidizing forest destruction. A program operated in the U.S. by the Forest Service and the Bureau of Land Management (BLM) transforms forests in the Southwest into grazing land for leasing—at below-market rates—to cattle ranchers. . . .

From the jungles of Brazil to the southwestern U.S., special interest groups fuel forest destruction. Both projects would be unprofitable without governments' shifting development costs to taxpayers.

Destroying the Tongass National Forest

The same is true in the Tongass National Forest in Alaska, one of the world's last temperate zone rain forests. The Forest subsidizes logging operations in the Tongass rain forest, which lose 98 cents for every taxpayer dollar spent. Logging jobs bolster the local economy, but cost U.S. taxpayers an average of $36,000 for each job created. The benefits are concentrated, creating Forest Service and logging company jobs (and profits) in the area, while the costs are spread out among U.S. taxpayers.

In the Tongass National Forest, and in other U.S. forests, government-built roads subsidize logging, just as Brazilian government roads subsidize logging and burning in the Amazon. The U.S. Forest Service has built 342,000 miles of roads in the national forests.

According to a study by the National Center for Policy Analysis: "These roads, primarily designed to facilitate logging, extend into the ecologically fragile backcountry of the Rocky Mountains and Alaska, where they are causing massive soil erosion, damaging trout and salmon fisheries and causing other environmental harm. Because the costs of these logging activities far exceed any commercial benefit from the timber acquired, this environmental destruction would never have occurred in the absence of government subsidies."

Road building does create jobs, though, and increases Forest Service budgets. The programs are driven by the logic of special interests—the benefits are concentrated, while the costs are spread out.

Tongass logging, Southwest chaining, and Amazon burning are all uneconomical projects that probably never would have been started without subsidies. Either the land would have been left alone, or other less destructive practices would have been developed.

Indians in the Peruvian Amazon, for example, have apparently learned how to cultivate the rain forest in profitable and environmentally sound ways. *The Economist* (February 11,1989) cites a Peruvian study showing "the value of the products of a natural forest exploited sustainably for its fruit, rubber and timber, exceeded threefold the value of beef that the land would produce as pasture."

Free Market Needed

Many environmentalists, possibly influenced by Malthusian arguments, believe that overpopulation and economic growth alone force settlers into the Amazon rain forests, and into other tropical rain forests around the world. But if Brazil had an open economy, with sound money, free markets, and free trade, the opposite would likely happen: people would be drawn from the countryside into the cities, to take new jobs and share better living standards.

Cities can absorb an astonishing number of people, and when unshackled can transform low-cost labor into rapidly increasing prosperity. Singapore and Hong Kong are two recent examples of thriving cities creating wealth for their once-impoverished workers.

Accelerating the Destruction

The causes of rain forest destruction are more varied in the tropics than in temperate regions, with population pressures, landlessness, international debt, and large-scale cattle ranching, as well as commercial timber harvesting, playing a part. But both near and far from the equator, government policies are accelerating forest destruction beyond what social and economic pressures alone would accomplish.

John C. Ryan, *World Watch*, May/June 1989.

The mass migration of rural workers to urban areas has continued since the Industrial Revolution. People take advantage of the better jobs in and around thriving cities, leaving behind the agrarian life in isolated villages. Most Latin American economies, however, are neither free of inflation nor thriving.

Hampered by protectionism, taxes, regulations, and money-losing state-owned companies, Latin American cities have not been able to create the new jobs and prosperity needed to employ and enrich swelling urban populations. Brazilian politicians, instead of deregulating their economies, have dreamt up schemes to relieve urban pressure by shuttling the poor out to exploit the "hidden riches" of the Amazon.

Though eliminating government subsidies would make the current destruction of the Amazon rain forest (and Alaska's Tongass rain forest) unprofitable, private commercial development of the rain forests might someday be profitable.

Protection Through Ownership

If people want to stop future commercial rain-forest development (rather than just stopping subsidies for current unprofitable development), they should be willing to translate that desire into action. The Nature Conservancy did just that in Costa Rica with a $5.6 million debt swap that will finance nine local conservation projects, protecting some of Costa Rica's rain forest from development. Another debt/nature swap in Bolivia encourages ecologically sound development (rather than just setting aside virgin forests, which does little to enhance the local economy).

If Americans want more of Latin America's 1.6 billion forest acres set aside, they should consider buying the land, or purchasing long-term leases. In the same way, if Brazilians want to protect one of the world's last temperate zone rain forests from destructive logging, or protect piñon-juniper forests in the Southwest, they too should have the right to purchase or lease the land.

Unfortunately, as it now stands, the Brazilian government is no more likely to let Americans purchase and protect land in the Amazon's tropical rain forest, than is the U.S. government to let Brazilians purchase and protect land in Alaska's temperate rain forest.

"The only people that can really conserve the environment are our people."

Indigenous People Can Save Rain Forests

Santos Adam Afsua

Santos Adam Afsua, a Peruvian Indian, is a member of the Coordinating Body for the Indigenous Peoples' Organizations of the Amazon Basin (COICA). COICA, an international group, was founded in 1984 to defend the interests of the indigenous peoples of the Amazon Basin. In the following viewpoint, Afsua explains the position of COICA in an interview with *Multinational Monitor*, a liberal monthly magazine. Afsua decries the abuses against the rain forest and its people and argues that indigenous groups are the best guardians of the forest.

As you read, consider the following questions:
1. According to Afsua, how have the governments of the Amazon Basin responded to indigenous resistance to the use of the forest by "outsiders"?
2. What does Afsua think of multilateral development banks?
3. What is the problem with debt-for-nature swaps, according to the author?

"Indigenous Voices," an interview of Santos Adam Afsua. This interview first appeared in the December 1989 issue of *Multinational Monitor*, PO Box 19405, Washington, DC 20036, subscriptions, $22/year. Reprinted with permission.

Multinational Monitor: To what extent are indigenous rights respected by South American countries and to what extent are the indigenous peoples allowed self-governance?

Santos Adam Afsua: Historically, the governments of the countries in the Amazon Basin have never recognized our traditional organizations. They have considered the forest an empty space to use as they wish. That has been their excuse to promote so-called development, which has led to the destruction of our forest.

Because of our persistence in opposing this penetration of the forest by national or multinational organizations or companies, we have been seen as obstacles to the government. As a result, the indigenous people have been subjected to incredible levels of repression, massacres, torture, jailings, abuse and mistreatment. Facing that situation, we have seen the need to further organize to be able to better struggle against these abuses [and] these new forms of colonialism. We have organized to be able to defend the resources, to defend the inhabitants and to defend the homeland.

And this is one of the reasons why we have decided as an international organization to take the initiative . . . and talk directly with bank officials, to multilateral development banks, to environmental organizations: to explain directly how the intervention affects us.

Protecting the Forest

MM: How do you view the rainforest?

Afsua: You must understand that we try to maintain the forest as our ancestors have maintained, protected and taken care of it. That is extremely important because the destruction of the forest would not only ruin our homelands but would have a worldwide effect. The issue is not just to protect the forest; the issue is also to [rely on] the people that are able and have for millennia been able to protect and maintain the forest. There is no time to lose, and bank officials and others must understand that we are not only talking about ourselves, but about the future of the world.

It is important to point out that the forest is not just the forest in itself, is not just the trees or animals, it is also the people who live in it. We have to look at the integrated form.

The attacks on the forest are not only taking place in the Amazon Basin in Peru. The same problems that we face are being faced by our brothers in Ecuador, Colombia, Brazil and Bolivia. And that's why we needed to organize an international coordinating body: to be able to express common problems and to seek common solutions.

In trying to maintain the forest, the banks and environmental groups are trying to commercialize it through so-called "debt for nature swaps" without realizing that there are Indian people who have been able to conserve these spaces, to protect the forest. The only areas in the Amazon that have not been affected by the overall destruction and that are still left with certain ecological and environmental balances are the areas and territories where we live.

Part of the Ecosystem

We are part of the ecosystem, and our ancestors are the ones who protect its resources. And if we're thrown out, who is going to defend the Amazon? National parks are not an answer. That's an outsider's solution. A park created by law can also be done away with by law. This has nothing to do with indigenous peoples—just like the debt-for-nature idea.

We think that instead of debt for nature, we should be talking about debt for indigenous control—creating large new extensions where Indians can live, to protect our culture while also protecting the land.

Evaristo Nugkuag, *Mother Jones,* July/August 1990.

We live to protect the forest with the best ecological and environmental knowledge that we possess, a knowledge we inherited from our ancestors. We do this with the understanding that we will continue living there, and we have to protect this forest because we have to think of future generations.

Without Our Consent

MM: Have any governments treated the indigenous people well?

Afsua: All governments [fail to] take the Indians into consideration. The governments come and go and they bring different ideas, and they each bring different plans. All of this is geared to the same destruction, to destroy our lives. So we have no hope, no matter who is in government.

MM: The assassination of Chico Mendes of the rubber tappers received a lot of publicity. Have the indigenous leaders received similar international attention for their work and for the harassment to which they have been subjected?

Afsua: We have been the object of a different type of attention. Different types of actions that indigenous peoples have done have received certain levels of international attention. Two years ago, because of the struggles that we have been waging, COICA received the alternative Nobel Peace Prize. But it is very difficult for us to get that type of attention, that type of treatment; that is why we came to the U.S. to speak directly [to decision-makers and the people of other countries].

MM: What has been the indigenous peoples' experience with multilateral banks?

Afsua: A lot of the loans from the multilateral development banks which have gone to the governments in our region have been used for specific political purposes. They have never reached the people and the people have never benefited from them. We do not have anything to do with all these debts. We are not part of that and we should not be responsible for resolving the problem.

Many of the projects sponsored by the multilateral development banks involve providing credits so that people, colonists, can come to our forest. These credits have been used to invade our territories, without respect for our spaces. These loans have been made without our having been consulted and without our consent, and that is totally inappropriate. That is why we have taken this initiative [to visit the United States]; because we need to engage in a dialogue to stop this type of destruction. We are here to raise the conscience of the people who are in charge of making these loans. They don't know about this reality, they don't know about what they are doing to our lives.

Multinational Companies

MM: Are multinational corporations the driving force behind your land being taken away and misused? Or do you feel the problem is more with governments and multilateral banks?

Afsua: It is all connected; the multinational companies are connected with the banks. The companies open up roads when they do exploration for different types of [raw materials]. These companies destroy the ecological balance through the pollution they produce; they destroy the water; they destroy the air; they destroy the soil.

MM: In 1982 the World Bank published a paper on tribal people and economic development. At that time the Bank said that it was going to start paying more attention to the concerns of indigenous people. Did you note any change around that time? Did the paper make any difference at all?

Afsua: Since that publication there has been a real gap, a lack of real change by the Bank. In 1986 the president of COICA met directly with the president of the World Bank to talk about the need to stop the loans which harm us. We have, since then, been able to slow down or stop some of the projects. Of course, this has been to our favor, and has worked against the interests of the big developmentalists, so we see that there have been some improvements.

However, we still do not see any change from the World Bank's notion of economic development, a notion which is totally different from our concepts of development.

MM: How successful have your recent meetings with the World Bank been?

Afsua: We have been able to meet with some Bank officials. We could not meet with the president of the World Bank, as we had hoped to do. However, we have been able to meet with the vice president for Latin America, and some officials of various departments, especially the environmental department of the World Bank. In these meetings we have expressed our concerns, and we have put forward specific positions. We have submitted and we have discussed. Now time will tell what will happen.

MM: What sort of things did you want to communicate to the environmental group?

Afsua: We have come to meet with the different environmental organizations to tell them, first of all, that the only people that can really conserve the environment are our people.

Defending the Forests

Indigenous peoples are actively defending their forests, their cultures and their ways of life, not merely in a few isolated incidents but in places as distant and different as Brazil and Malaysia. Their heroic efforts are often undertaken at great personal risk, even under the threat of death. More than one person per day has died while attempting to prevent the invasion and destruction of the world's tropical forests; many more have been arrested, persecuted or forced to flee their forest homes.

Jason W. Clay, *Cultural Survival Quarterly*, vol. 13, no. 1, 1989.

The environmental organizations usually contract a bunch of experts that go to our regions to do their studies; but we have realized that these people misinterpreted the reality, our reality.

In our meetings with the environmental organizations, we believe that they have taken our points very seriously. We have said that the environmental organizations and the indigenous organizations need to communicate and coordinate directly.

MM: Several of the environmental organizations have advocated "debt for nature" swaps in which environmental groups pay off some of a country's debt in exchange for guarantees that some of that country's rainforest will be preserved. How do the indigenous peoples' organizations view the debt for nature swaps?

Afsua: We believe, first of all, that the debt has been created by a total mismanagement of foreign loans, of foreign capital. The governments are responsible for this poor management and use of resources. Now the governments are trying to find ways to pay their interest and to pay back the debt. They have looked at alternatives [to direct payment], like the debt for nature swaps.

This is one of the reasons we have met with the banks and the environmental organizations: to make them understand that the debt for nature swaps cannot take place with our land because that debt is not ours; we have not contributed in any way to that debt.

MM: Do you think your meetings with the environmental groups were successful?

Afsua: Our meetings with the environmental organizations have helped to establish a linkage. Now we have decided that we are going to meet again. . . . We expect that all the environmental organizations with which we have been in touch will be able to come, so we can then start working on common programs.

MM: You want to form an alliance of indigenous people, environmental groups and the rubber tappers, nut gatherers and other people who use but do not destroy the forest. But there have been reports of conflict between indigenous people and the rubber tappers.

Afsua: Some conflicts exist between our groups and the rubber tappers, but many more exist with the colonists, the people who come to work on the big cattle ranches. They're the ones with whom we have the most problems.

*"[Fruit and latex] provide a more consistent
source of income and yield higher total revenues
than timber."*

Harvesting Rain Forests' Native Plants Can Stop Deforestation

Charles M. Peters

The destruction of tropical rain forests, Charles M. Peters contends, is both ecologically and economically unsound. Over the
long run, Peters argues, harvesting the rain forest's fruit, latex,
and other nonwood products provides much more income than
intensive logging, a leading cause of deforestation. While sustainably harvesting the rain forest's diverse bounty presents a
feasible alternative to deforestation, the author cautions that the
approach requires planning and support which is currently ab-
sent. Charles M. Peters is an assistant scientist at the New York
Botanical Garden.

As you read, consider the following questions:

1. According to Peters, what are the three steps involved in
   appraising a rain forest?
2. What do appraisers of the rain forest and investment bankers
   have in common, according to the author?
3. In the author's opinion, what are some of the potential
   problems with sustainable harvesting?

Tropical rain forests have recently received a lot of attention from the media, and anyone who watches television or reads news magazines can quickly outline the highlights of this story. Rain forests are some of the most complex and least-understood forest ecosystems on earth. They are a storehouse of biological diversity. They regulate climate, protect the soil, act as a watershed for some of the world's major rivers, and provide habitats for an incredible variety of plant, animal, and human populations. The bad news is that several million acres of tropical rain forest are destroyed every year. Tons of carbon are spewed into the atmosphere as these forests are burned; soil fertility and site productivity are drastically reduced; and countless plants and animals, many of which have yet to be described, are lost forever.

Conventional wisdom has it that tropical forests are being converted to cattle pastures, agricultural fields, or plantations of tree crops because these land-use practices, although ecologically disruptive, yield higher net revenues than those obtainable from natural forests. The key assumption in this argument is that, with the exception of a few valuable timber trees, primary rain forests simply are not worth very much money.

Two lines of evidence, however, appear to challenge the idea that destructive logging and forest clearing make good economic sense. In the first place, lumber and plywood are not the only useful products found in tropical forests. Rain forest trees also produce fruits, edible oils, spices, medicines, fibers, fodder, and a wide assortment of industrial compounds, such as resins, essential oils, gums, latexes, and dyes. Secondly, although many of these so-called minor forest products are collected solely for subsistence use, a substantial number of forest species are also sold in local markets, and a few, such as rattan, brazil nuts, rubber, and illipe oil (an important ingredient in cocoa butter and many cosmetics), are even traded internationally. These resources, together with the forests that produce them, are obviously worth something. The problem is that few attempts have been made to actually quantify these benefits.

How to Appraise a Rain Forest

Putting a monetary value on a tract of rain forest is essentially a three-step process that incorporates plant taxonomy, ecology, and resource economics. Step one is to identify all of the trees and shrubs occurring within the forest. This, in itself, can be a somewhat lengthy operation because accurate taxonomic identifications usually require a sample of the leaves, flowers, and fruits of each plant. Assuming that all collections are made and a complete list of species can be compiled for the forest, the next part of this step is to determine which of the trees produce useful products. Ethnobotanical studies and market surveys of the region are conducted to obtain this type of information.

The second step involves determining what economists call "production functions" for each of the economic tree species encountered in the inventory. For example, given that there are five species of native fruit trees in the forest, how much fruit does each tree produce every year? Or, how much annual diameter growth do the timber trees exhibit? Collecting these growth and yield data inevitably requires spending several years in the forest measuring tree diameters and counting and weighing all the fruits produced by different species.

Fruits of the Forest

The fruits of the forest, from allspice to chicle—the substance that makes chewing gum chewy—have commercial value, and are already being harvested for sale locally and overseas. . . . The extraction of fruit, far from being a threat to the wilderness, can in fact help preserve the forest in the long run, if it is done carefully.

Betsy Carpenter, *U.S. News & World Report,* June 4, 1990.

The final step is, as they say, the bottom line. Given an understanding of the abundance and productivity of different plant resources, current prices for each species are collected from local markets to estimate the total gross value of one year's harvest from the forest. This result, although extremely useful in some contexts, completely ignores the fact that forest resources must be harvested and transported to market before any real income is generated. These activities all incur a cost in either time or money, and this cost, therefore, must also be quantified and included in the appraisal. One last calculation, subtracting all the costs from all the benefits, yields the desired answer—the annual net financial worth of a limited tract of tropical rain forest. . . .

Accounting in Amazonia

From 1984 until late 1987, Alwyn Gentry, a botanist at the Missouri Botanical Garden, and I collected all of the information necessary to valuate a one hectare (2.45 acres) tract of primary rain forest in the Peruvian Amazon. . . .

The forest we appraised is located near the small village of Mishana, approximately 55 miles southwest of the city of Iquitos in Peru. The inhabitants of Mishana are detribalized indigenous people known as *ribereños* who make a living farming, fishing, and collecting a wide variety of forest products to sell in Iquitos.

Gentry painstakingly collected and identified every one of the 842 trees found on the Mishana study site. He was surprised to find that the forest contained more than 270 different species of trees, making it one of the most diverse or species-rich tropical forests ever inventoried. I was equally surprised to find that almost half of these trees yield products that are actually harvested and sold in local markets. Within a single hectare of rain forest at Mishana, there are 93 trees that produce edible fruits, 233 trees that produce marketable timber, and 24 trees that can be tapped for rubber. The diversity of native fruits alone on this site is overwhelming. There are oil-rich *aguaje* and *ungurahui* palm fruits, both of which are used locally to make delicious ice cream and beverages. There are *leche huayo* (milk fruit), *naranjo podrido* (rotten orange), *sacha cacao* (false chocolate), and *masaranduba* fruits, which have a creamy, custard-like pulp; and there are *tamamuri* and *charichuelo* fruits which possess a tart, acidic flavor. . . .

Figuring Monetary Value

As luck would have it, I had spent the previous two years in Peru collecting production and market price data for these fruit trees as part of my ecological research. I had also compiled a list of mill prices for the major timber trees in the region and had interviewed innumerable local people to find how much it costs to harvest and transport different forest resources. Without really meaning to, Gentry and I had already completed all three steps of the valuation process. All that was left to do was the arithmetic. To ensure that our math was correct, we solicited the help of Robert Mendelsohn, a resource economist at Yale University. By combining the inventory, yield, and price data collected for each species, we estimated that one hectare of Mishana forest produces about $650 worth of fruit and $50 worth of rubber every year. This material would generate a net annual revenue of about $422 upon delivery to the market in Iquitos. However, as Mendelsohn quickly pointed out, both fruit and latex can be collected every year from the forest, and consequently, the total financial worth of these resources is considerably greater than the market value of only one year's harvest. A more useful approach, he suggested, is to calculate the combined net present value, or NPV, of all future collections conducted in the forest. Although it sounds a little strange, investment bankers employ a similar analysis to determine the present value of long-term bonds that pay a certain dividend every year. Following this suggestion, we calculated that the NPV of the fruit and latex trees growing at Mishana is about $6,330 per hectare.

That hectare of Mishana forest also contains about 94 cubic meters of marketable timber. If liquidated in one felling, these logs would generate a net revenue of approximately $1,000 on delivery to the sawmill. A logging operation of this intensity, however, would inevitably damage many of the remaining trees in the forest and would greatly reduce, if not eliminate, any future revenues from the fruit and latex trees. In fact, the net financial gains from timber extraction would be reduced to zero if as few as 18 fruit trees were damaged by logging. Based on this finding, we concluded that clear-cutting is simply not a very good investment option at Mishana.

A better strategy would be to selectively log a small number of timber trees at periodic intervals. These harvests would be considerably less destructive to the forest and would still permit annual fruit and latex collections. Based on Gentry's original inventory data, we estimated that a maximum of 30 cubic meters of wood could be harvested from the forest every 20 years on a sustained-yield basis. Each of these harvests would yield a net revenue of about $310. Using a simple discounting procedure similar to that employed for fruits and latex, we calculated that the NPV of periodic timber harvests at Mishana is about $420.

Based on our assumption of sustainable timber harvests and annual fruit and latex collections, we estimate that the combined financial worth of the tree resources growing in one hectare of rain forest at Mishana is almost $7,000. Surprisingly, this result is more than three times the net recent value of a fully stocked cattle pasture in the Amazon and almost twice that of an intensely managed timber plantation. Far from being a worthless tangle of vegetation that must be eliminated to yield a profit, sustainable forest exploitation at Mishana would actually generate higher net revenues than almost any other type of land use. As can be appreciated, these findings make it extremely difficult to justify the idea that tropical deforestation is a good investment. They also raise serious questions about the uncontrolled logging currently occurring in the tropics.

The Importance of Minor Forest Products

In terms of economics, intensive logging at Mishana would be a little bit like killing and eating the goose that lays the golden egg out of ignorance about the price of precious metals. Fruits and latex represent more than 90 percent of the total market value of the forest. These resources provide a more consistent source of income and yield higher total revenues than timber. They can also be harvested with considerably less damage to the forest. Risking the destruction of more than $6,000 worth of nonwood products by conducting a logging operation designed to extract only $400 worth of lumber seems ludicrous. Unfortunately, this is exactly what is happening in many of the world's remaining rain forests.

I am convinced that the major problem here lies in the failure of public policy to recognize the actual value of these "minor" forest products. Tropical timber is sold in international markets and generates a substantial amount of foreign exchange. It is a highly visible export commodity that is controlled by the government and supported by large federal expenditures. Nonwood resources, on the other hand, are collected and sold in local markets by subsistence farmers, forest collectors, middlemen, and shop owners. These decentralized trade networks are hard to monitor and extremely easy to ignore in national accounting schemes. . . . Clearly, thousands of forest collectors each carrying a small basket of fruit to market are more difficult to census than logging trucks. This difficulty, however, does not lessen the total economic worth of the products collected by these people.

© Wicks/Rothco. Reprinted with permission.

In spite of the economic and ecological benefits afforded by this land-use practice, several problems must be overcome before promoting the increased collection and sale of nonwood forest products. For example, markets for many of these plant resources are localized and very small, and prices can drop rapidly in response to increased supply. There is a drastic need to expand existing markets, to open new markets at both the national and international level, and to develop innovative technologies for storing and processing these resources. . . .

Much remains to be learned about the ecology and productivity of rain forest resources. Picking up fruits in the forest is a relatively benign activity compared with timber harvesting, but it should be remembered that these fruits contain the seeds a tree needs to maintain itself in the forest. Without some idea of the regeneration and growth requirements of a tree species, intensive fruit harvesting could gradually cause the local extinction of a valuable resource. The fact that many stands of Brazil nut trees display a pronounced lack of seedlings and saplings suggests that this species may already have been overexploited. Simple management activities can be employed to remedy this situation, but only if the knowledge and local initiative exists to do so.

Destructive Harvesting Practices

Destructive harvesting practices are another problem that currently plagues the exploitation of nonwood forest products. Although simple and effective methods for climbing trees are available throughout the tropics, some forest collectors feel that this is either too time consuming or too labor intensive, and decide instead to fell the entire tree. This practice has virtually eliminated the aguaje palm from many of the forests surrounding Iquitos. Educating collectors about the ecological impact and economic cost of destructive harvesting is an obvious prerequisite to sustainable forest use.

A final problem has to do with securing land rights for the people who live in the forest and make a living collecting nonwood resources. Timber concessions are granted for logging operations and federal subsidies are allocated for the creation of cattle pastures, yet rarely have the activities of forest collectors received government support. They have no guaranteed collection rights to the forest, they are not eligible for government loans that could be used for management, and they receive no extension assistance concerning the collection, processing, or marketing of their products. The concept of extractive forest reserves as articulated by the rubber tappers in Brazil appears to be a particularly innovative response to this situation. An attractive logic is associated with the idea of giving legal control over the forest to people that have the largest vested interest in its conservation and sustained use.

The commercial exploitation of fruits, latex, and other nonwood products is not a panacea for tropical deforestation. It is, however, the land-use practice that looks the best on the balance sheets of both economists and ecologists. Policy makers, resource managers, and development planners in the tropics should try to do everything they can to promote this form of forest utilization. In the economy of the rain forest, any other course of action is just throwing money away.

5

"By leaving most of the trees standing, selective loggers can preserve the integrity of the ecosystem and allow the rainforest to survive."

Selective Logging Can Save Rain Forests

Scott Lewis

In the following viewpoint, Scott Lewis argues that the timber industry is cutting a "wide swath through the world's tropical forests." This destruction occurs, Lewis contends, even though innovative logging practices can ensure the survival of the rain forests. These techniques selectively remove trees so the forest can restore itself, the author says. To encourage reform in the tropical timber industry, Lewis calls on consumers of tropical woods to exert economic pressure on the governments and companies that benefit from logging. Scott Lewis is an energy and environmental policy analyst.

As you read, consider the following questions:

1. Why does Lewis think that logging can hurt a country's economy?
2. What does the author mean by the terms "selective logging" and "small-patch clear-cutting"?
3. In the author's opinion, why is local control of forest resources important?

Excerpted, with permission, from *The Rainforest Book* by Scott Lewis. Los Angeles: Living Planet Press, 1990.

Tropical hardwoods are valued for their beauty, strength, and durability. Resistant to wear, rot, and insect damage, hardwoods make excellent wall paneling, floorboards, and furniture. These characteristics have led to demand for tropical hardwoods in developed countries, including the United States. Tropical hardwoods also make their way into paper, packaging, and other uses for which alternative woods are equally suitable. For example, Japan uses much of its tropical hardwood imports for disposable molds that hold concrete during construction and are then thrown away.

While Japan imports primarily unprocessed logs, the United States is the leading importer of processed tropical timber. . . .

Widespread Logging

Commercial logging has cut a wide swath through the world's tropical forests. Not only has excessive tropical forest logging contributed to species extinction and the long-term loss of income to rainforest countries, it has caused severe human difficulties as well. In many countries different laws govern the land itself; underground resources, such as minerals, coal, and oil; and above-ground resources, such as timber. Often, legal claims by communities to local forests have been challenged by loggers who have been given legal title to the timber resources by the government.

In Bolivia, Guarani Indians who fought to obtain legal title to the land under one law were confronted by loggers who had been given timber concessions to the same land under a different law. This is permissible under the existing Bolivian legal structure, making it very difficult for local communities to gain control over their own forest resources.

The lack of local control has led to overcutting of many tropical forests. Africa was once the leading source of tropical hardwoods to the developed world, but overcutting there has depleted the majority of rainforests, and few remain productive. In Ghana and the Ivory Coast, for example, logging is one of the causes that have brought about the loss of up to 80 percent of the original rainforest. Gabon has already lost over 60 percent of its original primary rainforest cover, and logging concessions have been granted in three-fourths of the forests that remain.

Southeast Asia has eclipsed Africa as the leading supplier of tropical hardwood to the international market, but its rainforests, too, are becoming widely decimated by logging. Over 80 percent of Thailand's primary rainforest has been destroyed or severely damaged.

Recent studies show that timber harvesting can result in the loss of valuable economic revenue because of its impact on fisheries, tourism, and the loss of products that could have been extracted sustainably, such as nuts, fruits, latex, and oils. Deforestation has increased the sediment load of many tropical rivers, causing declines in both freshwater and saltwater fisheries. An economic analysis of the effects of logging versus fishing and tourism in Palawan in the Philippines found that a logging ban would save more than $11 million over 10 years, even taking into account the revenues from the logging operations.

The Destruction Continues

A flood exacerbated by deforestation that left hundreds dead in November 1988 finally convinced the Thai government to ban all commercial logging. Subsequent developments in Thailand underscore the difficulty of enforcing a timber ban. Loggers have managed to circumvent the Thai ban by cutting trees near the Laos and Myanmar (Burma) borders, taking the logs across the borders, and then importing them back into Thailand, as though they had originated in Laos or Myanmar.

The Timber Frenzy

Since the 1950s, logging has increased rapidly in rain forests worldwide. Rainforest countries have opened up vast tracts of land to international timber industries in order to generate capital. Too often, both the governments and timber industries have focused on quick profits, rather than the long-term survival and renewal of the rain forests. Driving this destructive timber trade are the demands of consumers in industrialized nations, including the United States.

Sierra Club, *Tropical Rain Forests: A Vanishing Treasure*, September 1990.

Indonesia, once a minor player in the tropical hardwoods market, now exports more hardwood plywood than any other country. By 1988 Indonesia was exporting over $3 billion worth of hardwood plywood annually; only oil generated more export earnings. Diminishing timber reserves led the Indonesian government to impose a ban on raw log exports in 1985. The ban has not been enforced, however. In the first five months of 1989, Indonesia exported nearly $1 million worth of tropical hardwood logs to the United States.

The Philippines, with less than 10 percent of its original forest cover remaining, also has banned timber exports. Malaysia banned raw-log exports from its mainland rainforest in 1985, but it still exports wood from its provinces of Sarawak and Sabah on the island of Borneo. The rainforests of these two provinces are the oldest in the world, but they may be gone in as little as seven years. Loggers there have access to 95 percent of the rainforest not already set aside in existing or proposed reserves. Japan, the world's largest consumer of tropical timber, takes most of the rainforest wood cut in Sarawak and Sabah; close to 90 percent of Japanese log imports comes from the two Malaysian states. Japan's voracious appetite for tropical timber is also responsible for the deforestation of large sectors of rainforest in Thailand, Indonesia, and the Philippines.

As reserves in Southeast Asia dwindle, timber companies are turning to even more remote rainforests, such as those in Papua New Guinea. There is also increasing interest in Latin American timber, and the region is poised for a great expansion in logging. In three months in 1987, Brazil alone exported more mahogany lumber to the United States than to all other countries combined for any 12-month period in the previous 10 years. The other important tropical timber producers in Latin America are Paraguay, Ecuador, Colombia, and Peru.

At the present pace of timber extraction, the revenues generated by commercial logging will be short-lived, however. Currently, the tropical timber trade produces roughly $6 billion annually for tropical countries. That figure is expected to drop to $2 billion by the turn of the century as supplies shrink due to poorly managed logging. By the year 2000, many tropical countries will be forced to become net timber importers.

Alternatives to Deforestation

This need not be the case. Alternatives to typical clear-cutting practices, such as selective logging and small-patch clear-cutting, can lead to sustainable timber harvesting. In selective logging, only the commercially desirable species are removed from a patch of forest. Out of the thousands of tropical hardwood species, only a few are sought after by commercial buyers.

Southeast Asia, for example, exports only about two dozen of its thousands of types of trees. By leaving most of the trees standing, selective loggers can preserve the integrity of the ecosystem and allow the rainforest to survive. Even so, most loggers clear-cut entire areas of forest and either burn undesirable species or leave them to rot.

Selective logging often creates its own problems, however. Because of the density of the trees and the vast entanglement of climbing plants and vines that wind from one tree to another, a falling tree can damage or destroy dozens of other trees. When the loggers drag the selected trees to the road, extensive soil damage results. A commercial logging operation using selective logging techniques may leave up to two-thirds of the remaining trees damaged, and almost a third of the soil left bare and permanently harmed. If care is taken to cut climbing plants and vines loose before trees are felled, and if trees are cut to fall at angles that will minimize the number of other trees they damage on the way down, much of this destruction can be avoided.

Another problem with selective logging is high-grading—the impoverishment of the forest through the removal of all the valuable species. Care must be taken to leave examples of some of the valuable species behind to serve as a source of seeds for forest regeneration. Selective logging also takes more time, thus raising the cost of logging. Given the right conditions, however, selective logging might be successful.

Appetite for Hardwood

Industrial countries' appetite for tropical hardwoods also contributes to forest destruction. This ready market encourages Third World countries to "mine" their forests to earn vital foreign exchange. For example, Malaysia—currently the leading tropical log exporter—gets all of its export logs from the states of Sabah and Sarawak. The rate of timber harvesting in Sabah is four times the rate of natural regneration, leading to forest depletion. Similarly, unsustainable logging in Côte D'Ivoire (Ivory Coast) has contributed to a halving of the nation's forested area over the last two decades. If this rate of destruction continues, the country's forests will be completely gone in 16 years.

Sandra Postel, *American Forests,* November/December 1988.

Small-patch clear-cutting is another promising technique for protecting the rainforest. Using this approach, loggers clear a small patch of forest but leave the surrounding areas intact. Natural forest growth eventually fills the holes back in, reseeding the patch with local species. Disruptions to wildlife, watershed, and climate are thereby minimized. . . .

Unfortunately, neither selective logging nor small-patch clearcutting is widely practiced. So far the idea of sustainable tropical forestry has proven to be elusive. According to the International Tropical Timber Organization (ITTO), sustainable tropical forestry has succeeded on less than one-eighth of 1 percent of all tropical forests. Worldwide, such efforts have had "negligible" success, according to ITTO.

Tree Plantations

A third technique being tried to reduce the pressure to cut timber from the virgin forests is the creation of tree plantations. These tree farms are designed to supply timber for domestic demand as well as export. Brazil has established almost 10 million acres of tree plantations over a 20-year period. In the process, the country has gone from being a net importer of pulp and paper products to exporting $365 million worth of plantation-grown products a year. In Southeast Asia, about 200,000 acres of hardwood plantations are established each year.

The trouble with plantations is that many growers clear the primary forest to start their projects, using the profits from the felled native timber to offset start-up costs. For example, in Ecuador and Colombia, there has been large-scale clearing of tropical forest for oil palm plantations. . . .

Social and economic disruption of local communities can be severe. In Karnataka, India, for example, rural communities were not allowed on common lands after the establishment of eucalyptus plantations, and this lack of access reduced their supply of fuelwood and fodder. The project, which required little labor, provided support to few in the communities. Rural poor in Karnataka eventually protested the plantations by uprooting the eucalyptus seedlings.

There are other problems with tree plantations. One important consequence is the loss of biological diversity and general ecosystem simplification. In cases where only one or a few species are planted, the trees become much more vulnerable to pest infestation, disease, and environmental change. Species diversity provides the genetic resources to adapt to environmental alterations and restricts the progress of fungal diseases and insects. There are numerous instances of tree plantations suffering massive losses from insect attack.

In degraded rainforest areas natural regeneration should be encouraged instead of tree plantations. Where the land has been severely degraded, regeneration should be undertaken by planting a large variety of native species to provide diversity and wildlife habitat.

A Sustainable Future

The challenge is for tropical timber importers to design a system that rewards and thereby encourages sustainable forest management without crippling tropical economies. We must encourage the companies and government officials who regulate and exploit the tropical hardwoods trade to reduce the level of cutting and to perform timber harvesting in a more ecologically sound fashion. Our ultimate goal must be that rainforest hardwoods only be taken from sustainably managed forests.

In the long run, tropical forestry projects will neither be sustainable nor provide substantial benefit to local communities until legal control over forest resources is placed in the hands of the local communities. Only in this way will those managing the forests have a stake in their long-term health and sustainability; only then will the financial revenues benefit local economies.

One way the United States can promote this outcome is through the wise use of market influence. Consumers of tropical hardwoods must seek to determine the origin of hardwoods and purchase only those that come from well-managed systems. Identification could be made easy through the imposition of labeling requirements by our government and the governments of importing countries.

At the same time, the federal government should be encouraged to restrict imports of both processed and unprocessed tropical hardwoods except from countries and operations that meet the criteria of sustainability. This could be accomplished through the establishment of a tariff system, where countries that demonstrated progress toward sustainable forestry would be rewarded with lower tariffs or no tariff restrictions. Among the criteria for favorable tariff treatment must be control by communities over local forests and their resources, including the planning and implementation of timber sales and forest management; forestry projects that don't displace or interfere with local land tenants and that protect the land rights of native tribes; and timber harvesting that does not result in significant soil erosion, loss of biological diversity, or decreased forest productivity.

6

"Nature tourism has become critical to saving endangered animal habitat and preserving the world's rainforests. "

Tourism Can Save Rain Forests

Edward Warner

Visiting areas of natural beauty and value, known as "nature tourism," can contribute to the preservation of these areas, according to Edward Warner, the author of the following viewpoint. When they visit rain forests, tourists provide income to the local communities, Warner says. Because tourism and the income gained from it depends on the forest's preservation, the author reasons, local communities will want to protect the nature around them. While there are potential problems with nature tourism, they are relatively minor and are being addressed by an environmentally conscious industry and clientele, Warner contends. Edward Warner is a freelance writer.

As you read, consider the following questions:

1. What are the characteristics of "ecotourism," according to Warner?
2. What does the author say are the possible disadvantages of nature tourism?
3. In the author's opinion, why must local inhabitants benefit from nature tourism?

Edward Warner, "Ecotourism," *Environmental Action,* September/October 1989. Reprinted with permission.

At first it seemed serendipity, the happy confluence of two trends: On one hand, the rainforests and animal habitats of the world are being destroyed. On the other, tourists from North America and Western Europe are travelling to nature-oriented destinations like never before.

Could increased tourism give the people who live in these wild regions a reason to stop the logging, poaching and slash-and-burn farming? Could it even give them new and better-paying jobs in a tourist economy?

But problems have cropped up: Deforestation to heat lodges in Nepal, oil spills from tourist boats in Antarctica, tribal people forsaking their native music and dress to listen to U2 on Walkmans and wear Reeboks.

A New Kind of Tourism

The purest bloom may be off the orchid for nature tourism, but many believe these early errors are part of the learning experience leading to a new kind of nature tourism, an "ecotourism" where travelers are schooled in cultural and ecological sensitivity before they board the plane, where their tour company supports conservation and cultural enhancement projects in the host nations, and where a large share of the cash remains in the rural areas of the host country. In sum, a brand of tourism that enhances the natural environment and the lives of local people.

Some say ecotourism is here already, pointing to the fact that, whatever its excesses, nature tourism has become critical to saving endangered animal habitat and preserving the world's rainforests, which are being decimated at a rate of 140,000 acres a day.

All the world's people have something at stake in this because trees eliminate much of the carbon dioxide from the world's air and increased carbon dioxide levels have been blamed for triggering a global warming trend that could flood cities and turn farmland into deserts.

The people of the industrialized world—specifically their cars and electric power plants—have caused the carbon dioxide buildup, but don't expect their governments to start buying up the world's rainforests as buffer zones against First World pollution. In post-Reagan America, where a $7 billion foreign aid budget has remained largely unchanged since 1984, government purse strings are drawn tight.

For the individual who wants to take action to curb global warming, one option is a birding trip to Costa Rica, or rafting in the Amazon jungle.

Not a bad way to atone for one's sins of energy use.

Nature tourism has already seen success in preserving pristine animal habitat, which the Nature Conservancy estimates is being destroyed so fast that it will be gone from tropical regions in 30 years. In the developing African nation of Rwanda, for instance, visitors to the Parc Nacional des Volcans pay $170 each to view the mountain gorillas made famous by Dian Fossey and the movie, "Gorillas in the Mist." The fee revenue is used to protect habitat and prevent poaching, and helps make tourism Rwanda's second-biggest source of foreign currency.

New Trends in Travel

Tourism presents another attractive and sustainable alternative to rainforest logging. "Ecotourism" is a growth industry: the number of foreign tourists arriving in Manaus, Brazil, the heart of the Amazon rainforest, increased to over 70,000 in 1988 from 12,000 in 1983. In an effort to draw tourists, Costa Rica now advertises the wonders of its rainforests and other natural resources in U.S. magazines.

It stands to reason that if countries realize the economic benefits of preserving their rainforests in order to attract tourist dollars, they will do much to protect them.

Scott Lewis, *The Rainforest Book,* 1990.

Rwanda's ecotourism gains are cited by the World Resources Institute in an upcoming report on different means of financing international conservation efforts. The report says: "Although some 7,000 protected areas exist throughout the world, comparatively few enjoy de facto protection, and most of those in developing countries that do, can attribute their survival to the revenue they earn from tourism."

Translation: One of the rainforests' best hopes may be a thousand points of ecotouristic light.

Currently in Effect

A major proponent of using tourism to protect a region's ecology is Wilbur Garrett, editor of *National Geographic Magazine.* Since a 1987 meeting with the president of Guatemala, Garrett has promoted a plan called *"La Ruta Maya",* or The Mayan Route in English. As Garrett explained in an interview with *Environmental Action,* this circular system of existing trails and roads (some unpaved) links the Mayan archaeological sites on Mexico's Yucatan peninsula with those in Guatemala, Belize and Honduras. It also takes tourists to rainforests, beaches and coral reefs now far off the beaten track.

Garrett views La Ruta Maya as a continuing effort that has already begun—without any official opening ceremony, new treaties or expected date of completion. The governments of all four adjoining countries have told Garrett they support his brainchild. And *National Geographic* will promote this tourism concept through a major feature article.

What La Ruta Maya is not, Garrett maintains, is a large-scale development scheme. Lodges will be established (preferably by local businessmen) as the need arises rather than in response to any government's master plan. No new roads must be built, though some need improving, and a road connecting Honduras and Guatemala would be helpful, he says.

Efforts to preserve the lands through which La Ruta Maya passes are also showing signs of success. Mexico, Belize and Guatemala have agreed to place about 5 million acres into a United Nations-designated "biosphere." Farming and tourism, but not deforestation, are allowed within such protected areas. Besides committing 1.7 million acres to the biosphere, Guatemala recently created 44 national parks.

Other strategies that will help preserve the region's wildlands can be incorporated into La Ruta Maya, Garrett says, pointing to small-scale agriculture as an example. Over 100 potential cash crops thrive in the rainforest, including cacao, and the route could help farmers get their goods to market. . . .

A Growing Phenomenon

Even rough figures on how many tourists travel on nature-oriented journeys to developing nations aren't available, but Liz Boo, a program officer with the World Wildlife Fund, says "it's a growing phenomenon."

The coordinator of the Nature Conservancy's three-year-old tour programs, Bridget Bean, says 200 tourists traveled on her trips in 1989, twice as many as the year before. She expects the total to double again. And overall, more Americans are travelling outside U.S. borders—the 12.5 million U.S. citizens who did so in 1988 represented a 29 percent leap over the 1983 level.

Ecotourism isn't confined to the United States either. Canada has seen a rise in overseas travel, with more travelers taking adventure-oriented tours in Third World settings. And at least two lesser-developed nations—Peru and Costa Rica—are promoting ecotourism to their own population, hoping to build a constituency of nature lovers and preservers.

Costa Rica has the potential to become the world's leading ecotourism destination. Tourism and parks are already a money maker, the nation's second-biggest source of foreign currency after the agricultural sector.

One-tenth of the world's bird species—around 850 species—live in or migrate through this country the size of West Virginia. Costa Rica also has 1,200 species of orchids and 1,500 species of butterflies. Prior to 1969, however, Costa Rica had not a single national park and just one nature preserve; today, 11 percent of the country's landmass is in national parks. In an indication that it is seeking tourists other than the Club Med sun-and-fun set, ads for Costa Rica's national airline feature the bright green Quetzal bird, and a brochure depicts the nation's wildlife.

Uneven Benefits

After completing a five-nation study on nature tourism for the World Wildlife Fund, Liz Boo's assessment is that benefits will vary around the world because "not every park's going to be a big money maker."

Heavy reliance on tourism by Costa Rica and other developing countries has some worrying that these economies will become hostage to the sometimes fickle tastes and roller-coaster national economies of Western powers.

For some nations, the question already has vital importance. In Nepal, for instance, *National Geographic*'s Garrett maintains that if "you take all the tourism away, they'd be broke." In the meantime, the great number of foreign trekkers in Nepal has driven up food and lodging costs, notes *Natural History* magazine, so that locals must hustle to keep pace with inflation.

Nor is nature tourism an evenhanded substitute for foreign aid. Its dollars typically go to nations or regions where few people live. The rainforest thrives in Belize, but not in neighboring El Salvador, largely because, though of equal size, the former has only 160,000 citizens while the latter has about 5 million.

On the other hand, ecotourism is not being touted as a source of income that is any more stable or long-term than, say, oil refining or iron mining—just a lot less polluting.

And, while it may benefit neighboring nations unevenly, the economic transaction at its heart is at least human-faced: Travelers meet local tourism workers personally, which may bring these workers better treatment than they'd get, say, working for a textile assembly plant.

A human face does not guarantee humane behavior, however. According to expert Jason Clay, if indigenous people are made to feel inferior or backward in their encounter with tourists, they may give up their culture for the pursuit of all the consumer goods that tourist income can buy. Tribal cultures don't need to be "protected" from Western culture, stresses Clay, research director for the nonprofit human-rights group Cultural Survival based in Cambridge, Mass. Rather, they need "the room and the time to make the choice."

Environmental Backfire?

Another potential pitfall has a certain irony to it: Nature-seeking visitors to a pristine wild area sometimes cause as many environmental problems as they solve.

In Nepal's Annapurna Range, a 1987 study reported in *Natural History* counted approximately 50 travelers' lodges, whereas there had been almost none prior to 1970. Thanks to the lodge operators' demand for wood and fuel, the tree line had been lowered by several hundred feet, and no trees were left in the adjoining Annapurna Sanctuary, a wildlife preserve.

Worries over the environmental impact of nature tourism accelerated in 1988 when an Argentinian tour boat went aground off Antarctica, spilling most of its 250,000 gallons of fuel. In the aftermath, a report presented to the parliament of Australia (which claims 42 percent of Antarctica as its territory) said boats were still the best way to transport and house Antarctic tourists, but stricter regulation was needed. In any case, a 1988 Environmental Defense Fund report says that scientists, not tourists, are the biggest pollution problem for the icy continent. Though approximately 2,500 tourists visited Antarctica in the 1987-88 season, the study found that the chief danger is garbage and toxic wastes discarded in pits, burned and dumped in the ocean by Antarctica's 57 scientific research stations.

Compelling Arguments

The arguments in favor of developing nature-based tourism are compelling. For one, it brings in crucial foreign exchange. In Costa Rica, Ecuador, the Philippines and Thailand, tourism ranks among the top five industries and brings in more foreign currency than wood exports. Secondly, from a conservation perspective, nature-based tourism places a monetary value on habitat preservation—a spur to governments, the local community and tourists alike to recognize that any disturbance to the environment is detrimental.

Judith Gradwohl and Russel Greenberg, *Saving the Tropical Forests,* 1988.

Worldwide, nature tourists are typically tidy travelers, say tour operators such as Jean Shollian, a destination coordinator at International Expeditions Inc. "These people are into the environment and protecting it," she notes, adding that ecotourists see unpaved routes and un-airconditioned lodgings as part of the package.

Nature tourists and their tour operators also often generously fund conservation efforts in the regions they visit. The Nature Conservancy, for example, raised $150,000 for the Darwin Research Station in the Galapagos Islands by mailing a fundraising appeal to those who signed the station's guest log. That organization also requests a $300 contribution from each person on its tours to fund the host nation's conservation efforts.

To ensure that nature tourism results in environmental preservation and the protection of indigenous cultures, experts roundly say one factor is crucial: That local people receive most of the economic benefits. Unless the local economy improves through ecotourism, the local powers and the national government will have little incentive to fight off poachers, or land-clearers, or hydroelectric dams.

Forests and People

"The forest has to survive in harmony with the people who live there," observes Fred Van Bolhuis, senior associate at the World Resources Institute. "Unless they benefit substantially from the tourism, [the forest] is not going to survive."

The flipside is also that local citizens who are financially committed to ecotourism will act to protect their resources. Lodge keepers in Nepal responded to the dire 1987 tree census by converting to kerosene for heating and by regulating lodge development and forest use, according to *Natural History*. To mitigate the inflation impact, a conservation organization was established that levies fees on tour operators—money that has since funded a school, the region's first clinic and a nursery of trees for fuel.

Local regulation has worked especially well, conservationists say, in the Galapagos Islands, which had virtually no tourism before 1970 and now receive 36,000 visitors annually. "In the Galapagos, tourism control is extremely strict and hinges primarily upon a system of licensed naturalists who work for private tour companies, but are held personally responsible for the action of their passengers," nature writer Tui De Roy, a Galapagos native, told *Bioscience*. Tourists can only travel in groups led by a naturalist and are restricted to specific sites and well-marked trails.

Clearly, ecotourism represents one of what may be dozens of solutions to saving endangered forests and habitat. Yet it is one of the few solutions that is here now, awaiting no action by any government or massive spending effort by any organization. It is also one of the few that is small-scale, based on the travel decisions of citizens in one nation and on the rise of a tourist economy in another.

No one will deny that ecotourism is a pragmatic approach. If the price of this triage for the rainforest can be kept to a Coke can beside a jungle path, or a tribal chieftain with a boombox, or the loss of some nature *au naturel*, then that price will be small indeed.

Recognizing Statements That Are Provable

We are constantly confronted with statements and generalizations about social and moral problems. In order to think clearly about these problems, it is useful if one can make a basic distinction between provable statements for which evidence can be found and unprovable statements which cannot be verified because evidence is not available, or the issue is so controversial that it cannot be definitely proved.

Readers should be aware that magazines, newspapers, and other sources often contain statements of a controversial nature. The following activity is designed to improve your skill at distinguishing between statements that are provable and those that are not.

The following statements are taken from the viewpoints in this chapter. Consider each statement carefully. *Mark P for any statement you believe is provable. Mark U for any statement you feel is unprovable because of the lack of evidence. Mark C for any statement you think is too controversial to be proved to everyone's satisfaction.*

If you are doing this activity as a member of a class or group, compare your answers with those of other class or group members. Be able to defend your answers. You may discover that others come to different conclusions than you do. Listening to the reasons others present for their answers may give you valuable insights into recognizing statements that are provable.

P = *provable*
U = *unprovable*
C = *too controversial*

183

1. Tropical forests house one-half to three-quarters of all living species.

2. By 1988 Indonesia was exporting over three billion dollars worth of hardwood plywood annually.

3. The road-building projects that first drew Brazilians into the Amazon were subsidized by the World Bank.

4. If indigenous people are made to feel inferior in their encounters with tourists, they will give up their culture.

5. Ecotourism will succeed if local communities benefit from it.

6. Rain forest trees produce many fruits, fibers, and industrial compounds.

7. The Brazilian government is unlikely to let Americans purchase and protect land in the Amazon's tropical rain forest.

8. The tropical timber trade produces roughly six billion dollars annually for tropical countries.

9. Deforestation can be traced to the expanding populations of tropical countries.

10. Marginal lands can support the increased populations of the future, at acceptable living standards.

11. A lot of the loans from the multilateral development banks which have gone to the governments in the Amazon Basin have been used for specific political purposes.

12. Tropical forestry projects will not be sustainable until legal control over forest resources is placed in the hands of local communities.

13. Deforestation in Brazil would be unprofitable without government subsidies and incentives.

14. Biological diversity is a goal worth fighting for.

15. The murder of Chico Mendes of the rubber tappers received a lot of publicity.

16. We must encourage the government officials who regulate the tropical hardwoods trade to reduce the level of cutting.

17. Tourism and parks earn more foreign currency for Costa Rica than any other sector of the economy except agriculture.

18. Harvesting rain forests' nonwood products will generate more income than logging them.

19. Rain forests act as a watershed for some of the world's major rivers.

20. The foreign debts of Third World countries are the result of poor management by Third World governments.

Periodical Bibliography

The following articles have been selected to supplement the diverse views presented in this chapter.

Bruce Babbitt	"Amazon Grace," *The New Republic*, June 25, 1990.
Henry R. Breck	"Rain Forests for Rent," *Newsweek*, December 5, 1988.
Betsy Carpenter	"Faces in the Forest," *U.S. News & World Report*, June 4, 1990.
Douglas Foster	"No Road to Tahuanti," *Mother Jones*, July/August 1990.
Gawain Kripke	"The Destruction of the Southeast Asian Rain Forest," *Multinational Monitor*, November 1989.
Dena Leibman	"Default or Deliver," *Sierra*, September/October 1990.
Michael D. Lemonick	"Hot Tempers in Hawaii," *Time*, August 13, 1990.
Eugene Linden	"Playing with Fire," *Time*, September 18, 1989.
Ariel E. Lugo	"The Future of the Forest," *Environment*, September 1988.
Mac Margolis	"Rain Forest Crunch," *World Monitor*, November 1990. Available from The Christian Science Publishing Society, 1 Norway St., Boston, MA 02115.
Robert C. Repetto	"Deforestation in the Tropics," *Scientific American*, April 1990.
Hannah Finan Roditi and James B. Goodno	"Rainforest Crunch," *Dollars & Sense*, November 1990.
Philip Shabecoff	"Loss of Tropical Forests Is Found Much Worse than Was Thought," *The New York Times*, June 8, 1990.
Roger D. Stone	"The Global Stakes of Tropical Deforestation," *USA Today*, March 1988.
Nira Broner Worgman	"Brazil's Thriving Environmental Movement," *Technology Review*, October 1990.
Clemens P. Work and Geri Smith	"Using Red Ink to Keep Tropical Forests Green," *U.S. News & World Report*, March 6, 1989.

How Can Sustainable Agriculture Be Promoted?

Chapter Preface

For most of human existence, people lived as hunters and food gatherers. Agriculture, the intentional growing of plants for food, began only about ten thousand years ago. Early farmers would select a field to be cleared, burn off the shrubs and trees, and then use the ashes to fertilize the first crop. After a few seasons, as the soil's nutrients became depleted and harvests began to decline, the farmers would abandon the field and select another to start the process over again. The old field would slowly begin to regenerate and shrubs and trees would gradually reseed the area, returning nutrients to the topsoil and restoring the land's fertility. After fifteen or twenty years, the field would be ready for the next generation of farmers to burn and cultivate.

This bush-fallow system of agriculture, also called swidden or shifting cultivation, is one of many forms of traditional agriculture still found in Third World nations. It is a sustainable method—that is, it provides enough food to support farm communities while still allowing the land to replenish its nutrients. Such practices supported indigenous people for thousands of years—as long as populations remained small.

Third World populations have increased, however, and farmers—needing to produce more food for more people—now return to the abandoned fields before the land can regenerate. As increasing acres of this overcultivated land become unusable, farmers clear more forested areas for cultivation. This has resulted in deforestation and the erosion and depletion of the soil. Much of the land cultivated in this traditional way is now infertile because of overuse, and can no longer support Third World farmers and their families.

The Third World must develop a new type of sustainable agriculture to protect the land and provide enough food to feed the region's people. But how this can be accomplished is controversial. The authors of the following chapter discuss and debate a variety of ways to promote sustainable agriculture.

"Farmers successfully adopting these systems generally derive significant sustained economic and environmental benefits."

Alternative Agriculture Will Achieve Sustainability

National Research Council

The National Research Council is an independent adviser on scientific and technical questions of national importance to the U.S. government. The following viewpoint is taken from a committee report on alternative farming methods. The report reviews the scientific and economic knowledge of alternative agriculture and the policies that influence its adoption. It concludes that, although much needs to be done to encourage wider adoption, alternative agriculture practices will benefit farmers, the economy, and the environment.

As you read, consider the following questions:

1. Why do the authors of the report contend that alternative agriculture is not a single system of farming practices?
2. How can farmers reduce pesticide use, according to the authors?
3. What policies discourage adoption of alternative agriculture, according to this viewpoint?

Excerpted from the executive summary of *Alternative Agriculture*, a 1989 report of the Committee on the Role of Alternative Farming Methods in Modern Production Agriculture, Board on Agriculture, National Research Council. Excerpted with permission.

In the 1930s, crop yields in the United States, England, India, and Argentina were essentially the same. Since that time, researchers, scientists, and a host of federal policies have helped U.S. farmers dramatically increase yields of corn, wheat, soybeans, cotton, and most other major commodities. Today, fewer farmers feed more people than ever before. This success, however, has not come without costs.

The U.S. Environmental Protection Agency (EPA) has identified agriculture as the largest nonpoint source of surface water pollution. Pesticides and nitrate from fertilizers are detected in the groundwater in many agricultural regions. Soil erosion remains a concern in many states. Pest resistance to pesticides continues to grow, and the problem of pesticide residues in food has yet to be resolved. Purchased inputs have become a significant part of total operating costs. Other nations have closed the productivity gap and are more competitive in international markets. Federal farm program costs have risen dramatically in recent years.

Because of these concerns, many farmers have begun to adopt alternative practices with the goals of reducing input costs, preserving the resource base, and protecting human health. The committee has reviewed the dimensions and structure of U.S. agriculture, its problems, and some of the alternatives available to farmers to resolve them.

Many components of alternative agriculture are derived from conventional agronomic practices and livestock husbandry. The hallmark of an alternative farming approach is not the conventional practices it rejects but the innovative practices it includes. In contrast to conventional farming, however, alternative systems more deliberately integrate and take advantage of naturally occurring beneficial interactions. Alternative systems emphasize management; biological relationships, such as those between the pest and predator; and natural processes, such as nitrogen fixation instead of chemically intensive methods. The objective is to sustain and enhance rather than reduce and simplify the biological interactions on which production agriculture depends, thereby reducing the harmful off-farm effects of production practices.

Definitions

Alternative agriculture is any system of food or fiber production that systematically pursues the following goals:

• More thorough incorporation of natural processes such as nutrient cycles, nitrogen fixation, and pest-predator relationships into the agricultural production process;

• Reduction in the use of off-farm inputs with the greatest potential to harm the environment or the health of farmers and consumers;

189

- Greater productive use of the biological and genetic potential of plant and animal species;
- Improvement of the match between cropping patterns and the productive potential and physical limitations of agricultural lands to ensure long-term sustainability of current production levels; and
- Profitable and efficient production with emphasis on improved farm management and conservation of soil, water, energy, and biological resources.

"We don't bother buying pesticides anymore. We just spray the crops with our groundwater."

Simpson/Rothco. Reprinted with permission.

Alternative agriculture is *not* a single system of farming practices. It includes a spectrum of farming systems, ranging from organic systems that attempt to use no purchased synthetic chemical inputs, to those involving the prudent use of pesticides or antibiotics to control specific pests or diseases. Alternative farming encompasses, but is not limited to, farming systems known as biological, low-input, organic, regenerative, or sustainable. It includes a range of practices such as integrated pest management (IPM); low-intensity animal production systems;

crop rotations designed to reduce pest damage, improve crop health, decrease soil erosion, and, in the case of legumes, fix nitrogen in the soil; and tillage and planting practices that reduce soil erosion and help control weeds. Alternative farmers incorporate these and other practices into their farming operations. Successful alternative farmers do what all good managers do—they apply management skills and information to reduce costs, improve efficiency, and maintain production levels.

Some examples of practices and principles emphasized in alternative systems include:

- Crop rotations that mitigate weed, disease, insect, and other pest problems; increase available soil nitrogen and reduce the need for purchased fertilizers; and, in conjunction with conservation tillage practices, reduce soil erosion.
- IPM, which reduces the need for pesticides by crop rotations, scouting, weather monitoring, use of resistant cultivars, timing of planting, and biological pest controls.
- Management systems to control weeds and improve plant health and the abilities of crops to resist insect pests and diseases.
- Soil- and water-conserving tillage.
- Animal production systems that emphasize disease prevention through health maintenance, thereby reducing the need for antibiotics.
- Genetic improvement of crops to resist insect pests and diseases and to use nutrients more effectively.

Adaptability of Alternative Systems

Alternative systems are often diversified. Diversified systems, which tend to be more stable and resilient, reduce financial risk and provide a hedge against drought, pest infestation, or other natural factors limiting production. Diversification can also reduce economic pressures from price increases for pesticides, fertilizers, and other inputs; drops in commodity prices; regulatory actions affecting the availability of certain products; and pest resistance to pesticides.

Alternative farming practices can be compatible with small or large farms and many different types of machinery. Differences in climate and soil types, however, affect the costs and viability of alternative systems. Alternative practices must be carefully adapted to the biological and physical conditions of the farm and region. For example, it is relatively easy for corn and soybean farmers in the Midwest to reduce or eliminate routine insecticide use, a goal much harder for fruit and vegetable growers in regions with long production seasons, such as the hot and humid Southeast. Crop rotation and mechanical tillage can control weeds in certain crops, climates, and soils, but herbicides may be the only economical way to control weeds in others.

191

Substituting manure or legume forages for chemical fertilizers can significantly reduce fertilizer costs. However, a local livestock industry is often necessary to make these practices economical. . . .

Findings

Based on its study, the committee arrived at four major findings.

1. A small number of farmers in most sectors of U.S. agriculture currently use alternative farming systems, although components of alternative systems are used more widely. Farmers successfully adopting these systems generally derive significant sustained economic and environmental benefits. Wider adoption of proven alternative systems would result in even greater economic benefits to farmers and environmental gains for the nation.

Hooked on Drugs

If American agriculture checked into a chemical dependency center it would certainly be diagnosed as a serious addict. Hooked on a nasty array of pesticides, antibiotics, and synthetic fertilizers, its health deteriorating, its economic house in disorder, American agriculture would be recommended for a program of immediate detoxification. . . .

And American agriculture would certainly flunk a "urine" test: detectable traces of 60 different types of agricultural pesticides can be found in the groundwater of 30 states. In many regions, agriculture is also the biggest contaminator to surface water.

Sandra Steingraber, *Food First News*, Winter 1990.

---

2. A wide range of federal policies, including commodity programs, trade policy, research and extension programs, food grading and cosmetic standards, pesticide regulation, water quality and supply policies, and tax policy, significantly influence farmers' choices of agricultural practices. As a whole, federal policies work against environmentally benign practices and the adoption of alternative agricultural systems, particularly those involving crop rotations, certain soil conservation practices, reductions in pesticide use, and increased use of biological and cultural means of pest control. These policies have generally made a plentiful food supply a higher priority than protection of the resource base.

3. A systems approach to research is essential to the progress of alternative agriculture. Agricultural researchers have made

important contributions to many components of alternative as well as conventional agricultural systems. These contributions include the development of high-yielding pest-resistant cultivars, soil testing methods, conservation tillage, other soil and water conservation practices, and IPM programs. Little recent research, however, has been directed toward many on-farm interactions integral to alternative agriculture, such as the relationship among crop rotations, tillage methods, pest control, and nutrient cycling. Farmers must understand these interactions as they move toward alternative systems. As a result, the scientific knowledge, technology, and management skills necessary for widespread adoption of alternative agriculture are not widely available or well defined. Because of differences among regions and crops, research needs vary.

4. Innovative farmers have developed many alternative farming methods and systems. These systems consist of a wide variety of integrated practices and methods suited to the specific needs, limitations, resource bases, and economic conditions of different farms. To make wider adoption possible, however, farmers need to receive information and technical assistance in developing new management skills.

Incentives for the Adoption of Alternatives

Major segments of U.S. agriculture entered a period of economic hardship and stress in the early and mid-1980s. This period followed more than 30 years of growth in farm size and production following World War II. Export sales after 1981 slumped well below the record levels of the late 1970s. This was caused by the rising value of the dollar, a period of worldwide recession, high and rigid federal commodity program loan rates, and increases in agricultural production and exports from developed and certain developing countries. As food surpluses grew in some regions of the world, the industrialized nations promoted agricultural exports with a variety of subsidies. Many U.S. farmers, particularly specialized producers of major export crops such as corn, soybeans, cotton, and wheat, suffered financial hardship.

Some farmers, caught by the abrupt downward turn in commodity prices and land values, were unable to pay debts. Many were forced to leave farming. A substantial increase in federal price and income support payments beginning in 1983, coupled with stronger export demand, has helped insulate row-crop and small-grain producers from further economic losses. Nonetheless, tens of thousands of farms are still struggling, particularly middle-sized family farms with little or no off-farm income.

Apart from economic hardship, other adverse effects of conventional agriculture are being felt in some regions. Specialization and related production practices, such as extensive synthetic chemical fertilizer and pesticide use, are contributing to environmental and occupational health problems as well as potential public health problems. Insects, weeds, and pathogens continue to develop resistance to some commonly used insecticides, herbicides, and fungicides. Insects and pathogens also continue to overcome inbred genetic resistance of plants. Nitrate, predominantly from fertilizers and animal manures, and several widely used pesticides have been found in surface water and groundwater, making agriculture the leading nonpoint source of water pollution in many states. The decreasing genetic diversity of many major U.S. crops and livestock species (most notably dairy cattle and poultry) increases the potential for sudden widespread economic losses from disease. . . .

More Acceptable to Farmers

Once the term was synonymous with the dreaded *O* word—a farm-belt euphemism for trendy organic farming that uses no synthetic chemicals. But sustainable agriculture has blossomed into an effort to curb erosion by modifying plowing techniques and to protect water supplies by minimizing, if not eliminating, artificial fertilizers and pest controls. "Sustainable agriculture used to be something you said under your breath," jokes Indiana farmer Jim Moseley, agricultural consultant to the U.S. Environmental Protection Agency. "Now the definition has broadened so that it's politically acceptable to a greater range of people, and that has opened up an opportunity for dialogue."

J. Madeleine Nash, *Time,* May 21, 1990.

Farmers who adopt alternative farming systems often have productive and profitable operations, even though these farms usually function with relatively little help from commodity income and price support programs or extensions.

The committee's review of available literature and commissioned case studies illustrates that alternative systems can be successful in regions with different climatic, ecological, and economic conditions and on farms producing a variety of crops and livestock. Further, a small number of farms using alternative systems profitably produce most major commodities, usually at competitive prices, and often without participating in federal commodity price and income support programs. Some of these farms, however, depend on higher prices for their products. Successful alternative farmers often produce high per acre yields with significant reductions in costs per unit of crop harvested. A wide range of alternative systems and techniques deserves further support and investigation by agricultural and economic researchers. With modest adjustments in a number of federal agricultural policies many of these systems could become more widely adopted and successful.

Alternative farming practices are not a well-defined set of practices or management techniques. Rather, they are a range of technological and management options used on farms striving to reduce costs, protect health and environmental quality, and enhance beneficial biological interactions and natural processes.

Farmers adopting alternative practices strive for profitable and ecologically sound ways to use the particular physical, chemical, and biological potentials of their farms' resources. To these ends, they make choices to diversify their operations, make the fullest use of available on-farm resources, protect themselves and their communities from the potential hazards of agricultural chemicals, and reduce off-farm input expenses. Instead of rejecting modern agricultural science, farmers adopting alternative systems rely on increased knowledge of pest management and plant nutrition, improved genetic and biological potential of cultivars and livestock, and better management techniques. . . .

Well-managed alternative farming systems nearly always use less synthetic chemical pesticides, fertilizers, and antibiotics per unit of production than comparable conventional farms. Reduced use of these inputs lowers production costs and lessens agriculture's potential for adverse environmental and health effects without necessarily decreasing—and in some cases increasing—per acre crop yields and the productivity of livestock management systems.

Farmers can reduce pesticide use on cash grains through rotations that disrupt the reproductive cycle, habitat, and food supply of many crop insect pests and diseases. By altering the timing and placement of nitrogen fertilizers, farmers can often reduce per acre application rates with little or no sacrifice in crop yields. Further reductions are possible in regions where leguminous forages and cover crops can be profitably grown in rotation with corn, soybeans, and small grains. This usually requires the presence of a local hay market. Fruit and vegetable growers can often dramatically decrease pesticide use with an IPM program, particularly in dry or northern regions. . . .

Farmers will also have to acquire the new knowledge and management skills necessary to implement successful alternative practices. If these conditions are met, today's alternative farming practices could become tomorrow's conventional practices, with significant benefits for farmers, the economy, and the environment.

Editor's note: This is an edited version of the executive summary of the Board on Agriculture-National Research Council report Alternative Agriculture. *The 448-page report is available from the National Academy Press, 2101 Constitution Avenue, Washington, DC 20418. Call toll free: 1-800-624-6242.*

"The evidence is insufficient to conclude that the effects of conventional agriculture practices. . . are destructive enough to threaten the sustainability of U.S. agriculture."

Alternative Agriculture Will Not Achieve Sustainability

Pierre Crosson and Janet Ekey Ostrov

Pierre Crosson is a senior fellow at Resources for the Future in Washington, D.C. Janet Ekey Ostrov is a former research assistant for the same organization. Resources for the Future is a member of the Renewable Natural Resources Foundation, an organization concerned with promoting renewable natural resources and public policy alternatives. Crosson and Ostrov contend that it is too early to predict if alternative agriculture can be profitable for most farmers. They conclude that a large-scale shift to alternative agriculture would actually increase costs, reduce crop yields, and increase soil erosion.

As you read, consider the following questions:

1. Why do the authors believe that alternative agriculture is less profitable than conventional agriculture?
2. In what ways does alternative agriculture require more management skills than conventional agriculture, according to Crosson and Ostrov?
3. How do the authors rationalize relying on fossil fuels?

Pierre Crossan and Janet Ekey Ostrov, "Sorting Out the Environmental Benefits of Alternative Agriculture," *Journal of Soil and Water Conservation*, vol. 45, no. 1, January/February 1990, © 1990 Soil and Water Conservation Society. Reprinted with permission.

Proponents of alternative agriculture contend that it has significant environmental advantages over the conventional system now followed by most crop and animal producers in the United States. Farmers do not adequately reflect these advantages in their economic calculations because most of the advantages, such as reduced off-farm damages to soil and water quality, accrue to others. . . .

We use alternative agriculture here to mean the wide range of practices indicated by terms such as "low-input," "organic," and "regenerative" agriculture. The U.S. Department of Agriculture (USDA) definition of organic farming describes the system we have in mind: ". . .a production system which avoids or largely excludes the use of synthetically compounded fertilizers, pesticides, growth regulators and livestock feed additives. To the maximum extent feasible organic farming systems rely upon crop rotations, crop residues, animal manures, legumes, green manures, off-farm organic wastes, mechanical cultivation, mineral bearing rocks and aspects of biological pest control to maintain soil productivity and tilth, to supply plant nutrients, and to control insects, weeds and other pests."

Farm Comparisons

Most of the literature on the comparative economics of alternative agriculture is cast at the farm level; typically, the short-term profitability of alternative farms is compared with that of conventional farms. . . . The studies we reviewed showed that the alternative farming systems were less profitable than the conventional systems. . . .

In the studies reviewed, the most obvious reason for the lower profitability of the alternative systems was the yield penalty imposed as a result of committing large amounts of land to low-value rotational uses, both to provide nutrients and to control pests. The studies are less clear about other causes of the yield penalty, but difficulties of controlling pests without pesticides, particularly weeds, is a likely factor. . . . The Council for Agricultural Science and Technology cites a number of sources indicating that organic farmers name weed control as their number one problem (as it is of most conventional farmers, according to CAST). . . .

Herbicides control fast-growing weeds that compete with emerging corn and soybean plants when soil temperatures are cool, thus permitting earlier planting in the spring than would be possible if weeds were controlled by cultivation. R.S. Fawcett also asserts that herbicides give farmers greater flexibility in the timing of cultivation, and perhaps more important, although Fawcett does not label it so, herbicides permit continuous cropping. Herbicides permit farmers to keep more of their land in relatively high-value uses more of the time than would be possible using a rotational system of weed control. . . .

The CAST report gives considerable weight to banning fungicides in alternative systems of producing some fruits and vegetables. According to the report, foliar fungicidal sprays are the only feasible means of disease control for such plants as apples and tomatoes. The CAST report also notes that pesticides allow control of disease and insect damage in fresh fruits and vegetables after harvest, making it more possible to store and ship them over longer distances than is feasible for the same crops grown organically. Thus, the ban on using these materials may make the market for alternatively produced fruits and vegetables smaller than that for their conventionally produced competitors.

A Misconception About Fertilizers

There is a popular misconception that simply reducing the use of agricultural chemicals and fertilizers would automatically reduce the contamination of water resources and food supplies, while improving the sustainability of U.S. agriculture as an industry. This belief is often based more upon emotion and philosophy than on science and experience. It is based on small-scale demonstrations that cannot necessarily be extrapolated to mainstream agriculture.

Paul E. Fixen, Potash & Phosphate Institute *News & Views*, August 1989.

Another question is whether substituting organic for inorganic sources of nutrients contributes significantly to the yield difference between alternative and conventional systems. Although there is agreement that manure and crop residues are the major sources of organic fertilizers used in alternative agriculture, scientists disagree whether such practices exact a yield penalty. . . . Data from the Rodale farm in Kutztown, Pennsylvania, assert that "the potential for meeting crop nitrogen needs from legumes in rotation has been grossly underestimated by American scientists.". . . Kent D. Olson and colleagues, however, estimated the yield effect of substituting organic for inorganic sources of nutrients on field crops and found it to be substantially negative. . . .

Obstacles to Adoption

When asked to list obstacles to adopting alternative farming systems, the farmers surveyed most often named lack of information about practices; lack of marketing information, especially about the availability of markets offering premium prices for alternatively produced output; and the need for more research, particularly about weed control in alternative farming systems. Some also indicated that the supply of organic fertilizers and other inputs was a problem.

Roger Blobaum did not consider the management requirements of alternative agriculture as a barrier to conversion. Management was not prominently discussed in the literature on economics we reviewed. Clearly, however, alternative agriculture requires more management time and skill than conventional agriculture. In a discussion of some of the key characteristics of successful organic farmers, Patrick Madden asserted that they are "superb managers" with complete knowledge of their farm operations. Eliminating inorganic fertilizers and pesticides means that the farmer must have enough understanding of the complex relationships among crops, weeds, insects, diseases, and determinants of soil fertility to suppress those things that threaten the crop and encourage those things that make it thrive. Organic farmers also must be more careful about the timing of their operations. . . .

The more demanding management requirements of alternative agriculture may be a barrier to its more widespread adoption. Time spent in acquiring managerial skills and then applying them on the farm is time not available for other purposes. Many farmers work part-time off the farm, and for them more on-farm work has an opportunity cost measured by lost off-farm income. More on-farm work also means less time available for recreation, for family life, and for other pursuits of value to the farmer. . . .

At the farm level alternative agriculture, as it is now practiced, is less profitable than conventional agriculture. This is not a surprising finding. If it were not so, alternative agriculture would have already replaced conventional agriculture or would be well on its way toward doing so—which it is not.

Alternative agriculture is less profitable because what it saves in fertilizer and pesticide costs is not enough to compensate for the additional labor required and for the yield penalty it suffers relative to conventional farming. The main reasons for the yield penalty appear to be the necessary rotation of main crops with low-value legumes and the difficulty of controlling weeds without herbicides.

Inadequate Study

What would the economics of alternative agriculture look like if the system were to wholly displace the existing system? The question has been inadequately studied. Madden says that at present the economic consequences of a large-scale shift to alternative agriculture have no credible evidence. . . .

CAST estimated that a complete shift to alternative agriculture would reduce yields of most crops 15 to 25 percent, partly because organic sources of nitrogen would be inadequate to support current yields and partly because of losses from weeds, resulting from the ban on herbicides. CAST argues that to maintain production with a 15 to 25 percent yield reduction would require an increase in cropland of 18 to 33 percent if the land were of the same quality as land currently in production. . . .

CAST concluded that a wholesale shift to alternative agriculture would increase production costs, drive up supply prices, reduce amounts demanded (and hence production), and make farmers as a group economically better off at the expense of the rest of society. CAST also considered distributional effects among regions and farmers and concluded that the corn, soybean, and cotton-growing areas of the South and Southeast would be relatively disadvantaged because organic systems for combating the severe weed and insect problems in those regions would be less effective than in the Midwest and other areas growing those crops. Regions having inadequate supplies of manure or where growing legumes is uneconomical, as in dryland wheat-growing areas, also would be negatively affected.

Limits of Alternative Agriculture

CAST also concluded that because the switch to alternative agriculture would require more cropland, erosion would increase. Finally, land prices would rise, reflecting the increase in net farm income, and farm employment and wages would rise because of the relatively labor-intensive nature of alternative agriculture. . . .

A closely related issue concerns the relationship between the conditions of supply of organic matter and wholesale adoption of alternative agriculture. As noted earlier, crop residues and animal wastes are the principal sources of organic wastes potentially available to agriculture. . . .

If 100 percent of the nitrogen in crop residues and animal wastes could be made available to farmers on economical terms it would not be enough to replace nitrogen fertilizers, unless the losses of nitrogen in waste material were substantially less than the losses of fertilizer nitrogen.

This raises two important questions. First, could all of the nitrogen content of crop and animal wastes be made economically available to farmers? Second, are the losses of nitrogen from wastes less than from fertilizer?

Because an estimated 70 percent of crop residues already is returned directly to the soil, the nitrogen in this source is already available to farmers. The issue, therefore, is the economics of using the nitrogen in animal wastes, 61 percent of which is excreted in unconfined habitats, most of it on rangeland and pastureland rather than on cropland. Because of the high (75-90 percent) water content of animal waste, the cost of collecting and transporting it is high relative to the price of an equivalent amount of nitrogen in fertilizer at current prices.

With respect to the second question, estimates of nitrogen loss from fertilizer typically range from 30 to 50 percent or more. The nitrogen, as nitrate, is leached to groundwater, carried away in runoff, and volatilized by denitrification. Losses of nitrogen from animal wastes, however, appear to be high as well. CAST cites the 1978 USDA study on use of organic wastes as indicating that 63 percent of the nitrogen in manure now returned to the land is lost to volatilization and leaching, and that at best this could be reduced to 45 percent. According to CAST, this would increase the available amount of nitrogen from collectible manure from about 9 percent to 12 percent of the amount now supplied in fertilizer.

The only source of organic material that has much promise for replacing nitrogen fertilizer on a significant scale over the next decade or so is leguminous crops. This, of course, is what alternative agriculture proposes to do. Apart from whether these crops can produce enough nitrogen to replace that now available in fertilizer—an unsettled question—the necessity of including these crops in rotation with main crops is the primary reason for the lower yields of the latter per acre of land in the rotation. And this yield penalty is a principal reason for the conclusion of all the studies consulted that wholesale conversion to alternative agriculture would drive up the costs of agricultural production, increase the amount of land in crops, and have unfavorable (except for farmers) macroeconomic consequences.

On balance, we conclude that a wholesale shift to alternative agriculture under current conditions would have unfavorable macroeconomic consequences. . . .

Sustainability Comparisons

A sustainable agricultural system is one that will indefinitely meet rising domestic and foreign demand for food and fiber at constant or declining real economic and environmental costs of production. A principal tenet of the alternative agriculture movement is that the current U.S. agricultural system is not sustainable in this sense. The reasons are that the existing system (a) generates enough erosion to seriously threaten the long-term productivity of the soil; (b) destroys useful biota in the soil through its heavy use of inorganic fertilizer and pesticides, again posing a threat to the soil's long-term productivity; and (c) relies heavily on fossil fuel sources of energy, which in time will be exhausted.

Studies of the long-term effects of erosion on soil productivity. . .agree that continuation of present rates of U.S. cropland erosion for 100 years would reduce crop yields at the end of that period by, at most, 5 to 10 percent from what they otherwise would be. If technological advances increase yields over that period at only half the annual rate experienced over the last 40 years, the negative yield effect of erosion would be offset several times over.

Returning Soil to Earlier Conditions

The term "regenerative agriculture," is frequently used synonymously with sustainable agriculture. This concept means "the capacity of the natural environment to recover from disturbance." As applied in the present sense, this concept seems to propound a return to the "natural" physical, chemical, and biological conditions of the soil. To deplete present soil nutrient levels to their native state, inactivate current drainage systems, and otherwise work toward returning soil conditions to those in Illinois before farming began, would not only take years, it would also be absurd.

Robert G. Hoeft and Emerson D. Nafziger, *Better Crops with Plant Food,* Spring 1988.

If USDA is right in expecting the amount of land in crops to decline over the next 50 years, erosion will decline also, probably proportionately more than the decline in cropland because production will tend to concentrate on less erodible land. In this case, the long-term threat of erosion to soil productivity would be even less than presently estimated. . . .

The evidence is insufficient to conclude that the effects of conventional agricultural practices on soil biota are destructive enough to threaten the sustainability of U.S. agriculture. . . .

The soils of organic farmers are usually richer in soil biota than are the soils of conventional farmers. It is not clear, however, that the difference raises an issue of long-term sustainability. It is extensively documented that badly eroded, biotaimpoverished soils can be restored to rich fertility over a period of some years by adopting management techniques—such as those of alternative agriculture—that build soil organic matter. The process takes time and involves some expense, but it is not rare. Consequently, even though conventional agriculture severely reduces soil organic matter and related biota—which it may but does not necessarily do—the losses need not be permanent. If economic conditions favor it, the soils can be restored. Restoration, of course, costs something, but that is an issue of the comparative economics of alternative and conventional systems. It is not an issue of long-run sustainability.

The nitrogen fertilizer used in the United States is produced from natural gas, and most pesticides are petroleum-based. Because petroleum and natural gas are exhaustible resources, they will someday become more expensive than they are now, and eventually their price will become so high as to exclude them from any except the most high-value uses. Therefore, their continued use by the existing agricultural system would be inconsistent with the earlier definition of long-term sustainability.

The issue, however, is one of timing. As long as the cost of fossil fuels, taking account of the future opportunity cost of the resource, is less than the cost of the alternatives, it is in the social interest to use fossil fuels. As supplies are used up and their cost rises, it will be in the social interest at some point to switch to cheaper energy sources and to invest in research to develop those sources so that they are available when costs of fossil fuels begin a long-term rise.

At that point, renewable sources of energy, such as those used in alternative agriculture, almost surely will become economically more important. One can argue, therefore, that to maintain the sustainability of American agriculture into the indefinite future a shift from the present system to something like alternative agriculture eventually will be necessary. But "eventually" is not now.

Conclusions on Sustainability

The argument that American agriculture should shift to the alternative system over the near term because the existing system is not sustainable is not well-supported. Soil erosion under the existing system is not a serious threat to long-term productivity. The existing system may reduce soil biota, in some cases severely, relative to alternative agriculture, but there is no evidence that the damage is permanent. Finally, the dependence of the existing system on exhaustible energy sources implies that the system eventually must be abandoned for one, such as alternative agriculture, that relies mainly on renewable energy sources. But the relative prices of exhaustible and renewable energy sources clearly indicate that "eventually" is not now.

"Sustainable agriculture is possible only with biotechnology and imaginative chemistry."

Biotechnology Can Promote Sustainable Agriculture

Howard A. Schneiderman and Will D. Carpenter

Howard A. Schneiderman is senior vice president and chief scientist of Monsanto Company, a private chemical corporation. Will D. Carpenter is vice president of Monsanto's technology division and adviser on biotechnology to the U.S. House of Representatives Science and Technology Subcommittee on Natural Resources, Agriculture, Research and Environment. In the following viewpoint, Schneiderman and Carpenter contend that the Third World must increase the productivity of its agriculture to meet word food needs. They argue that using modern technology to develop new disease-resistant plants, enhance protein production in livestock, or produce fertilizers that are environmentally friendly is crucial to sustainable agriculture.

As you read, consider the following questions:

1. Why do the authors argue that biotechnology will increase agricultural productivity?
2. Why do Schneiderman and Carpenter believe that biotechnology is important to sustainable agriculture?
3. According to the authors, how is sustainable agriculture important to the Third World?

Howard A. Schneiderman and Will D. Carpenter, "Planetary Patriotism: Sustainable Agriculture for the Future." Excerpted in large part, with permission, from *Environmental Science & Technology*, April 1990, vol. 24, no. 4, 466-73. Copyright © 1990 American Chemical Society.

Somewhere on this planet, probably in Mesopotamia in what is now Iraq, lies a plot of land that has been farmed continuously for 5000 years. Clearly, that was *sustainable agriculture*. But can today's intensive agriculture survive into future millennia?

Demand for food will be driven by population growth and the need for an upgraded diet in newly industrializing countries. Future agriculture must meet these burgeoning needs without damaging the environment and must also supply feedstocks —the raw materials for the world's chemical industries—when conventional petrochemical supplies become exhausted. That will require sustainable agriculture.

What Is Sustainable Agriculture?

The American Society of Agronomists in 1988 wrote: "A sustainable agriculture is one that *over the long term* enhances environmental quality and the resource base on which agriculture depends, provides for basic human food and fiber needs, is economically viable, and enhances the quality of life for the farmer and for society as a whole" (emphasis added).

The time dimension is critical. It implies the ability to meet current needs and to endure indefinitely with appropriate evolution. Sustainable agriculture must evolve as world population doubles and the demand for animal protein increases during the next 40 years. Production of animal protein requires more agricultural resources than the production of plants: For example, it takes 5 or 6 times as much energy to produce a calorie of pork as a calorie of grain. By 2030, the world must produce more than twice the food it does today. . . .

Sustainable agriculture. . .reduces the use of chemical pesticides and synthetic fertilizers and also provides farmers with a profitable livelihood. It provides consumers with high-quality, abundant food while treating the environment gently.

Biotechnology is one key to sustainable agriculture because it allows farmers to reduce their use of herbicides, insecticides, and fungicides and to control pests that elude present technology. It may take another 20 years for today's basic advances in biotechnology to be widely used for production of seeds and animal protein enhancers. But it will happen, and the benefits will be enormous. Biotechnology promises lower input costs for farmers, lower pesticide exposure for farm workers, lower pesticide residues for consumers, and reduced chemical load for the planet.

During the next 20 years many of today's chemical pesticides will become obsolete. Certain environmentally friendly herbicides, like glyphosate, will still be used, often in combination with biotechnology, to replace less friendly herbicides. New crop chemical formulations will be target-specific, require

205

smaller doses, and protect nontarget organisms. Chemical innovations will enable farmers to use the new products at a fraction of an ounce per acre, instead of a pound per acre. Biotechnology may make certain crops more efficient in using soil nutrients, but the big news in fertilizer efficiency will be new controlled-release formulations of synthetic fertilizers. In the long term, soil microbes may be genetically designed to enhance the tilth of soils. Biotechnology will be embraced by farmers in less-developed countries. . .because it can sustainably enhance production, productive efficiency, and incomes. . . .

Agriculture's Urgent Challenge

There are those who wonder about agricultural biotechnology: Why be concerned about producing more food when we are now awash in surpluses, and farmers' prices are too low? Well, first, we are not awash in surpluses everywhere around the world. Further, we have a knowledge base for a much smaller world than we will have soon. And you don't just crank out knowledge on demand when you awaken to a screaming need. It has taken us 6,000 years or so to get agriculture where it is today. We don't have 6,000 years. We have maybe a dozen.

Gerald S. Still, *Agricultural Biotechnology and the Public,* 1988.

Today, farmers worldwide are searching for resource-efficient, cost-efficient, more profitable production systems, and the world is looking for environmentally friendly and sustainable agriculture. Biotechnology is particularly suited to fill this need through genetic engineering, that is, the transference of genes by nonsexual procedures. Scientists can take genes from one organism and insert them into a different organism, such as a bacterium, producing a bacterium with new genes that carry instructions to manufacture a new protein. For example, the gene for human insulin has been inserted into bacteria, and these genetically transformed bacteria now produce human insulin for diabetics.

In other experiments, scientists have inserted various foreign genes into plants and endowed these transgenic plants with desirable new traits such as resistance to pests. It is becoming possible to transfer traits that are controlled by many genes, such as drought resistance. By the mid-1990s, several useful transgenic seeds will be available to farmers, and by the year 2000 dozens should be available. Gene transfer is just a natural extension and acceleration of plant breeding. . . .

Genetically modified soil microbes, both bacteria and fungi, may become valuable as substitutes for some pesticides and soil

206

supplements. Microbial pesticides are particularly attractive because they are less capital-intensive than many products traditionally used in less-developed countries.

Making each acre of farmland in less-developed countries more productive will slow the destruction of rain forests, a vital source of genetic diversity. The plants, trees, insects, and microbes there contain a huge variety of traits that is essential to help us keep pace with the evolution of diseases and pests. If we continue to destroy our genetic library—a library as yet largely unread—we will be plowing under future human productivity and health.

Biotechnology and Animal Agriculture

Probably the first and most widespread farm application of biotechnology is the use of somatotropins, or growth hormones, to enhance the efficiency of protein production in livestock. Somatotropins, proteins normally produced by the pituitary glands of domestic animals, can now be produced synthetically by genetically transformed *E. coli* bacteria.

Four-year tests of bovine somatotropin (BST) on 20,000 dairy cows have shown a 10-20% boost in milk production and a 10% reduction in feed consumed. Forty cows treated with BST twice a month can produce as much milk as 50 untreated cows, while using 10% less feed. Porcine somatotropin (PST), a similar protein for hogs, can boost feed efficiencies as much as 20% and produce leaner, protein-rich hogs. In China, where 300 million overfat hogs are the animal-protein mainstay, PST could lead to an upgrading of the national diet. PST significantly reduces the feed grain needed to produce a pound of pork. . . .

Another important application of biotechnology is the production of powerful vaccines for foot-and-mouth disease, scours, shipping fever, and other animal illnesses. Direct gene transfer to chickens, swine, and cattle is also possible: Domestic animals someday may be born resistant to diseases.

Minimum-Till Agriculture

In many parts of the United States a pound of topsoil is permanently lost for every pound of soybeans or corn grown. That is a heavy price to pay, and it is certainly not sustainable. This erosion is caused by many factors, including tilling to control weeds. In many places, minimum-till agriculture could reduce soil erosion. For example, if crops could be designed to be tolerant to an environmentally friendly herbicide like glyphosate, farmers could control weeds with less tilling, reduce water loss, and eliminate harsher herbicides. Such an approach is environmentally sensible, saves time and gasoline, and can enhance yields. . . .

The pollution of surface water and groundwater by the nitrates in synthetic fertilizers presents an enormous challenge.

Crops need fertilizers. . . .

One promising avenue for research is the development of con-trolled-release formulations of synthetic fertilizers. In addition, biotechnology may produce plants or microorganisms that make more efficient use of soil nutrients. Still another strategy is to design crop plants that can fix atmospheric nitrogen for their own growth. That approach did not advance appreciably in the past, in part because fixing atmospheric nitrogen is so energy-demanding that yield suffers.

Third World

The less-developed world presents special problems for sus-tainable agriculture. Most of the 5 billion additional people on this planet in 2030 will live in the less-developed countries of the humid tropics. Because of food distribution problems, the tropics need sustainable agriculture that is indigenous and highly productive. The slash-and-burn agriculture often used there now cannot support high-density populations. Most nutri-ents are stored in vegetation rather than in soil, which leaves the soil infertile within a few years.

Promises of Biotechnology

We have good evidence that the world population will double in the next thirty years. Those people must be fed or allowed to starve. . . .

Biotechnology already promises to make each dairy cow more ef-ficient, reducing the total capital and labor input required to pro-duce the dairy products we need.

Biotechnology promises the development of new resistant vari-eties of plants which will need far fewer synthetic chemicals for their protection.

It promises DNA modified microorganisms which will control many of the plant pests which are now controlled wholly by chemicals.

Richard McGuire, *Vital Speeches of the Day*, December 15, 1989.

Another obstacle to sustainable agriculture in the humid trop-ics is economic development itself. Development tends to gener-ate exploitative forms of production; long-term sustainability is often sacrificed for short-term income. Poor soil requires both skilled farming and thoughtful political and economic action by government if it is to be farmed indefinitely. The problem is made even more complex because national agricultural policies often favor the spread of capitalized, monocultural cash-cropping and extensive ranching. The lure of immediate economic advantage and short-term security promotes exploitative land use rather than sustainable agriculture. Only when people in less-developed countries can feed themselves and enjoy reasonably good health will they join the world's economy as steady producers and consumers. For both economic and humanitarian reasons, it is in the best interests of the developed world to help them.

Improved agricultural practices and biotechnology can alleviate some of the more urgent problems. In fact, plant biotechnology was identified by UNESCO [United Nations Educational, Scientific, and Cultural Organization] and other scientific groups as a top priority for less-developed countries. For example, agroforestry, intercropping, perennial crops, and minimum tillage will help secure more durable yields from poor tropical soils. Genes for increased protein can be transferred into important root crops such as cassava and taro. Genes for resistance to viruses, insects, and fungi can be inserted into cassava, sorghum, millet, and cotton to enhance yields and reduce input costs. The technology of plant gene transfer must be developed where it will be used, to ensure that it will respond to local conditions and be readily accepted by the people.

The foregoing ideas are not a quick technology fix for the problems of agriculture in the humid tropics or for world hunger. The less-developed countries need economic and political reform, education, land reform, debt relief, an agricultural infrastructure, a strict deforestation policy, realistic government food subsidies, family planning, and many other things. But the new technologies are powerful and necessary tools to help ensure a sustainable supply of food.

Conclusion

A principal problem facing agriculture during the next 40 years is that current techniques cannot provide the food output and diet improvement that the world will need. . . . We must squeeze greater yields from existing acres in ways that will remain environmentally friendly indefinitely. . . .

Sustainable agriculture and the continuous innovations that it demands must become a fact of daily life. Farmers must continue to innovate, as they have for the past 11,000 years. Sustainable agriculture is possible only with biotechnology and imaginative chemistry; it is simplistic to advocate sustainable agriculture while eschewing biotechnology. Unless the whole world goes back to farming, biotechnology is our best hope for sustainable agriculture. And it seems to have arrived in time to do some good.

"The new biotechnologies are almost completely in the hands of private industry. And that suggests that the primary consideration is not the interests of Third World farmers."

Biotechnology Can Harm Sustainable Agriculture

Miriam Reidy

In the following viewpoint, Miriam Reidy writes that biotechnology negatively affects Third World agriculture. Quoting from a report by Church and Society, a subunit of the World Council of Churches, Reidy argues that most technologies are owned by large corporations that control the marketplace and exploit developing countries. She writes that farmers cannot afford to purchase new inventions, synthetic substitutes are replacing field crops, and genetic diversity is severely threatened. Reidy is an editorial assistant for *One World,* a publication of the World Council of Churches.

As you read, consider the following questions:

1. In the author's opinion, how have synthetic substitutes affected Third World farmers?
2. How do transnational enterprises control biotechnology, according to Reidy?
3. What does the author believe Third World countries can do to limit the negative impact of biotechnology?

Miriam Reidy, "Monitoring the Impact," *One World,* June 1990.

Modern biotechnology is "an effort to combine the scientific analysis of biological processes with technical ingenuity to cultivate and modify single cells and tissue probes in order to use their metabolic capacities for medical and industrial purposes".

Besides its applications to human reproduction—prenatal genetic diagnosis, artificial insemination, *in vitro* fertilization, embryo freezing—biotechnology is being used in agriculture and animal breeding.

Manipulation and Control

Opinions about what biotechnology can or will do vary widely.

Hailed by some as the ultimate solution to virtually all the serious problems facing humanity, it is branded by others as a tool for creating a "brave new world" where life itself can be manipulated and engineered. . . .

Biotechnology is "not a solution in itself, but rather a very powerful tool that can be used in several ways".

In fact, biotechnology is something farmers have done from time immemorial. What is new is the extent to which it can be manipulated and controlled.

Advances in genetics, molecular biology and biochemistry have made technologies like gene transfer, tissue culture and enzyme immobilization not only more efficient but economically viable.

A striking aspect of contemporary biotechnology is that most manipulating and controlling is done by transnational enterprises (TNEs). . . .

Ten of the top fifteen agricultural biotechnology research enterprises are TNEs—not, as is sometimes supposed, small research and development (R&D) "boutiques".

One feature of this TNE dominance is the integration of laboratory and marketplace.

For example. . .the use of biotechnology to make plants withstand herbicides enables a single company to sell two products together, by precoating proprietary seeds with their own pesticides or fertilizers or growth regulators.

The use of animal growth hormones to raise milk and meat production will often increase the need for veterinary products produced by the same company.

TNE control over biotechnology is reinforced through patenting. Although such patents have existed in the North for at least 20 years, "plant breeders' rights" typically granted less exclusive control than industrial patents.

Now corporate plant and animal breeders using biotechnology want much stronger patent protection for all biological products and processes—plants, animals, micro-organisms, human cell lines and individual genes. . . .

If adopted, proposals now being discussed in the UN [United Nations] and the European Community would mean that "the only innovations that will not be patentable under international intellectual property conventions will be those of the world's poor".

Negative Impacts

Speculating about the effects of biotechnology on Third World agriculture is risky since its results have yet to flood the market-place.

Nevertheless, past experiences allow some forecasting of how biotechnology will affect markets, economies, nations and people.

In theory, it could help small farmers in the Third World to produce crops and livestock better adapted to their soil and climatic conditions and farming systems, and to conserve and use indigenous germ-plasm at the local level.

Export Product Substitutions

A. . . type of economic risk that may be associated with biotechnology involves rapidly shifting export markets. Research is likely to permit industrialists and agriculturalists in the developed countries to produce many raw materials and final products that they formerly purchased chiefly from the tropical developing countries. . . .

The product substitution process has been going on for many years, of course. What is different about genetic engineering is that it is likely to allow substitutes to be developed and adopted much more quickly than before, leaving less time for national economies to adjust and find new markets in which to compete.

Anne Hollander, *Conservation Foundation Letter*, No. 6, 1988.

However, unlike the Green Revolution, which was mainly developed and promoted by public institutions, the new biotechnologies are almost completely in the hands of private industry. And that suggests that the primary consideration is not the interests of Third World farmers.

The first direct impact on Third World countries is likely to be export product substitution, as field crops are replaced by "natural" factory production in the North, quality and quantity requirements for raw material are reduced and crop production is shifted to temperate zones.

Already, for example, biotechnology produces millions of completely identical oil palm clones a year. Estimates are that palm oil could satisfy the world's entire vegetable oil demand, making other vegetable oil crops like cocoa and coconut obsolete.

Sugar was one of the first crops to be affected by substitution. It is reckoned that sugar prices fell 59 per cent on the world market after 1975 due to increasing use of substitute sweeteners by the food industry. Ten per cent of all sugar consumption has now been replaced by biotechnologically engineered high fructose syrups from corn, potatoes and cassava.

Several other crops like cocoa, pyrethrin, vanilla, gum arabic and medicinal plants are also on the verge of being replaced by tissue culture substitutes produced in Northern biotechnology factories. . . .

About US$20,000 million in Third World exports is imperilled by new biotechnologies.

The impact of this, not only on the farmers and workers who produce and process these crops, but on whole economies that depend on them for export earnings, can only be disastrous.

Third World Farmers

A second likely impact of the biorevolution is further reduction of the power of Third World farmers. As freely donated biological resources are privatized (and patented) by the North and agricultural biotechnology is concentrated in TNE hands, farmers will have to pay fees to corporations each time they reproduce a patented seed instead of saving part of their harvests for the next year's sowing.

As genetic engineering develops, patenting may allow a few large companies to take over animal husbandry as they have seed production.

Action groups campaigning against the legalization by European Community member states of patents on life point out that having to pay for patented "inventions" aggravate Third World nations' debt burdens and the marginalization of the poor.

They see such patenting as "a total denial of farmers' rights in the South [Third World] to compensation for all the work they do in providing the world economy with rich and useful genetic diversity".

This points to a third likely impact of biotechnology on agriculture in the South. Most of the world's genetic diversity is found in the Third World, where plants have evolved into a huge biological treasure chest and farmers for thousands of years have been breeding and maintaining the genetic diversity on which agriculture and world food security depend.

As traditional plant varieties and animal breeds are replaced by modern, high-tech ones, the genes that the former carry, as well as access to and control over them, are lost.

This genetic erosion is already hitting small farmers in the Third World harder than anyone else.

213

Current methods of improving crops have already depleted crop varieties (up to 5000 varieties of potato have disappeared in Bolivia and Peru alone). Genetic engineering will accelerate this trend.

Similarly, the introduction of new breeds of livestock via embryo transfer may drastically reduce indigenous breeds.

Another issue is the effect on human and environmental health of releasing biotechnology "products"—transgenic plants and animals, new microbial fertilizers or so-called "bio-pesticides"—into the ecosystem.

Because they are alive, genetically engineered products are inherently more unpredictable than chemical products. They can reproduce, mutate and migrate.

If plants with newly inserted genes for herbicide resistance are grown in the farmer's field, might those genes be transferred to weeds, making them resistant to herbicides as well?

If bacteria modified to lower the freezing temperature of crop plants mutate in the environment, might this cause atmospheric changes?

Public concern about such risks may push First World governments to adopt stringent safety regulations, moving the testing of biotechnology products to places where there are no such controls.

An example was the secret release of a biotechnologically produced rabies vaccine in Argentina by a US firm. Before the experiment was halted, farmworkers as well as test cows were contaminated. . . .

Ethical Considerations

There is also a profound theological issue at stake: the manipulation of forms of life—human and otherwise—according to a reductionist conception which removes the distinction between living and non-living things. . . .

"The scientific perspectives undergirding biotechnology function according to a mechanistic worldview where living organisms. . .can be snipped, programmed, cloned, designed, replicated and manipulated at will."

Such a mechanistic view contradicts the sacramental, interrelated view intrinsic to a theology of the integrity of creation.

A related question is whether life should be so treated (and patented) for economic benefit.

"It often seems that the primary goal. . .is not the welfare of the global biosystem, nor even the welfare of the human species within it, but rather the maximizing of material advantages for those few most able to appropriate and profit from the extraction of the earth's resources," says the report.

Questions about First World removal and control of Third World genetic resources and the loss of genetic diversity are relevant here. Both threaten Third World farmers and the rural poor who depend on biological products and processes for 85 per cent of what they need to survive. . . .

Third World Advantages

What are the chances of preventing or at least limiting the negative impacts of biotechnology on Third World agriculture, economies and people?

Pat Mooney. . .directs a Canadian organization called the Rural Advancement Fund International (RAFI). . . .

Mooney thinks that because genetic resources and biological materials are found mainly in the South, Third World negotiators in UN forums still have "a fighting chance".

At a recent discussion with scientists, nongovernmental organizations and governments, representatives of TNEs indicated an interest in paying US$500 million a year for access to Third World germ plasm, Mooney says. The offer was refused.

Third World Gene Drain

Over the past ten years there has been a massive gene drain from farmers' fields in the South to laboratories and gene banks in the North. An estimated 90 p.c. of all germ plasm currently held in these banks in fact came from the third world. It was gathered at no cost, but after manipulation in the laboratory it can be marketed under trade patent protection for enormous sums.

Iftikhar Ahmed, *Update,* June 1988.

Mooney lists other grounds for thinking that despair is premature: . . . Biotechnology laboratories haven't yet been entirely taken over by TNEs, industry doesn't yet present a united front, parliaments haven't yet legislated, and the average person doesn't like the thought that human life could be manipulated in this way."

In most industrialized countries, Mooney says, the question of whether life forms should be patentable is still under discussion.

Moreover, he adds, "if the US insists that *all* intellectual property regimes be included under GATT [General Agreement on Tariffs and Trade] rules, then the South can argue for the implementation of the joint UNESCO [United Nations Educational, Scientific, and Cultural Organization]/WIPO [World Intellectual Property Organization] Model Law on Folklore."

Now being prepared as an international convention at UNESCO, this law recognizes that "communities" invent, that their "inventions" are often evolutionary, that they have ongoing rights to their ongoing innovations and that "folklore" is the "knowledge of the common people".

Implementation of such a law, says Mooney, would give the Third World legal patent control over almost all of the world's biological diversity. But he thinks grassroots action is even more important than international negotiations.

Numerous initiatives have begun to fortify local control over genetic resources and seed production. In the Philippines, India, Brazil and Nicaragua, farmers are trying to conserve and develop plant genetic resources for local use.

Over the past decade, several networks have been created to raise critical awareness, press for better international regulations and challenge unethical marketing practices of industry.

These include the International Baby Food Action Network (IBFAN), Health Action International (HAI), Pesticide Action Network (PAN), Seeds Action Network (SAN), Joint Action Coalition on Biotechnology (JACOB). . .and others. . . .

Citizens' groups can have a pivotal influence on the course of biotechnology and its social, economic and environmental impacts by monitoring industry practices, forecasting impacts, informing and mobilizing public opinion, influencing research priorities, helping the Third World raise concerns and stimulating grassroots activities.

So there is some reason to hope that it is not too late to counteract the negative impact of the biorevolution on Third World agriculture.

> *"To eliminate hunger, the poor of the world —indeed most people—should obtain their protein from the proper proportion of vegetables and grain."*

Vegetarianism Promotes Sustainable Agriculture

J.W. Smith

Environmentalists criticize large-scale beef production because it is an inefficient use of land. In addition, cattle raising contributes to a loss of topsoil and wastes edible grain. In this viewpoint, J.W. Smith argues that if more people became vegetarians, world hunger would end and world resources would be conserved. Smith is the author of *The World's Wasted Wealth— The Political Economy of Waste.*

As you read, consider the following questions:

1. What does the author mean by the phrase "a protein factory in reverse?"
2. What does Smith believe must be done to encourage vegetarianism?
3. In Smith's view, how would worldwide land reform help promote sustainable agriculture?

J.W. Smith, "Absurdities in World Agriculture," *The Animals' Agenda,* September 1990. This article was excerpted from *The World's Wasted Wealth* by J.W. Smith, New Worlds Press, 1990. Reprinted with permission.

The often heard comment (one I once accepted as fact) that "there are too many people in the world, and overpopulation is the cause of hunger," can be compared to the same myth expounded in 16th-century England and revived continuously since. Through repeated acts of enclosure, the peasants were pushed off the land so that the gentry could make money raising wool for the new and highly productive power looms. They could not do this if the peasants were to retain their historic entitlement to a share of production from the land. Massive starvation was the inevitable result of this expropriation.

Much as today, there were then serious discussions in learned circles about overpopulation as the cause of this poverty. This was the accepted reason because a social and intellectual elite were doing the rationalizing. It was they who controlled the educational institutions that studied the problem. Naturally the final conclusions (at least those published) absolved the wealthy of any responsibility for the plight of the poor. But the absurdity of suggesting that England was then overpopulated is clear when we realize that the total population of England in the 16th century was less than in any one of several present-day English cities.

The hunger in underdeveloped countries today is equally tragic and absurd. Their European colonizers understood well that ownership of land gave the owner control over what society produced. The most powerful simply redistributed the valuable land titles to themselves, eradicating millennia-old traditions of common use. . . .

The Wealthy Control Nature's Resources

The problem is that, at bottom, nature's wealth was, and is, being controlled to fulfill the needs of the world's affluent people. The U.S. is one of the prime beneficiaries of this well-established system. Accordingly, our great universities search diligently for "the answer" to the problem of poverty and hunger. They invariably find it in "lack of motivation, inadequate or no education," or some other self-serving excuse. They look at everything except the cause—the powerful own the world's social wealth. . . .

Allowing for (let alone sponsoring) an egalitarian distribution of land around the world would give our own land and resources a respite. With undisturbed access to their own land, no people in the world (except in unusual emergencies) would need our food. Then there would be no reason to plant the one-quarter of our crops that are for export. Hence, under different circumstances, the work expended for this $36 billion worth of exports would be unneeded, allowing those resources to be freed for other uses, or let alone as a form of enlightened payback to the biosphere.

Frances Moore Lappé, who was pursuing her education in

community organizing, was frustrated by the realization that she was not learning anything that would affect the underlying reasons for poverty and hunger. She quit. She then undertook to educate herself by mastering basic source material ignored in academic circles. She insists that all the necessary information is available to prove clearly that every country in the world can feed itself. Lappé became a leading authority on food and nutrition and *Diet for a Small Planet* was her first effort to share this knowledge with a hungry world. One dramatic consequence is that Mexico and Norway have tried to plan their food programs around her teachings.

Lappé learned that: (1) The human body can manufacture all the amino acids that are the building blocks of protein, except eight. These are called the essential amino acids. (2) These nutrients are found in grains and vegetables but not all eight in any one, except for soybeans. (3) If any essential amino acid is missing or short in a person's diet, that sets the limit on the body's ability to build protein. And (4) it is only necessary to eat a meal of vegetables and grain that include most of these eight in adequate amounts for the body to build its own protein. For fulfilling the need for human protein, an amino acid is an amino acid whether it is in meat or vegetables.

Our preferred source of protein is beef. Knowing this, Lappé studied the efficiency of beef production. She was astounded to learn that a cattle feeder intent on producing "prime beef" must feed his steers 16 pounds of perfectly edible human food in the form of grain to produce one pound of beef.

She recognized this was "a protein factory in reverse." Delving into this waste of grain, Lappé's research showed that the proper combination of leafy-vegetables produces, on the average, 15 times more protein per acre than grain-fed beef, while peas, beans, and other legumes produce ten times more, and grain, five times. To eliminate hunger, the poor of the world—indeed most people—should obtain their protein from the proper proportion of vegetables and grain.

If people throughout the world could be taught how to obtain cheap protein, and had access to their land, there would be no need for hunger in any country. Global production exceeds 3,000 calories of food per day for each person, while the daily need is only 2,300 to 2,400 calories, and recent studies show that even this may be excessive. Counting the grain required to produce the meat they eat, the consumption by the well-to-do of 8,000 to 10,000 calories per day is a major cause of world hunger.

Teach Sensible Nutrition

How to effect these changes? There needs to be a change in public education on food to correspond with the training to be responsible for one's own health. Sensible nutrition should be taught in every school. The gain in health from reducing meat consumption is well established, but more education is needed on the principles of cheap and adequate protein as presented by Lappé. With this knowledge, most people would be able to make intelligent choices and thus regain control of this critical area of individual and social well-being. Society's health and the quality of life would rise accordingly. And the cost would be lower, not higher, as the purveyors of misinformation would have us believe.

Because animal fat is the primary reason for cholesterol build-up, heart attacks, and other cardiovascular diseases, many people are already reducing (or eliminating) their meat consumption and lowering their food costs. Heart attacks decreased 26 percent from 1970 to 1983, and total cardiovascular diseases were down 40 percent as of 1987. If the availability of cheap and nutritious sources of protein were promoted—just as beef has been for 50 years—there would be a mass defection of what Lappé calls the "Great American Steak Religion." In fact, shifting to vegetables—for health, political, and moral reasons—may open people to an exciting culinary experience. After all, there are only a few kinds of meat available, whereas an estimated 350,000 vegetables can be developed for food.

The Inefficiency of Meat Production

The production of one pound of beef requires 2,500 gallons of water. It takes less water to produce a *year's* worth of food for a pure vegetarian (a vegan, one who consumes no meat, eggs, or dairy products) than to produce a *month's* worth of food for a meat-eater.

Raising animals for food is an extremely inefficient way to feed a growing world. The U.S. livestock population consumes enough grain and soybeans to feed more than *five times* the country's entire human population. One acre of pasture produces an average of 165 pounds of beef; the same acre can produce 20,000 pounds of potatoes.

If Americans reduced their meat consumption by only 10 percent, it would free 12 million tons of grain annually for human consumption. That alone would be enough to feed the 60 million people who starve to death each year.

People for the Ethical Treatment of Animals, "Vegetarianism: Eating for Life," 1988.

In the design of all this waste in agriculture, there was no conspiracy or intention to harm people. When this country was being settled, it was the dream of every settler to own his or her own land. Here was all this "virgin country" and few people. With the vitality of people pursuing a vision of "manifest destiny" farmers cleared the land and improved farming methods while scientists genetically increased agriculture's productive potential. But to survive economically (especially since equipment, support drugs, and fertilizers began to rise sharply in cost), farmers eventually pressed politicians to find ways to market the growing heap of unneeded food. Much of this ended up as "fed beef" consumed by Americans. But a significant share began to be exported to dispossessed people who no longer controlled their own land, and thus could not feed themselves. We loaned their governments money to buy this food and this further enforced upon them the extraction and export of their natural resources to pay back this debt.

In this light, it's evident that much of U.S. agricultural production for export is unnecessary, if not downright harmful to the very people we profess to be helping. In 1974 we exported over 60 million tons of grain, of which only 3.3 million tons were aid, and most did not reach the starving. For example, from

1984 to 1990, 84 percent of our agricultural exports to Latin America was given to the local governments to sell to the people. This undersold local producers, destroyed their markets, and reduced their production. What we often believe to be aid is actually destroying those countries' local economies. And many cases of outright "gifts" of food for nations undergoing political turmoil are simply pacifiers designed to buy short-term stability for a friendly regime at the expense of the U.S. taxpayer.

Unnecessary Farm Production for Export

A large share of the world's food problem originates in the fact that we must sell, rather than they must buy. This places a heavy burden on those already impoverished countries. But the cost to our own economy is also high. The U.S. is losing one percent of its topsoil every year due to intensive farming practices. The value of this fertility loss is estimated at 20 dollars per acre per year. At that rate, America's soil fertility will be exhausted in 100 years. Further, 32 million acres are irrigated by groundwater, and in over half, the water table is falling over six inches per year. The giant Oglala aquifer irrigates almost half of these acres, and in north Texas, it is already almost totally depleted. It is predicted that two-thirds of U.S. groundwater supplies will be gone by the year 2020.

In this context, the elimination of both unnecessary farm production and the manufacturing capacity to produce and support so much unrequired economic activity would result in the saving of valuable natural resources. It would also reduce the pollution (including "biological pollution" derived from animal-injected drugs) created by these activities. . . .

All of which brings us to another point. U.S. agriculture is reputed to be the world's most productive. But as the preceding analysis shows, much of this bountifulness is artificial, unrequired, and caused by social processes in need of careful examination and revision. The facts seem to suggest that eliminating the 35 percent of U.S. agricultural output that is damaging other economies and America's health would still leave farming twice as efficient as any sector of the economy we care to look at. And yet, there's a catch-22 here, too. The problem with American-style agriculture is that it is tremendously resource intensive. Where most segments of the economy waste labor, agriculture squanders a lot of capital and natural assets—both foreign and domestic.

Great changes must come in the near future if humanity is to insure a viable path of survival for itself, its oft-forgotten fellow creatures, and the fount of all life: the constantly plundered biosphere.

"Cattle are more 'environmentally friendly' and more efficient in their use of land, grain, water and energy than. . . is claimed."

Meat Consumption Promotes Sustainable Agriculture

National Cattlemen's Association

The National Cattlemen's Association is the primary resource organization of the beef cattle industry. In this viewpoint, the Association challenges several common notions about beef production. The authors argue that the cattle industry does not threaten sustainable agriculture, but actually enhances sustainability. They contend that cattle graze land that is too poor to grow cultivated crops and so do not compete for land available for food crops. In their view, there is no evidence that beef consumption causes destruction of tropical forests.

As you read, consider the following questions:

1. Why do the authors believe that it is unnecessary to change to a vegetarian diet to promote sustainable agriculture?
2. According to this viewpoint, why don't cattle contribute to the world hunger problem?
3. What are the primary causes of tropical forest destruction, according to the authors?

Excerpted, with permission, from "Twelve Myths and Facts About Beef Production," a 1990 factsheet of the National Cattlemen's Association.

Myth: By "eating lower on the food chain" (eating less meat), Americans would improve the environment, and they would free land and other resources for the production of food crops rather than meat and other animal products.

Fact: The optimum use of natural resources in the U.S. as well as other parts of the world involves use of both animals and plants to produce the nutrients which humans require. For example, about half the land area of the U.S. is strictly grazing land—not suitable for crop production. That land would be of no use as a food resource if it were not for grazing livestock.

Cattle are more "environmentally friendly" and more efficient in their use of land, grain, water and energy than sometimes is claimed. Only through ruminant (four-stomach), grazing animals can we harvest food from the more than 1 billion acres of range and pasture land in the U.S. At least 85% of the grazing land is too high, too rough, too dry or too wet to grow cultivated crops. The availability of grazing cattle more than doubles the U.S. land area that can be used to produce plants for food purposes.

Cattle production is not preventing production of plant-source foods for domestic and overseas use. The U.S. has more than enough cropland to grow both feed grains and food crops. In fact, because of grain surpluses, government crop programs involve removal of land from grain production.

Cattle are fed just enough grain, in feedlots, to make beef production highly efficient and to make beef more affordable. Grain feeding makes beef more palatable. Feedlot feeding helps even out the beef supply, avoiding the seasonal gluts and shortages which occurred when beef was produced only on forage and roughage. If cattle had to spend more time on grass, the size of the cattle herd would have to be reduced, beef supplies would be smaller, and costs would be higher.

Actually, the nutrient values of plant and animal-source foods cannot be directly compared. Livestock serve as a means of gathering, concentrating and storing nutrients essential to human health. In the U.S., foods from animals supply 68% of the protein, 35% of the energy, 83% of the calcium, 60% of the phosphorus, 42% of the iron, 89% of the vitamin B-12 and large amounts of other essential nutrients.

Soil and Land Conditions

Myth: Livestock raising in the U.S. is largely responsible for loss of topsoil. Overgrazing is causing deterioration of western rangeland.

Fact: Cattle production is not a major factor in U.S. soil erosion. In fact, production of forage (as opposed to cultivated crops) and use of grazing animals to produce food from the forage are one way to conserve soil. For more than 50 years, steps—including managed livestock grazing—have been taken to improve range conditions. Experts agree that the rangelands, including publicly owned rangelands in the West, are in better condition than they have been since the turn of the century.

Grazing Improves Land

But saying cattle don't belong in the Rockies is crazier than a piebald pinto. Much Western land is good for little else. As several scientists have observed, most ranch land is in better shape than Yellowstone National Park. Ecologists such as Allan Savory have shown that grasslands survive better with moderate grazing than without it.

Alston Chase, *The Washington Times*, October 30, 1990.

Most of the nation's cropland is used to produce crops for human food use and for export. Only 19% of total cropland is used to produce feed grains. It is estimated that production of grains and harvested forages for all beef cattle accounts for only 5.8% of soil erosion from non-federal rural land. However, soil erosion is a possible problem in producing any crops. That is why cattle producers as well as other farmers and ranchers are now involved in soil conservation programs. Use of conservation tillage practices continues to grow. Grass is used as a protective cover for soil.

Western range conditions suffered in the early 1900s because of drought and over-grazing. Since then, livestock producers, range scientists and federal land managers have worked to improve conditions. In a report, the Bureau of Land Management pointed out that public rangelands were in better condition than at any time in this century. The trend on more than 87% of BLM rangeland is stable to improving. Managed grazing results in better grass conditions than would exist if there were no grazing. The grazing improves vegetation health and diversity—it's similar to mowing a lawn.

In a survey of cattle producers, 52% of producers said that the condition of their pasture or range had improved since 1980—because of various management practices. Only 13% said that conditions had declined, and that was because of drought.

Whether land is public or private, it is in a cattleman's own best interest to promote regeneration of forages and to take proper care of the resources for which he is responsible. Grazing management is the main job of a producer with pasture or range. A producer must be a good steward of the land if he is to be successful and if he is to pass his business on to the next generation.

Myth: Cattle consume excessive amounts of grain—grain that otherwise could help feed hungry people.

Fact: 1 An average of 4.5 lbs. of grain (compared to a claimed 16 lbs.) is used in producing a pound of beef (retail weight).

2 The world hunger problem is a result of poverty, lack of buying power and food distribution problems—not meat eating in the U.S. The grain whose use is debated would not even be produced unless there was a market for it. To get more grain to the poor and hungry, taxpayers or other organizations must buy it and distribute it.

Beef cattle spend all or most of their lives on pasture and range. At least 80-85% of the nutrients consumed by cattle come from non-grain sources—feedstuffs not edible by humans. These feedstuffs include grass, roughage, food processing by-products and crop aftermath.

Less than half the dry matter produced by crops is edible by humans. Millions of tons of nutrients would be wasted—to say nothing of waste disposal problems—if it weren't for the fact that livestock can make use of food processing by-products and crop residues like corn stalks. . . .

The U.S. continues to produce more grain than can readily be sold. For most of the last three decades, U.S. grain surpluses have increased, even with an expanding animal agriculture. That is why acreage reduction has been part of government grain programs. The increase in grain supplies has not helped alleviate world hunger. If grain were not fed to livestock, more grain would not necessarily be available to feed the hungry. Relief programs and/or economic development in poor countries, providing the ability to produce or purchase and distribute more food, are needed to help solve hunger problems. . . .

Water Use

Myth: It takes 2,500 gallons of water to produce a pound of meat.

Fact: The total amount of water used in on-farm production of grain-fed beef averages 200 gallons per pound of carcass beef. For all beef (not just feedlot-fed beef), the average is lower. That is because more than 30% of all beef is from cattle consuming little or no grain (some of which may be irrigated). Water for cattle production is not "used up." It is quickly recycled as part of nature's hydrological cycle.

The claim that 2,500 gallons of water are used to produce a pound of beef has to be based on incorrect feeding and crop irrigation assumptions. Data on livestock drinking water use and on hay and grain crop irrigation indicate that water use for beef production is significantly less than claimed. That is true even if one assumes that most of the grain fed to cattle is from irrigated cropland (because of more feeding and more grain crop irrigation in the arid West).

Mature cattle consume 8 to 15 gallons of water per day, depending on temperature, humidity and type of feed consumed. Most of this water returns to the soil. Most water used in beef production is for irrigation of hay, silage and grain in arid regions. Total use of water to produce an 1100-lb. grain-fed slaughter animal, with 682 lbs. of carcass beef, is estimated at 200 gallons per pound of carcass beef. The average for all beef is significantly less because more than a third of U.S. beef is from cattle getting little or no grain.

The average citizen in Fort Collins, Colo., uses 81,450 gallons of water for drinking, waste disposal, bathing, laundry, lawn watering, etc. in a year's time. . . .

Deforestation

Myth: U.S. beef consumption is causing deforestation of land in the U.S. and destruction of tropical rainforests in Latin America.

Fact: There is no evidence that livestock grazing has been a significant factor in deforestation of U.S. land. And there is little or no relationship between U.S. beef consumption and destruction of tropical rainforests. The U.S. imports no fresh beef (for hamburger or any other use) from Brazil or other South American countries. Imports of beef from Central America amount to only 0.4% of beef used in the U.S. . . .

Grazing is practiced on some deforested land in Latin America, but the primary causes of excessive rainforest destruction are not related to beef production. Most of the forestland conversion has been for crop and timber production. The U.S. imports no fresh beef from South America. Because of animal health regulations, the U.S. permits importation of only cooked and canned beef (and the amount is limited) from South America. . . . Imports represent only a small part of U.S. beef consumption.

Only 0.4% of beef used in the U.S. comes from Central America. Avoiding U.S. fast food hamburgers or other beef will do nothing to halt rainforest destruction.

Methane Production

Myth: U.S. cattle produce large amounts of methane, a "greenhouse" gas, thereby contributing significantly to possible global warming problems.

Fact: Methane represents only 18% of the world's greenhouse gases, and only 7% of world methane production is attributable to cattle. Beef cattle in the U.S. account for only 0.5% of world methane production and only 0.1% of total greenhouse gases.

Because of highly efficient production methods, U.S. beef cattle emit much less methane per animal unit than do cattle in other countries.

It has been said that the world's 1.3 billion cattle produce almost 100 million tons of methane a year. However, cattle's contribution to the possible methane and greenhouse gas problem is less than sometimes stated. An analysis shows that, because of the carbon dioxide produced, driving six miles each way to buy a hamburger would result in 100 times as much greenhouse gas as the methane generated in producing a hamburger in the U.S. Controlling methane emissions from cattle, even if it could be done, would provide little or no benefit from the point of view of global atmospheric chemistry and global warming. The major sources of methane are rice paddies, wetlands, biomass burning, fossil fuel exploration, landfills and coal mines. . . .

Diet and Health

Myth: The risk of death from heart disease and other diseases can be greatly reduced if a person avoids eating a meat-centered diet.

Fact: Lean beef is regarded by leading health organizations and agencies as a valuable and appropriate part of American diets. The American Dietetic Assn., the American Heart Assn., the National Heart, Lung and Blood Institute, and other organizations generally recommend 5 to 7 oz. of lean, trimmed meat daily. Nutrition authorities point out that trimmed beef provides large amounts of essential nutrients—such as iron, zinc, vitamin B-12 and balanced protein.

Livestock Farming Is Sustainable

Mixed crop-livestock farms make sustainable farming easier by providing diverse crops, manure to cycle nutrients, value-added livestock to sell and year-round employment for farmers.

Mark Honeyman, *The New Farm*, September/October 1990.

Excess fat, from any source, can contribute to the development of illness in some people. But beef and fat are not necessarily synonymous. Trimmed beef has been part of diets which have contributed to improved health and to continuing increases in the longevity of Americans. Government statistics show that red meat alone provides 28% of the protein, 23% of the iron, 36% of the zinc, and 52% of the vitamin B-12 which Americans consume. It is a nutrient-dense food, supplying large shares of essential nutrients in relation to the calories it supplies. . . .

Research on fatty acids has shown that, on average, only 27% of the total fat in a serving of beef has the potential to elevate blood cholesterol levels. Also, beef has no more cholesterol than chicken. The amounts of fat, saturated fat and cholesterol in lean, trimmed beef are low enough that beef is included in low-fat diets recommended by scientific organizations.

Properly balanced vegetarian diets can meet nutrient needs, scientists note, but such diets are not easy to formulate. For most persons, animal as well as plant products have been important parts of diets for thousands of years. . . .

Pesticides in Food Production

Myth: Use of pesticides is causing environmental and human illness problems. Meat contains more pesticides than do plant-source foods.

Fact: Government data indicate that, for both plant and animal foods, there is no evidence of chemicals at anything more than a fraction of tolerance levels proven to be safe. USDA's official report for 1989 on residue monitoring of meat showed no violative pesticide residues in beef. . . .

Residues do not accumulate "up the food chain," in meat as opposed to plant foods. That is because living organisms do not just take up chemicals. They also detoxify, metabolize, biodegrade and excrete any chemicals. As a consequence, only a small fraction of any chemical absorbed is even temporarily deposited in tissues. Actually, animals provide a useful function by biodegrading chemicals, whether natural or man-made. The Food and Drug Administration's total diet studies show that foods supply less than 1% of allowable dietary intakes of crop chemicals. FDA samplings in 1988, together with total diet studies, continued to demonstrate that dietary intakes of pesticide residues are well below standards set by the Food and Agriculture Organization/World Health Organization.

"Natural" production systems do not result in crops without potentially toxic chemicals. Plants naturally produce "pesticides" to help fight off parasites, insects, birds and animals. In addition, organisms living on plants, such as fungi, may produce toxins.

Use of modern technology makes possible the production for Americans of a more bountiful, more healthful, safer, less costly supply of food.

Understanding Words in Context

Readers occasionally come across words they do not recognize. And frequently, because they do not know a word or words, they will not fully understand the passage being read. Obviously, the reader can look up an unfamiliar word in a dictionary. By carefully examining the word in the context in which it is used, however, the word's meaning can often be determined. A careful reader may find clues to the meaning of the word in surrounding words, ideas, and attitudes.

Below are sentences adapted from the viewpoints in this chapter. In each entry, one word is printed in italicized capital letters. Try to determine the meaning of each word by reading the entry. Under each item you will find four definitions for the italicized word. Choose the one that is closest to your understanding of the word.

Finally, use a dictionary to see how well you have understood the words in context. It will be helpful to discuss with others the clues which helped you decide on each word's meaning.

1. Farmers have practiced biotechnology from time *IMMEMORIAL*. They have always tried to improve the quality and quantity of their crops.

   IMMEMORIAL means:

   a) recently
   b) extending beyond the reach of memory
   c) without a patent
   d) management

2. Citizens' groups can have a *PIVOTAL* influence on the course of biotechnology by changing people's opinions and improving public policy.

   PIVOTAL means:

   a) harmonious
   b) toxic
   c) crucial
   d) connecting

3. Sustainable agriculture is possible only with biotechnology; it is simplistic to advocate sustainable agriculture while *ESCHEWING* biotechnology.

   ESCHEWING means:

   a) confronting   c) avoiding
   b) adapting   d) promoting

4. Future agriculture must meet the *BURGEONING* needs of an ever-increasing population that demands inexpensive, environmentally safe produce.

   BURGEONING means:

   a) decreasing   c) procrastinating
   b) example   d) expanding

5. Reducing the use of chemicals in farming would not reduce environmental damage. Improvements from chemical reduction occur on a small scale and cannot be *EXTRAPOLATED* to the entire agricultural industry.

   EXTRAPOLATED means:

   a) consumed   c) rejected
   b) invented   d) projected

6. A principal *TENET* of the alternative agriculture movement is that the current U.S. agricultural system is not sustainable.

   TENET means:

   a) undertaking   c) selection
   b) belief   d) tractor

7. With *EGALITARIAN* distribution of land, wealthy landowners would lose land while the poorer farmers gained it, but everyone would have enough food.

   EGALITARIAN means:

   a) racial   c) unpleasant
   b) unequal   d) equitable

8. Grain feeding makes beef more *PALATABLE*. Chemical substitutes for grain make beef taste bad.

   PALATABLE means:

   a) tasty   c) uncomfortable
   b) affordable   d) healthy

9. The increase in grain supplies has not helped *ALLEVIATE* world hunger. Although the world continues to increase the amount of food produced, more people are starving.

   ALLEVIATE means:

   a) relieve   c) consume
   b) believe   d) ability

Periodical Bibliography

The following articles have been selected to supplement the diverse views presented in this chapter.

Michael J. Dover and Lee M. Talbot	"Feeding the Earth: An Agroecological Solution," *Technology Review*, February/March 1988.
Evan Eisenberg	"Back to Eden," *The Atlantic Monthly*, November 1989.
Environmental Action	"Farm Animals and Meat," May/June 1990. Available from Environmental Action, 1525 New Hampshire Ave. NW, Washington, DC 20036.
Marsha Freeman	"New Technologies to Feed a Growing World," *21st Century Science and Technology*, January/February 1989. Available from 21st Century Science Associates, PO Box 17285, Washington, DC 20041.
Orville L. Freeman	"Meeting the Food Needs of the Coming Decade," *The Futurist*, November/December 1990.
Mark Honeyman	"Whole-Hog Management Benefits the Whole Farm," *The New Farm*, September/October 1990. Available from Rodale Institute, 222 Main St., Emmaus, PA 18098.
Thomas Kiely	"Appropriate Biotech," *Technology Review*, August/September 1989.
Jon R. Luoma	"Soil Is Not a Factory," *Audubon*, November 1989.
Richard McGuire	"Biotechnology and Agriculture," *Vital Speeches of the Day*, December 15, 1989.
Peter A. Oram	"Building the Agroecological Framework," *Environment*, November 1988.
John P. Reganold, Robert I. Papendick, and James F. Parr	"Sustainable Agriculture," *Scientific American*, June 1990.
Robert Rodale	"Beyond Purity," *Organic Gardening*, May/June 1989.
Jim Schwab	"The Attraction Is Chemical," *The Nation*, October 16, 1989.
Emily T. Smith	"Farmers Are Learning New Tricks from Mother Nature," *Business Week*, November 6, 1989.

6 CHAPTER

What Policies Would Help Conserve Global Resources?

Chapter Preface

Conserving global resources is a stated goal of many of the world's nations and leaders. But while it may be easy to support conservation in theory, it is often difficult to establish policies that produce results. In the words of the Worldwatch Institute's 1990 *State of the World* report, "Building an environmentally sustainable economy requires specific steps and tough choices." Whether the policy is preserving forests, controlling population, or reducing the greenhouse effect, nations have difficulty deciding who should make these tough choices.

Since the quality of earth's air, water, and land are issues that affect all nations, many experts favor a multinational approach. For example, Jonathan Porritt, director of the British chapter of Friends of the Earth, asserts that protecting resources "will require an international agency with enforcement powers" to ensure a united effort by all nations.

But, as with any complex issue, it is often difficult to achieve any international consensus on environmental issues. A report by the United Nations' World Commission on Environment and Development (WCED) stated, "The earth is one but the world is not. We all depend on one biosphere for sustaining our lives. Yet each community, each country, strives for survival and prosperity with little regard for its impact on others." Alston Chase, a columnist who writes on environmental issues, believes that "asking federal or international governments to compose coherent regulations for natural preservation is like expecting the Incredible Hulk to perform brain surgery: His fingers are too clumsy to tie the knots."

All nations share earth's resources, and all have a stake in their preservation. Barber Conable, president of the World Bank, believes that to conserve resources, "We must reshape . . . the customs and ingrained attitudes of hundreds of millions of individuals and of their leaders." The authors in the following chapter discuss how this goal can best be accomplished.

234

"Today's environmental challenges require that all nations, North and South, make difficult commitments to themselves and to each other in order to secure their common future. "

International Policies Will Conserve Global Resources

James Gustave Speth

In this viewpoint, James Gustave Speth argues that developed and developing countries must cooperate and adopt mutually beneficial policies to conserve world resources. He contends that far-reaching policies are needed to stop global warming and forest destruction, promote sustainable development, and establish and manage biological reserves. Speth is president of the World Resources Institute, an independent center for policy research on natural resources and the environment.

As you read, consider the following questions:

1. According to Speth, what are the responsibilities of First World countries in making international environmental policies?
2. What does the author mean by coordinated policy reform and complementary national initiatives?
3. How can the Third World contribute to successful international policies, according to Speth?

James Gustave Speth, "Coming to Terms: Toward a North-South Compact for the Environment," *Environment*, June 1990. Reprinted with permission.

If we take seriously today's major environmental challenges—including global-scale atmospheric pollution, loss of biological diversity, and resource degradation in developing countries—we have to ask seriously what must be done to meet them. Finding all the answers to this question will be the work of years, but one precondition already seems clear. None of these challenges can be met without a new era of heightened cooperation and agreement between industrial and developing countries. These North-South understandings must transcend the traditional environmental agenda and incorporate initiatives in policy areas as diverse as international trade and debt, development and assistance, energy, technology transfer, and population. These agreements, once reached, would be nothing less than a global compact between North and South for environmental protection and economic progress.

Consider the North-South links inherent in today's gravest environmental problems, and the need for such understandings is evident.

Global warming now threatens to disrupt weather patterns and raise sea levels around the Earth. Containing the greenhouse effect will require major reductions in emissions of the three most prominent greenhouse gases—carbon dioxide, methane, and chlorofluorocarbons (CFCs). Carbon dioxide, still the leading greenhouse gas, highlights the difficulty of control. To control emissions, industrial countries will have to cut back on their voracious fossil fuel consumption and developing countries will need to stem the deforestation that claims more than an acre a second in the tropics. Deforestation and other land-use changes now account for about one-third of the carbon dioxide produced by human activity and some of the methane.

As a practical matter, developing countries expect industrial countries to take the first and strongest actions on global warming. These developing nations want to see the seriousness of the threat validated, and they conclude correctly that industrial countries are largely responsible for the problem and have the most resources to do something about it. But carrying this argument too far could lead to a tragic stalemate. Developing countries already account for about 45 percent of humanity's yearly contribution to the greenhouse effect, and their share will grow as they industrialize. . . .

Genetic Diversity

The loss of species and genetic variety is now proceeding at rates unmatched since the mass extinction episode 65 million years ago that wiped out two-thirds of all species. Today's losses center largely in the remaining tropical forests of Latin America, Asia, and Africa that are home to nearly half the species on

Earth. Every day, another hundred species die out. Deforestation is the principal culprit, but poaching and overharvest-
ing for food and profit also take their toll. Unless we act deci-
sively now to reverse habitat destruction, one-fourth of the
Earth's 5 to 30 million species could die out over the next few
decades, leaving our posterity—and our planet—incalculably
poorer.

A Global Mentality

I believe that the threats to the global environment have the potential to open our eyes and to make us accept that North and
South will have to forge an equal partnership. The threats to the
global climate prove beyond doubt that, if everyone does as they
please in the short run, we will all be losers in the long run. We
need to develop a more global mentality in charting the course
toward the future, and we need sound scientific advice and firm
political and institutional leadership.

Gro Harlem Brundtland, *Environment*, June 1989.

As with preserving climate, North-South cooperation is essential to preserving biodiversity. Leaders of developing countries
do not deny the legitimacy of concern about biodiversity; some
share this concern strongly. But they have difficulty giving it the
attention needed to reverse today's trends. New land for farming and ranching and timber for export are more immediate priorities, and the forests offer both. Fighting against poachers and
homesteaders puts leaders at odds with their own people. In
short, if the wealthy countries want to save threatened flora and
fauna, they will have to work with developing countries to
counter the forces leading to biotic impoverishment and also to
create powerful new incentives favoring protection of critical
ecosystems.

The decline of productive natural resources is rapidly emerging as a major threat to development prospects in much of the
Third World. Developing countries are many times more dependent than industrial countries on their natural resources—their
soils, fisheries, forests, and minerals. And within developing
countries, the poor are most dependent of all. Yet, this resource
base is eroding rapidly under pressure from unprecedented population growth, deep-seated social inequities, and misguided
policies.

For Third World leaders, resource deterioration is a more immediate challenge than global warming or biodiversity loss, and
most are showing increased concern. But even though nascent
efforts to protect the environment in developing countries are

now common, lack of commitment from political leaders, limited financial resources, inadequate training, and other constraints remain the rule rather than the exception.

As one measure of what resource erosion means for the future, the United Nations Food and Agriculture Organization predicts that between 1985 and 2000, rain-fed cropland in the developing world will become 30 percent less productive, while the number of people to be fed will swell by more than one billion. Unless the synthesis of environmental and economic imperatives called sustainable development becomes a reality, billions of people in the developing world will eventually lack the basic natural resources needed to sustain them at healthy levels. . . .

Equally pertinent for the North to recognize is its sometimes unwitting complicity in resource degradation in the South. Too often, Northern investment schemes and development aid finance large-scale projects that ignore environmental settings and local needs. Making matters worse is the development assistance community's historical neglect of projects that would enhance the conservation and sustained productivity of natural assets.

Similarly, industrial country management of the Third World's external debt has riveted attention on the immediate need to provide debt servicing, to the detriment of environmental, social, and other economic concerns. It also has resulted in economic stagnation that has further marginalized the poor, intensifying pressures on erodible soils, fuelwood supplies, and other resources.

Third World Challenges

Today's environmental challenges require that all nations, North and South, make difficult commitments to themselves and to each other in order to secure their common future.

Consider first the key elements of the South's contribution to solving these problems. Far-reaching initiatives will be needed to stop forest destruction, establish and manage biological reserves, pursue environmentally sustainable energy strategies, and conserve land and water resources for food production. Pursuing this ambitious agenda will require leaders to take steps with political and social risks, such as land tenure reforms, major efforts to curb population growth and improve the lot of the rural poor, and adoption of cutting-edge technologies that can leapfrog the destructive industrialization patterns of the North.

The leadership to make these changes must come from developing countries themselves, but industrial countries can help. . . .

Second, developing countries will expect industrial countries to show through their own domestic and international actions that they take these environmental challenges very seriously.

238

Yet, many industrial countries are not demonstrating such commitment. The United States is a case in point, as shown by such indicators as its energy consumption, its forest management practices, the fate of its biodiversity, the state of its foreign aid, and, at this writing, its general lack of environmental leadership internationally.

First World Requirements

The initiatives required of industrial countries are also far-reaching and difficult. Four areas stand out as priorities.

First, these countries must launch major national and international efforts to reduce greenhouse gas emissions. As the world's largest emitter of greenhouse gases, the United States' single most important step at this point is a national commitment to gains in energy efficiency that are large enough to push fossil-fuel use and releases of carbon dioxide steadily downward. . . .

Environment Is International

Environment is an international issue, to be pursued through international institutions, to be linked to all aspects of international relations. Conservation is each nation's task. But it is a task that can be accomplished only in the setting of a cooperative world order.

Rajiv Gandhi, *Issues in Science and Technology,* Winter 1988.

Second, industrial nations must sharply increase the flow to the South of both new financing and new technology for environmental conservation, sustainable development, and population programs. Official development assistance now amounts to some $40 billion annually, and reforms ensuring that these billions are well spent are badly needed. But neither reform nor conservation is likely to gain sufficient momentum without major new financing. . . .

A World Resources Institute study, *Natural Endowments: Financing Resource Conservation for Development,* identified promising ways to attract additional. . . funding. These include a global environmental trust, which might be funded by taxing industrial countries' greenhouse gas emissions, and an international environmental facility, which would collaborate with developing countries' governments and international aid agencies to identify the most urgent conservation needs, provide "pre-investment" funding to help generate well-designed projects to meet those needs, and bring projects into being by arranging financing, including loan guarantees, from a variety of existing sources.

Third, industrialized nations must relieve the burden that ex-

239

ternal debt imposes on developing countries. . . . Forgiving debt outright might be the North's most reasonable response to the poorest nations, whose loans come mostly from industrial governments rather than from commercial banks.

Finally, the wealthy nations must establish new programs to provide developing countries access to technical assistance, training, technology transfer, and planning grants to increase their capacity to manage environmental and energy challenges. The United States could contribute to this goal by launching a new program of international cooperation with developing countries. Such a program would not be limited to the poorest countries, which are eligible for assistance from the U.S. Agency for International Development (AID), but would extend to middle-income countries like Brazil and Mexico, where international environmental and energy cooperation is essential.

A Common Destiny

Such economic and environmental initiatives can be combined in many ways to spur concerted action between North and South. Perhaps the most successful steps will be those in which one country or region reciprocates positive steps taken unilaterally by another. As mutual confidence and concern grow, the process can spread. . . .

Countries must quickly develop better means to reach understandings and make mutual commitments that can sustain the Earth and its people. Fortunately, environmental concerns are steadily pushing nations to a sense of shared responsibility and common destiny that may soon be the most powerful force binding the world together.

"In dealing with global environmental problems. . .we must pay attention to local indigenous practices if we hope to avoid the traps and failures of many development projects of the past."

International Policies May Damage Global Resources

David Brokensha and Bernard W. Riley

David Brokensha is professor of anthropology and Bernard W. Riley is professor of geography and environmental studies at the University of California, Santa Barbara. In the following viewpoint, Brokensha and Riley write that international environmental policies aimed at conserving Third World resources oftentimes end up destroying these resources. They argue that these policies frequently do not involve local people and so fail to achieve their intended objectives.

As you read, consider the following questions:

1. What examples do Brokensha and Riley give as projects that failed because local people were not consulted?
2. Why is the Chipko movement important, according to the authors?
3. What suggestions do the authors have for international environmental planners to assure success for their policies?

From David Brokensha and Bernard W. Riley, "Managing Natural Resources: The Local Level," in *Changing the Global Environment: Perspectives on Human Involvement,* Daniel B. Botkin et al., eds. San Diego: Academic Press, Inc., 1989. Copyright © 1989 Academic Press, Inc. Excerpted with permission.

Local Natural Resource Management (NRM) is important, both for those who plan for development in the Third World and also for those whose local resources are affected. . . . Not only are some of our global environmental problems centered in regions of the Earth where there are many developing nations, but also plans for the study of the biosphere tend to be made in the developed nations with the assumption that all other nations will follow. Third World environments are generally deteriorating. During the last decade, most international and national agencies have realized that new approaches are necessary and that attempts must be made to find new institutions that will incorporate local people in development planning. During most of human history, the local community has been the basic unit for production and consumption of useful resources. Local systems of NRM (despite their variety) have been characterized by a high degree of social integration, low capital, and high labor inputs. They have also been dynamic, diversified, adaptive, and generally appropriate for their specific social and physical environments. As long as populations were small and technology limited, there was a balance. In the last century this was distorted by many forces, especially by rapid population increase. In Kenya, for example, an annual population increase of nearly 4 percent puts great pressure on the natural resource base. Introduction of new technologies, as well as development projects generally, have also altered the social and environmental balance, inducing a dependence on the state and erosion of local initiative. During the colonial period (which most Third World countries experienced), there was a tendency towards centralization. Government claimed ownership of basic natural resources such as land, forest, fish, and game. These claims further discouraged local responsibility, even though the state was seldom able to exercise effective control. Foreign interference was not the major problem since independent governments have further increased the level of centralization, and they too have often lacked effective management skills.

Local Administration

In recent years there have been modest signs in some countries and resource areas of a trend toward decentralization. . . . Local NRM—if it is to be effective—should mean administration by a small group of people familiar with the area and with each other, who are united by historical and social bonds.

Another critical factor has been exploitation of resources for commercial purposes, when previous use had been mainly for subsistence. In the case of forestry, fisheries, and game, outsiders (either exotic ethnic groups or people of European descent) with sophisticated technology (such as shotguns, nylon nets, outboard motors, chain saws) engaged in wholesale resource base destruction. . . .

We [know] how societies evolved workable rules for managing their natural resources, taking examples from water management, fisheries, forestry, and wildlife. In all cases, we are concerned with rights and duties, that are specified for individuals or groups and that are enforced. In contrast to common property regimes, many government-sponsored "top-down" projects leave local people unclear about their rights and responsibilities regarding maintenance, distribution, enforcement, and other matters. People need to be certain about costs and benefits (including, of course, social costs and benefits, often regulated by technicians and planners) before they will invest time or money in a project. . . .

Native Wisdom

Environmental regeneration is only possible if we learn to respect native wisdom and local decision-making. To paraphrase what Gandhi once said about India, the Third World lives in its village communities. The environment can be saved only if these village communities can be strengthened. In other words, if village decision-making and village democracy is strengthened.

Anil Agarwal, *Ambio,* April 1990.

We do not advocate in any way an abandonment of Western technology—small is not always beautiful—nor do we romanticize local NRM, recognizing that many of these systems are no longer effective because of inexorable distorting influences already mentioned. For example, one recent model examines "long-term persistence of communal tenure systems in Amazonia and recent dissolution of those systems." Government policy provided a direct incentive—granting individual title to land—to Indians who "improved" parcels of forest by establishing *permanent* fields or pasture. This was a clear instance of government intervention—attempting to increase resource extraction and promote agricultural colonization—destroying the previously sustainable system. New systems of land tenure mean that some Indians adopt destructive slash-and-burn techniques, abandoning their old sustaining agriculture. Many other examples could be cited. We are trying to demonstrate that the local people do not live in a state of ignorance about their natural world; unless they had a detailed and systematic knowledge of their environment, they would not survive. It is still necessary to demonstrate this because many officials and planners, both expatriates and developing country people, need to learn its truth.

The hazards of huge hydroelectric projects, like the Aswan Dam in Egypt, are well known; problems regarding health, effects on downstream fisheries, resettlement of displaced people, siltation, and weeds have been well described, as have the disappointing results of irrigation. Rather than reiterate the problems of big dams, we consider briefly the Kano River Project, a large-scale, capital-intensive project that was designed to irrigate 58,000 acres in northern Nigeria. According to T. Wallace, the Nigerian development planning process was generally "technocratic, economic, and authoritarian," human and social aspects being ignored. Some 13,000 people were relocated, and this was done in a way that soon reduced them from self-sufficient peasant farmers to government dependents. Most large-scale irrigation projects have been costly (up to $20,000 per hectare) and seldom produced anticipated benefits (the value of increased crop production). Further, benefits have been unequally distributed, with higher income farmers capturing a disproportionate share.

The promise of irrigation to increase agricultural productivity leads governments and international donors to continue promoting irrigation. Because of problems associated with large-scale projects, some planners are beginning to look at possibilities for small-scale irrigation, building on existing local systems. Another reason for looking at small-scale irrigation is that the easiest locations for large projects have already been used. . . .

Government irrigation agencies need to learn to work with local people, to use existing organizations, or to encourage new bodies, and to do this before beginning actual construction. The planners and engineers should try to understand the daily lives, problems, and opportunities of the people. Then, together they can develop appropriate ways of tackling problems and of enhancing long-term benefits of the project. In most cases, it is preferable to work with existing organizations than to create new ones, even if the distribution of benefits is imperfect. For example, cooperative societies for production, marketing, and services have been promoted—in irrigation and in other domains—as a solution, but they have seldom worked well, partly because inappropriate models from Europe or North America have been introduced to Third World communities without regard to local socioeconomic conditions. . . .

Fisheries

Artisanal, or small-scale fisheries, account for one-third of the total catch of fish worldwide and for 90 percent of the fishing population in Africa and Asia. The global figure of those engaged in these fisheries is 30 million, according to FAO [U.N. Food and Agricultural Organization]. Fisheries represent a major source of employment and income. Fish are also an important source of protein. Generally labor-intensive with relatively little imported technology, small-scale fishing has been often overlooked or dismissed by "experts" because of its "primitive" equipment and techniques. Yet these fishermen often operate at a more favorable cost-benefit ratio than do the larger fisheries, which cannot operate in all areas where small-scale fishing is carried out. Despite the large numbers involved, small-scale fisheries receive less than one-fifth of the total technical international assistance given to the fishing industry. . . .

Citizen Participation in Decision Making

Grass-roots action against poverty and for the environment comes down to the rights of people to shape their own destiny. The United Nations-sponsored World Commission on Environment and Development is unequivocal on this question. In the landmark report, *Our Common Future,* the commissioners write, "The pursuit of sustainable development requires a political system that secures effective citizen participation in decision making." Translated, that means democracy.

For those of us in industrial nations, the lesson is simple. If we want to help citizens of the Third World save their environment, our top priority should be to help protect their human rights. They, in their hundreds of thousands of local organizations, will take care of the rest.

Alan B. Durning, *The Amicus Journal,* Summer 1990.

Local management of fisheries is still, despite the distortions of the systems, deserving of study because of the detailed knowledge of fish and the waters that traditional fishermen have. In addition, upgrading what is already there is likely to be of more lasting benefit than attempting a radical transformation using what may well be an inappropriate model. Upgrading can focus on equipment (crafts, nets), processing, distribution, and training of men and women in the fishing industry. Local people must be integrated into management of their resources from the design stage of any project, which must be suitable for local institutions and beliefs. Access to the fishery may have to be restricted to ensure a sustainable system. Institutional development is vital to any project; it demands imagination, with ability to experiment, since existing institutions, whether modern or traditional, are seldom adequate. A special Fisheries Development Unit should be set up to deal with the needs of small-scale fisheries; progress should be step by step in accordance with long-term plans, and local people must be consulted at every step. . . .

Concern with global environmental problems is leading to proposals for international programs and actions. In general, plans for these are made in the developed nations for all nations. In addition, some key global environmental issues focus on parts of the world that are predominately Third World nations. For example, much of the tropical rainforests that receive so much interest are in Third World nations. In dealing with global environmental problems and in proposing the use of advanced technology, we must pay attention to local indigenous practices if we hope to avoid the traps and failures of many development projects of the past.

Before any planning is started that involves developing nations, it is essential first to examine existing institutions and practices, and to see how these can be improved, rather than simply introducing a radical new institution. . . .

Recognizing Different Priorities

Those concerned about global environmental issues who seek the participation of Third World governments must realize that government and local people have different priorities in research use, different objectives regarding that use, and different ways of resolving conflicts. For example, in forestry, government foresters think in terms of yields, inventories, and harvesting schedules, whereas locals place more importance on qualitative ecological aspects. It is necessary to take all viewpoints into account. Local national resource management has a strong social component, which needs to be understood before changes in resource management are proposed. . . .

In many parts of the world local natural resource management systems have been replaced by large-scale projects that are often accompanied by a centralized bureaucracy. Many of these projects have failed to achieve their social and economic objectives and have had many deleterious environmental consequences as well. Although the rural poor in the developing nations suffer the immediate negative impacts of such resource planning errors, there is a cumulative effect on the global environment that may have a severe long-term impact. For example, the overexploitation of many coastal fisheries may lead to the extinction of some species. The same is true for forestry management. By recognizing the positive aspects of a local natural resources management system, development planners may be able to achieve their economic goals without degrading either the local or the global environment.

"*To achieve its full potential, energy efficiency must emerge from the obscure corners of Energy Ministries and rise to the top of planning agendas throughout government and industry.*"

Sweeping Energy Policies Are Needed to Conserve Global Resources

Christopher Flavin and Alan B. Durning

Christopher Flavin is coauthor of *Renewable Energy: The Power to Choose* and vice president of Worldwatch Institute, a research center concerned with environmental problems. Alan B. Durning is a researcher with Worldwatch Institute and coauthor of *State of the World 1988.* In this viewpoint, Flavin and Durning argue that the world's supply of fuels is threatened, and that more efficient use of energy is required to conserve remaining resources.

As you read, consider the following questions:

1. Why is it necessary to raise automobile fuel efficiency, according to the authors?
2. How can industrialized countries increase energy efficiency, according to Flavin and Durning?
3. What do the authors mean by poverty-induced conservation?

Christopher Flavin and Alan B. Durning, "The Limits to Energy Growth," *National Forum,* Summer 1988. Reprinted with permission of Worldwatch Institute.

In 1972, The Club of Rome warned that the world would run out of fuels and raw materials. To the contrary, the world today faces a glut rather than a shortage of fossil fuels, but that glut is itself a product of temporary shortages and soaring prices. Efficiency made it possible for the world to climb out of the severe 1981-82 recession and led to a 75 percent decline in the real price of oil between 1981 and 1986. But the global environmental limits now emerging may turn out to be far more stringent and dangerous, sorely testing the resolve of policymakers and citizens alike.

Investment in energy efficiency is the most effective response to those limits, for it is simultaneously an investment in lowered oil dependence, reduced air pollution, and climate protection. Doubling the fuel efficiency of a typical car to 50 mpg lowers its annual fuel bill by almost $400; significantly cuts emissions of nitrogen oxides, hydrocarbons, and carbon monoxide; and reduces carbon emissions by half, or 450 kilograms annually. A similar improvement for the world as a whole would cut carbon emissions by 6 percent, or almost 200 million tons annually, a substantial contribution to climate protection.

In 1986, oil imports in many countries rose for the first time in almost a decade—by more than 1 million barrels per day in the United States alone. If current trends continue, the United States will be importing more oil than ever by the mid-nineties. Meanwhile, the concentration of remaining petroleum reserves in the Persian Gulf grows ever more pronounced. By the late nineties, the United States and the United Kingdom are likely to be minor oil producers; a half-dozen Persian Gulf countries with at least 80 years' worth of remaining reserves will be back in control.

These growing imbalances in the world oil market jeopardize the energy security of importing nations and the collective security of the world community. If Middle Eastern oil production reaches 80 percent of capacity—as it did in 1973 and 1979—it will take only a minor political or military conflict to send prices soaring. The increases that follow could well exceed those of the seventies. With world consumption now rising about 1 percent annually and production plummeting in the United States, the danger zone is likely to be reached in the mid-nineties.

Investing in Energy Efficiency

The only realistic means of avoiding another oil crunch in the nineties is to invest heavily in energy efficiency—largely in transportation. One change alone—the increase in the average fuel efficiency of American automobiles from 13.1 mpg in 1973 to 17.9 mpg in 1985—cut United States gasoline consumption by 20 billion gallons per year, lowering oil imports by 1.3 million barrels per day, two-thirds of the peak production from the rich oil fields of Alaska.

Petroleum geologists agree that the United States is unlikely to find another oil field as large as Prudhoe Bay's, but the country could save another 1.9 million barrels per day by the year 2000 by raising new-automobile fuel efficiency to 45 mpg in 1995, according to a study by Deborah Bleviss of the International Institute for Energy Conservation. In general, most countries should strive for a minimum 1 mpg annual improvement in the fuel economy of new cars.

'It's Keith's contribution to saving the planet'

After a decade of control efforts, air pollution remains a growing problem in most cities. Improved efficiency has the potential to reduce emissions of most dangerous pollutants, though this depends to some degree on the technologies employed. A 1987 study by the American Council for an Energy-Efficient Economy concludes that increased energy efficiency could cut electricity consumption in the Midwest by 15 to 25 percent, making it possible to reduce use of the region's dirtiest coal-fired power plants and so limit acid rain. Because the efficiency savings are economical in their own right, the funds saved could be used to invest in additional pollution controls.

Climate change looms as the ultimate environmental threat. Its impact would be global and, for all practical purposes, irreversible. Improving worldwide efficiency by 2 percent annually would keep the world's temperature within 1 degree Celsius of current levels, avoiding the most catastrophic climatic effects.

Annual Goal of 2 Percent

Improving energy efficiency by 2 percent per year for several decades is challenging but feasible. Over 50 years it would reduce global energy intensity by almost two-thirds. Some industrial market countries have been achieving this rate during the past 15 years. Sustaining this pace through decades of fluctuating fuel prices will be a difficult task, however, requiring major institutional changes. Fortunately, many of the needed technologies are already in place, and some countries are showing the way. Buildings worldwide must become as efficient as Sweden's, and industry must become as efficient as Japan's. Automobiles must become as efficient as the best prototype models now found in the engineering facilities of Europe and Japan.

Priorities in energy efficiency vary among countries. Industry is the top priority in Third World and centrally planned nations since it is the largest energy user and is a key determinant of both environmental quality and economic competitiveness. In industrial countries, this sector probably needs less government attention than others. Transportation efficiency is crucial for most countries. Improved automobile fuel economy could be accomplished with a package of consumer incentives for the purchase of more-efficient cars, fuel efficiency standards, industry R&D programs, and fuel taxes. Automobile fuel efficiencies will eventually reach some practical limits, at which point it will be important to have developed economical alternative fuels and be well on the way to more-efficiently designed communities that rely mainly on walking, bicycling, and mass transit.

In industrial market countries, buildings are the most wasteful energy users and deserve the greatest attention from government programs. Improvements already made in buildings there spare the atmosphere 225 million tons of carbon emissions annually, but heating, cooling, and lighting those buildings still pumps out over 900 million tons each year—17 percent of world carbon emissions from fossil fuels. Whereas the energy requirements of automobiles and industry could be halved with available technologies, building energy requirements can be reduced by 70 percent or more when new buildings are constructed. To sustain a 2 percent annual rate of improvement over the long run, building efficiency will have to compensate for diminishing returns in industry and transportation.

The investments required to sustain a 2 percent rate of improvement in energy efficiency in the next decade or two can be justified on purely economic grounds. The world has achieved over $300 billion worth of annual energy savings since 1973, mostly as a result of private investment decisions. Each additional 2 percent of savings will reduce bills by about $20 billion annually. It is impossible to estimate how much has been invested in energy efficiency during this period, but even assuming a large payback, the annual investments in the early eighties must have reached at least $20-30 billion.

In market economies, improved efficiency falls primarily to the private sector, which pays for the big ticket items such as home weatherization and the modernization of industrial equipment. However, governments must ensure that institutions and incentives are in place to encourage the needed investments.

Superpowers' Commitment

The United States and the Soviet Union have pivotal roles to play in energy efficiency. The United States is the world's largest energy consumer and led other nations into the profligate energy practices of the postwar period. The Soviet Union is the least energy-efficient major industrial country, and its claim on global energy resources is among the fastest growing. Together the two countries, with 10 percent of the world's population, account for 42 percent of the carbon now entering the atmosphere from fossil fuels. A joint commitment to improved energy efficiency by the superpowers would make a major contribution to climate protection and might help mobilize action around the world.

There are indications that the Soviet Union may soon make improved energy efficiency a national priority. Senior officials have gone on record as saying that efficiency gains will be essential if the country's economic restructuring is to be successful. Already meetings have taken place with energy-efficiency experts in the West, including representatives of the Rocky Mountain Institute and the U. S. National Academy of Sciences. Yevgeny Velikhov, vice president of the Soviet Academy of Sciences and an advisor to General Secretary Gorbachev, appears to have put his personal authority behind these new efforts.

The Third World is also critical to any long-term energy scenario. Indeed, one of the most troubling features of recent forecasts is the assumption that industrial countries will continue to use a disproportionate share of the world's energy, despite the fact that developing countries will soon have three-quarters of the world's population. A 1981 study by the International Institute for Applied Systems Analysis was ostensibly attuned to global equity issues, yet it still assumed the Third World would use just 36 percent of the global energy supply in the year 2020.

Such scenarios imply that while Third World energy use grows, per capita energy use will stagnate, presumably making it impossible for most developing countries to follow the modernization path taken by the newly industrializing nations in recent years. Although many developing nations are burdened with unmanageable foreign debt and have been priced out of the oil market, this is a morally intolerable vision, inconsistent with the articulated goals of the international community. Poverty-induced conservation is not conservation at all. It is just plain poverty.

Alternatives to Oil

For the longer term, we should begin in earnest the process of weaning our transportation fleet from oil. So-called alternative fuels—including reformulated gasoline, methanol and compressed natural gas—aren't the long-term answer. Reformulated gasoline and methanol would still be imported, and domestic natural gas resources are inadequate to support a major increase in demand for motor-vehicle use. Moreover, all are fossil fuels, so all contribute to the buildup of carbon dioxide in the atmosphere. The next century will require cars that run on electricity or hydrogen made from renewable sources of energy.

James Gustave Speth, *Los Angeles Times,* August 19, 1990.

One of the greatest challenges will be to meet the energy needs of the poor without repeating the mistakes of the rich. Only rapid advances in energy efficiency and a decentralized, agriculturally based development path can allow the Third World to fuel improved living standards with limited energy supplies. In the poorer countries of Africa and Latin America, the rapid onset of an energy-efficiency revolution is critical. Some Asian countries, including China, with the world's largest coal reserves, have sufficient fossil fuels to last for many decades but face a critical environmental choice. Using energy efficiency to displace coal may be essential to protecting human health as well as the climate.

A global energy study developed by an international team and published by the World Resources Institute in Washington, D.C., points up both the challenge and the promise of increased energy efficiency in the Third World. It concludes that the world energy supply in the year 2020 can hover just above the current level if energy efficiency is employed both to halve per capita energy consumption in industrial countries and to keep Third World per capita energy use steady while boosting living standards to current European levels. Some of the most dramatic improvements in Third World efficiency are projected for rural areas, as fuelwood cooking systems are replaced by more-efficient devices run on renewable fuels.

This scenario is consistent with the goal of improving energy efficiency by 2 percent annually. It would help foster greater equality in material living standards between industrial and developing countries. And it would make it possible to avoid the worst consequences of a global warming. But such scenarios are far easier to model on computers than to achieve in practice. Third World and industrial countries alike will have to overcome political obstacles and begin ambitious efforts to improve energy efficiency.

Efficiency of Policy

To achieve its full potential, energy efficiency must emerge from the obscure corners of Energy Ministries and rise to the top of planning agendas throughout government and industry. The very term energy efficiency must be transformed from a watchword of specialists to a centerpiece of national—and international—economic philosophy. As an essential ingredient of economic and ecological progress, its status should be charted as closely as productivity or inflation. The Commission of the European Communities has suggested the need for such a commitment. At a 1986 meeting, national energy ministers agreed to a target of a 20 percent improvement in energy efficiency by 1995.

Energy-efficiency improvements are by nature fragmented and often unglamorous: thicker insulation and ceramic auto parts are not perhaps as intrinsically captivating as nuclear fusion or orbiting solar collectors. But infatuation with grandiose energy-supply options helped get us into our current predicament; focusing on the mundane may be the only way to get out. Indeed, perhaps no other endeavor is as vital to the goal of fostering sustainable societies. Without improved efficiency, it is only a question of which will collapse first: the global economy or its ecological support systems. With greater energy efficiency, we stand at least a fighting chance.

VIEWPOINT

"There is no reason to believe that the supply of energy is finite, or that the price will not continue its long-run decrease."

Energy Policies Are Unnecessary

Julian L. Simon

Julian L. Simon is business administration professor at the University of Maryland and the coeditor of *The Resourceful Earth: A Response to Global 2000*, which criticizes the environmental movement. In this viewpoint, Simon argues that there is no shortage of energy supplies. He contends that technology will make resources become more abundant and cheaper. If future scarcities should develop, he believes these problems will become opportunities that lead to alternative solutions or new resources.

As you read, consider the following questions:

1. What examples does Simon give to illustrate his belief that people will discover substitutes for a resource in response to increased demand?
2. How does the author measure the future supply of oil?
3. Why is the term "known reserves" important to future energy supplies, according to Simon?

Published by permission of Transaction Publishers, from *Population Matters* by Julian L. Simon. Copyright © 1990 by Transaction Publishers.

Energy is an emotional topic. When asked their number one worry in September 1978, seven times as many people said "inflation" as said "energy." By summer 1979, the numbers were roughly equal. In a 1979 Gallup poll of Americans who drive cars, 82 percent said that "the energy situation in the United States" is "very serious" or "fairly serious." Energy is also a topic about which it is extraordinarily difficult to get any agreement among people on different sides of the controversy.

Energy is the master resource because energy enables us to convert one material into another. As natural scientists continue to learn more about the transformation of materials from one form to another with the aid of energy, energy will be even more important. Therefore, if the cost of usable energy is low enough, all other important resources can be made plentiful. For example, low energy costs would enable people to create enormous quantities of useful land. The cost of energy is the prime reason that water desalination is too expensive for general use; reduction in energy cost would make water desalination feasible, and irrigated farming would follow in many areas that are now deserts. And if energy were cheaper, it would be feasible to transport sweet water from areas of surplus to arid areas far away. Another example: if energy costs were low enough, all kinds of raw materials could be mined from the sea.

On the other hand, if there were to be an absolute shortage of energy—that is, if there were no oil in the tanks, no natural gas in the pipelines, no coal to load onto the railroad cars—then our entire economy would come to a halt. Or if energy were available, but only at a very high price, we would produce much smaller amounts of most consumer goods and services.

Supply of Resources

Because energy plays so central a role, it is most important that we think clearly about the way energy is found and used. An analysis of the supply of mineral resources identifies four factors as being important: (1) the increasing cost of extraction as more of the resource is used, if all other conditions remain the same; (2) the tendency for engineers to develop improved methods of extracting the resource in response to the rising price of the resource; (3) the propensity for scientists and business people to discover substitutes for the resource in response to increasing demand; (4) the increased use of recycled material.

The supply of energy is analogous to the supply of other "extracted" raw materials with the exception of the fourth factor above; minerals such as iron and aluminum can be recycled, whereas coal and oil are "burned up." Of course this distinction is not perfectly clear-cut: quarried marble is cut irreversibly and cannot be recycled by melting, as copper can; yet even cut marble can be used again and again, whereas energy sources cannot.

The practical implication of being "used up" as opposed to being recyclable is that an increased rate of energy use would make the price of energy sources rise sharply, whereas an increased use of iron would not affect iron prices so much because some of the additional iron could be drawn from such previously used stocks as dumps of old autos. All of this may seem to make our energy future look grim. But before we proceed to the analysis itself, it is instructive to see how in the past, energy "shortages" have frightened even the most intelligent of analysts.

Technology Will Find Solutions

This anti-technology, hair-shirt mentality is wrong. Although conservation is a vital ingredient in any sound national energy policy, achieving ecological sustainability cannot be accomplished by making war on progress. . . .

Only through the help of technology can society hope to cope with multiplying environmental threats and the growing scarcity of oil. Our goal should not be to force people to live more primitive lives, but to ensure that modern living is made more environmentally benign. Once the simple life is gone, we can never bring it back. Nor should we want to.

Alston Chase, *The Washington Times*, September 18, 1990.

There is no reason to believe that the supply of energy is finite, or that the price will not continue its long-run decrease. This statement may sound less preposterous if you consider that for a quantity to be finite it must be measurable. The future supply of oil includes what we usually think of as oil, plus the oil that can be produced from shale, tar sands, and coal. It also includes the oil from plants that we grow, whose key input is sunlight. So the measure of the future oil supply must therefore be at least as large as the sun's seven billion or so years of future life. And it may include other suns whose energy might be exploited in the future—a belief that requires a lot of confidence that the knowledge of the physical world we have developed in the past century will not be superseded in the next seven billion years, plus the belief that the universe is not expanding—this measurement would hardly be relevant for any practical contemporary decision making.

Energy provides a good example of the process by which resources become more abundant and hence cheaper. Seventeenth-century England was full of alarm at an impending energy shortage due to the country's deforestation for firewood. People feared a scarcity of fuel for both heating and the vital iron industry. This impending scarcity led inventors and business people to develop coal.

Then, in the mid-1800s, the English came to worry about an impending coal crisis. But spurred by the impending scarcity of coal, ingenious and profit-minded people developed oil into a more desirable fuel than coal ever was. And today England exports both coal and oil.

This story is prototypical of the intertwined history of resources, population, and civilization. The resource problems that arise become opportunities, and turn into the occasions for the advances of knowledge that support and spur economic development. If berries, roots, and rabbits had not become scarce 10,000 years ago, we would probably still be eating wild rabbits and roots, though perhaps with a tastier sauce than they had then. We need more and bigger problems, rather than just having our problems solved, as conventional economics would have it.

And the story spreads out from the energy resources. There is a direct connection between the deforestation crisis in England in the 1600s and the possibility that you can now travel in a train or car, or in an airplane. The development of coal created the new problem of water in coal mines. This problem led to the invention of the first steam engine for the purpose of driving pumps, and afterwards to a series of much improved pumps. Then someone had the bright idea to put wheels under the engine and run it on rails. *Voilá*, the railroad and the steam automobile, and of course factories with central steam power and belts to transmit the power, and steam farm machines to cut back-breaking and expensive labor. Then someone else replaced the idea of steam power in autos with the internal combustion machine, and that meant you could get around without aid of a hayburner or shank's mare or a bicycle, for better or for worse.

This series of ever-extending developments stemming from the original wood energy crisis in England goes on and on, leading to new resources that are cheaper than the old resources as well as being the founts of additional developments. . . .

History of Energy Supplies

Running out of oil has long been a nightmare. In 1885, the U.S. Geological Survey saw "little or no chance for oil in California," and in 1891 it prophesied the same for Kansas and Texas. In 1908, the Geological Survey estimated a maximum future supply of oil that has long since been exceeded. And since then, similar gloomy official prophesies by the Geological Survey, the Bureau of Mines, the Interior Department, and the State Department have regularly been made and subsequently proven false. Of course this does not mean that every gloomy forecast about oil must be wrong. And forecasts can be over-optimistic, too. But it does show that expert forecasts often have been far too pessimistic. We therefore should not simply take them at face value.

A look at the statistical history of energy supplies shows that the trend has been toward plenty rather than toward scarcity. The relevant measures are the production costs of energy (as measured in time and money) and the price to the consumer; and the relevant data are historical. These data for coal, oil, and electricity show an unambiguous trend toward less scarcity and a great availability of energy.

Energy and Prices

The sharp rise of crude-oil prices in the 1970s does not contradict the long-run conclusion that energy will become more available and less costly. The recent rise was clearly caused by the cartel agreements of OPEC [Organization of Petroleum Exporting Countries]. It is the result of political power rather than of rising extraction costs. When consumers are reaching into their pocketbooks, of course, they are concerned about the market price of oil, not about the production costs. But if one is interested in whether there is, or will be, an *economic* shortage of oil, or if one wants to know about the world's capacity for producing oil, the appropriate indicator is the cost of production and transportation—and that cost, since the first OPEC embargo in 1973, has been only a small fraction of the world-market price.

During the years of the "energy crisis," the cost of oil production has not risen at all. It is far less than 1 percent of the selling price of crude—a cost of perhaps 5 to 20 cents a barrel, in comparison with a selling price of somewhere around $35 a barrel in 1980. For perspective, we should remember that energy prices to the consumer have been falling not only over the very long haul but also in the recent past, since World War II. Before the OPEC cartel went into action, oil prices had been declining relative to those of other commodities. The price of Iranian oil fell from $2.17 a barrel in 1947 to $1.79 in 1959, and the price of oil at Rotterdam was at its lowest point in history in 1969; an adjustment for inflation would show even more decline. . . .

The price history of electricity is particularly revealing because the price of electricity measures the price to the consumer, at home or at work. The ratio of the price of electricity to the average wage in manufacturing shows that the quantity of electricity bought with an hour's wage has steadily increased. Because each year an hour's work has bought more rather than less electricity, this measure suggests that energy has become ever less troublesome in the economy over the recorded period, no matter what the price of energy in current dollars. In short, the trends in energy costs and scarcity have been downward over the entire period for which we have data. And such trends are usually the most reliable bases for forecasts. From these data we may conclude with considerable confidence that energy will be less costly and more available in the future than in the past. . . .

Future Energy Supplies

We must first dispose of the preposterous but commonly accepted notion that the energy situation can be forecast with the aid of presently known reserves. This notion is an example of the use of misleading numbers simply because they are the only numbers available.

Solar Energy Not the Solution

Solar energy has been considered a potential limitless supply of energy since the time of Archimedes, and the idea has been revisited from time to time by various scientists, including the French government about 100 years ago. What these scientists discovered is exactly what today's solar scientists have found: Solar energy is too diffuse, too intermittent, and too costly. To hold out the hope that it will provide a large supply of bulk energy is really to mislead an uninformed public with promises that cannot be fulfilled.

Michael Fox, *Energy & Environment*, July/August 1989.

"Known reserves" are defined as the total amount of oil in areas that have been well prospected. Geologists are quite sure of their existence. Individuals, firms, and governments create known resources by searching for promising drilling areas long in advance of the moment when wells might be drilled—far enough ahead to allow preparation time, but not so far ahead that the investment in prospecting costs will not obtain a satisfactory return. The key idea here is that it costs money to produce information about what are called "known reserves," and therefore people will create only as many known reserves as it is profitable to create at a given moment. The quantity of known reserves at any moment tells us more about the expected profitability of oil wells than it does about the amount of oil in the ground. And the higher the cost of exploration, the lower will be the known reserves that it pays to create. This explains why the quantity of known reserves, as if by coincidence, stays just a step ahead of demand.

Known reserves are much like the food we put into our cupboards at home. We stock enough groceries for a few days or weeks—not so much that we will be carrying a heavy, unneeded inventory that ties up an unnecessary amount of money in groceries, and not so little that we may run out if an unexpected event, such as a blizzard, should descend upon us. The amount of food in our cupboards tells little or nothing about the scarcity of food in our communities, because it does not as a rule reveal how much food is available in the retail stores. Similarly, the oil in the "cupboard"—the quantity of known reserves—tells us nothing about the quantities of oil that can be obtained in the long run at various costs. This explains why the quantity of known reserves, as if by a miracle of coincidence, stays just a step ahead of demand.

A more sophisticated—and even more misleading—approach is to project present growth in demand, assuming the price will remain constant, and then to compare that projection to known reserves, thereby indicating that demand will apparently outstrip supply very soon. Even assuming that the growth in demand at present prices is reasonably estimated—and this would be difficult to do well—all that such a calculation would show is that price must rise in order to lower the demand and raise the supply until demand and supply meet, a basic economic way of looking at supply and demand. . . .

Matters in Dispute

The future supply of oil. Some technologists tell us that at present prices and rates of consumption, production of oil will peak around the year 1990 and decline thereafter. Other technologists confidently predict that vast new sources of oil will be found as needed. Also in dispute is the amount of oil and other fossil fuels that can be safely burned without creating excessive atmospheric levels of carbon dioxide.

The future supply of natural gas. The American Gas Association says that there is enough gas "to last between 1000 and 2500 years at current consumption." In stark contrast is the estimate quoted by President Carter in 1977. That estimate, made in 1974 by the U.S. Geological Survey, was "6.1 million million cubic meters, 10 years' supply . . . at 1974 technology and 1974 prices." The difference boggles the mind; 10 years' supply versus a 1000 to 2500 years' supply!

The potential effect of oil conservation measures. Some informed persons argue that it is possible to increase greatly the efficiency of oil use, that is, to waste less of it. Other informed persons are doubtful of any great benefits in this respect.

Whether the "alternative" energy sources are practical. Such possible sources as tidal power, ocean thermal power, geothermal power, wind power, fuel cells, conventional solar power, or geopressurized methane and alcohol might be able to compete with oil in the near or not-so-near future if the price of oil were to remain in the long run at the present level. On the other hand, they might not be important even if the price of energy were to double, triple, or quadruple. Tidal power seems the best bet of the lot, especially in Great Britain, where a variety of devices that the sea compresses or bumps to convert its movements into electricity are well into the testing stages. There is less dispute that shale oil, available in vast quantities in the United States and elsewhere, could be profitable at present energy prices.

Also speculative are the possibilities of a variety of new and radical ways to harness solar power, some of which promise energy at remarkably low costs if they are developed.

The danger from nuclear power. The mainline scientific position—expressed in the 1979 report of the National Academy of Sciences Committee on Nuclear and Alternative Energy Systems —concluded that "if one takes all health effects into account (including mining and transportation accidents and the estimated expectations from nuclear accidents), the health effects of coal production and use appear to be a good deal greater than those of the nuclear energy cycle.". . .

The most recent wide-ranging technological survey of long-run energy prospects is that of Herman Kahn and his associates. After surveying the technological, environmental, and cost characteristics of all likely energy sources on the horizon, they concluded, "Energy costs as a whole are very likely to continue the historical downward trend indefinitely. . . ." The basic message is this: "Except for temporary fluctuations caused by bad luck or poor management, the world need not worry about energy shortages or costs in the future."

Conclusions

Extrapolation of long-run cost trends seems to be the most reliable method for estimating future energy availability. Such extrapolation promises continually decreasing scarcity and cost, though this runs counter to popular opinion. At worst, the cost ceiling provided by nuclear power guarantees that the cost of electricity cannot rise far above present energy costs, political obstacles aside.

As to technological forecasts, the best we can do is examine the range of forecasts that are now available and try to learn from the history of such forecasts whether the higher or lower ones are more likely to be correct. In my judgment, Kahn and his associates do their homework best and are on firm technological ground when they say that energy costs are likely to decline indefinitely.

"We now know the concept works—politically, financially, environmentally—for the benefit of debtor countries and their nature."

Debt-for-Nature Swaps Promote Conservation

William K. Reilly

Many people argue that the indebtedness of developing countries prevents them from pursuing sound environmental policies. Supporters of debt-for-nature swaps believe they can help solve this problem. In these swaps, lending institutions cancel small amounts of Third World countries' debts in exchange for protecting threatened natural areas within their countries. In this viewpoint, William K. Reilly contends that debt-for-nature swaps are beneficial to everyone involved. They reduce Third World debt, pay back creditor banks, and help conserve global resources. Reilly is the head of the U.S. Environmental Protection Agency and is past president of the World Wildlife Fund-U.S.

As you read, consider the following questions:

1. According to the author, what role do international conservation organizations play in debt-for-nature swaps?
2. Even though the swaps pay back only a small portion of the debt, why does Reilly believe they are necessary?
3. How does Reilly think the number of debt-for-nature swaps can be increased?

William K. Reilly, "Debt-for-Nature Swaps: The Time Has Come," *International Environmental Affairs,* vol. 2, no. 2, Spring 1990. Reprinted with permission.

Having worked as a private conservationist on three debt-for-nature deals—in Ecuador, Costa Rica, and the Philippines—and then having moved into government, I have been able to view debt-for-nature from two perspectives. I am more than ever persuaded of the usefulness and practicality of the concept, and of the potential for debt-for-nature to make more than a marginal contribution to conserving what remains of the rich flora and fauna and natural systems of debt-burdened countries. . . .

An Idea That Works

Debt-for-nature swaps are an idea whose time has come. In the short span of two years, groups like WWF [World Wildlife Fund], the Nature Conservancy, Conservation International, the National Park Foundation of Costa Rica, Fundación Natura in Ecuador, and the governments of Sweden, Ecuador, Costa Rica, Bolivia, the Philippines, Madagascar, Zambia, the Netherlands, as well as the United States, have demonstrated first, and most simply, that swaps work. And second, that everyone can benefit.

They have reduced foreign debts by over $85 million. They have helped poor countries in Latin America, Asia, and Africa protect one of the few resources in which they are very, very rich. Forests and wildlife; birds and mammals; reptiles and insects; flowers, and trees, and plants of immense variety and untold, still unproven, untested usefulness—a veritable Noah's ark of species the tropical countries have stocked and now sell on behalf of all others. Developing countries burdened with large domestic and external debt often cannot pay for the equipment, planning, and other measures needed to protect valuable ecosystems. . . .Alvaro Umaña, Costa Rica's Minister of Natural Resources, Energy, and Mines has pointed out:

> Developing countries, where the debt burden means a net flow of capital to the creditor countries, are not able to take a long-term view of their resources and to invest in sustainable programs. This is why debt-for-nature swaps, even though they affect less than 1 percent of the total debt, are absolutely necessary. The interest alone from Costa Rican debt-for-nature swaps is several times more than the annual budget of our national park service. Under the austerity program that the International Monetary Fund and Costa Rica implemented, there would have been no money to purchase land bridges between parks, to start tree nurseries for farmers, or even to fight forest fires.

I want to make several points about these transactions. First, the resources involved remain very much in the debtor's ownership. The "swap" does not involve giving away a title interest—in land or anything else. Second, the swap does not "legitimize" debt or "impose" a foreign agenda on the debtor. The reason is simple: in the last analysis, it is the debtor's decision whether the transaction is appropriate. In fact, in Ecuador and Costa Rica, it was local people—government officials and conservationists in debtor countries—who conceived and initiated the proposal for the deals.

THE DEBTOR-DEFORESTATION CONNECTION

	Average annual deforestation in the 1980s (thousand hectares)	Total external debt in 1987 (billion U.S. dollars)
Brazil	2,323	109.5
Colombia	890	15.5
Mexico	615	82.8
Ecuador	340	10.4
Peru	270	16.6
Venezuela	245	29.0
Ivory Coast	510	10.3
Nigeria	400	28.4
Zaire	347	8.6
Indonesia	620	48.5
Thailand	379	17.6
Malaysia	255	21.1
India	147	42.9
Philippines	92	28.4

Source: Data from the UN Food and Agriculture Organization and the World Bank.

The first debt-for-nature agreement, in Bolivia, received some criticism that implied the deal was yet another debt-for-equity swap with a wildlife reserve passing into foreign ownership, much as an industrial plant or a company might in a debt-for-equity swap.

In fact, the debt-for-nature agreements negotiated thus far have been embraced enthusiastically by the governments and conservation groups in the debtor countries.

So we now know the concept works—politically, financially, environmentally—for the benefit of debtor countries and their nature. For conceiving the idea, and then demonstrating and testing it, WWF and its sister organizations deserve great praise and gratitude. We should not be surprised if WWF now turns to us in government, and to the banks and multilateral aid and lending institutions and says, in effect: "We've taken this as far as we can. We've shown how to do it. We've proved debt-for-nature works. Now you take over and put some real money into it."

To help achieve an order of magnitude increase in the resources committed to conservation through debt-for-nature trades, I would suggest six general propositions.

First, and most simply, when forgiving debt, for heaven's sake, get something for it. Many developing nations would happily increase their local currency expenditures on reforestation, park protection, wildlife conservation, and pollution control in return for some write-down and repatriation of debt. But nature conservation needs to be explicitly considered in debt negotiations.

Several countries—France, Canada, Belgium, West Germany, the United States, among others—have announced programs of official debt forgiveness for sub-Saharan and other countries totaling at least $5 billion. Countries contemplating future programs of this kind should not overlook conservation opportunities.

The second proposition is to recognize the need for a transformation of scale in conservation efforts in the developing world and work to turn as much debt as possible into productive, local currency-funded conservation activity. . . .

The Need for Pathbreakers

Third, in trying to execute a really sizable debt-for-nature agreement, look first to those nations most responsible in addressing their debt problems, those in a position to play a leadership role, with the confidence and cooperation of creditor countries and banks. They, I think, can become pathbreakers, and an energetic, enthusiastic head of government from one of these countries can do a great deal to advance, to legitimize, and to popularize this idea.

Fourth, broaden the ambit of programs and activities to be financed with the proceeds of repatriated debt. It is important to include projects regarded as intimately supporting development policies such as water conservation projects; investments in training, reforestation and reclamation of degraded lands; groundwater protection; and pollution control. Sometimes lender institutions such as the World Bank or regional banks are reluctant to support pure park and wildlife conservation. So enlarge the menu. Give them more to choose from, broadening the constituency both in the developed and also developing countries involved.

Fifth, be opportunistic. A relatively small nation like Costa Rica may have received a disproportionate share of conservation assistance over the years because of the alertness and ingenuity of its president, minister of natural resources, and conservation leadership. Never mind. If the opportunity arises to do a very large debt-for-nature deal with a country whose president uniquely appreciates the debt-conservation relationship, that opportunity should not be missed. Others will soon follow.

Sixth is a special message for nongovernmental organizations [NGOs] that have worked with local groups to identify and design conservation programs funded by debt-for-nature trades. In our enthusiasm for doing agreements, let us be very careful not to forget the purpose. We need to insure that the conservation promises made in debt-for-nature deals are in fact kept. The programs are monitored and their results policed. One critical role for local NGOs like Fundación Natura in Ecuador has been to provide that function. . . .Let us, particularly as conservationists, be careful to recognize that that will not be primarily the function of banks. That will be the function of alert and organized conservationists all over the world. There's still some demonstrating to do, a demonstration that debt-for-nature can enter the mainstream of debt discussions and solve really big problems.

Linking the Environment and Development

Debt-for-nature agreements are part of a new wave of thinking about the links between development and the environment and debt. . . .

The exciting—the challenging—thing about our present time is that the issues of the environment have joined with the issues of development—old and new. We cannot further the environmental agenda without attending to development, and vice versa. Nature conservation will require debt reduction and long-term development. Long-term economic development is impossible without shoring up and stabilizing the natural systems, the groundwater and watersheds, the forests, and fisheries, and soils on which developing countries are so heavily, so disproportionately dependent.

The term, "sustainable development,". . .captures this idea. It captures the idea that we cannot look upon nature as something to be mined indefinitely. We must see it as the capital and take no more than the interest that it can sustainably produce. Debt-for-nature is not just a modern alchemy. Its time has come.

"Debt-for-nature swaps. . . raise serious questions about both local and national sovereignty."

Debt-for-Nature Swaps Harm Conservation

Brian Tokar

Brian Tokar is an environmental activist and author of *The Green Alternative: Creating an Ecological Future*. In this viewpoint, Tokar argues that debt-for-nature swaps do not help conserve tropical forests. He contends they harm Third World resources by promoting destructive development projects and undermining national sovereignty. Environmental organizations that promote debt-for-nature swaps are being exploited, he concludes.

As you read, consider the following questions:

1. According to Tokar, how do conservation organizations benefit from debt-for-nature swaps?
2. Why does Tokar believe the swaps are harmful to indigenous people?
3. What role do the international banks play in exploiting developing countries, according to the author?

Brian Tokar, "Environment for Sale," *Z Magazine*, April 1990. Reprinted with permission.

Few international environmental issues in recent years have raised as much widespread concern or as much passion as the fate of the world's tropical forests. Tropical forests are the earth's greatest reservoir of biological diversity, housing up to three quarters of all living species. They hold massive amounts of organic carbon and release globally-significant quantities of oxygen. Their human inhabitants include many of the last remaining tribal peoples whose traditional ways have not been compromised by the intrusion of civilization. The crippling indebtedness of many tropical nations, especially Brazil, has brought pressure for a wave of new development schemes, in which vast tracts of rainforest are being destroyed to satisfy the demands of international banks. Rainforest activists predict that if the destruction continues at present rates, there will be no tropical forests left in just 20 or 30 years.

In the 1980s, several Third World countries began to resist continuing debt payments. Citing the effects of foreign debt on their national economies and the fact that many loans have already been paid several times over in exorbitant interest payments, several countries have threatened to default on their loans. Others have slowed debt payments to a trickle, forcing banks to admit that many Third World loans will simply never be repaid.

Anxious to keep these countries "in the system," the banks continue to loan countries money to support debt payments, while proposing new, more destructive development projects and imposing ever-stricter austerity measures. In an effort to squeeze some tangible benefit from these increasingly dubious loans, banks have become increasingly involved in international debt-swapping. They are directly trading portions of various countries' debt for equity in debtor countries, stakes in future development and, most significantly for environmentalists, commitments for the preservation and "sustainable management" of parcels of tropical forest land. Organizations like the World Wildlife Fund, Conservation International, and the Nature Conservancy are actively sponsoring so-called "debt-for-nature swaps," promoting them as vehicles for '"The Greening of International Finance."

Vehicle for Exploitation

The first, and by far the best publicized, of these "swaps" was launched in 1987 when the Frank Weeden Foundation of Connecticut granted $100,000 to Conservation International for the purchase of $650,000 in unpaid debt from a Citibank affiliate in Bolivia. In exchange, the Bolivian government had agreed to support the expansion of the Beni Biological Reserve, an ecologically unique area containing some of the world's largest remaining reserves of mahogany and tropical cedar. The Reserve itself would become protected "to the maximum extent possible under Bolivian law," according to CI, and would be surrounded by a much larger "multiple use and conservation" buffer zone, for a total of almost 4 million acres. The Bolivian government agreed to allocate $250,000 (mostly from funds generated through US-sponsored food aid) toward the management of the project. CI would provide training, technical support and other forms of international assistance for the project, and advise local agencies on the "sustainable use" of the precious mahogany forests.

Education of Local People

Debt-for-nature swaps have not yet proven themselves. Simply demanding the preservation of land cannot inculcate in the local population the value of conservation or the importance of irrigation and crop rotation. Money will have to be spent developing education and social programs if any future exchanges are to bring long-term economic and environmental solutions.

Laura Caldwell, *Christian Science Monitor*, September 11, 1990.

Supporters of the project assert that the entire area might have been stripped of trees before the next century had Conservation International not intervened, while critics argue that the entire project is merely a vehicle for the more rational exploitation of the area. Some accounts report that logging in the buffer zone has increased tremendously since the project began: twice as many mahogany trees were removed in 1988 as in 1987, for example. Contracts for seven new sawmills in the area were approved immediately before the debt swap went into effect. Residents of the area were not consulted before the debt-swap agreement was signed, even though much of the land was already in dispute between logging companies and the area's 5,000 native inhabitants.

Experts in so-called "sustainable development"—one of the key catchphrases of corporate environmentalism—have carved the land up into experimental parcels which will experience varying degrees of tree harvesting, from the most limited to the most intensive. For the native people, these are trees that would have been used to build homes and canoes, and to shelter local wildlife for countless generations to come. The Moxeno and Chimane people have seen environmentalists thwart their efforts to manage the land as a community—the project's needs were apparently better served by continuing the Bolivian government's practice of maintaining native lands in isolated private plots, the preferred model in much of Latin America.

Debt-for-nature swaps, like the equity swaps upon which they were modeled, raise serious questions about both local and national sovereignty. The land ostensibly remains under the host country's control, but patterns of use are determined by international organizations. . . . Of course, most of the countries involved remain indebted to international banks to the tune of many billions of dollars.

African Concerns

Concerns about the impact of such schemes have arisen in Africa, where several countries are discussing plans for future debt-for-nature arrangements. Africans have already had some difficult experiences with North American conservationists. In 1909 Teddy Roosevelt went there and reportedly shot a third of the rhinos in Uganda. Groups like the World Wildlife Fund, with encouragement from wealthy big game hunters and safari enthusiasts, have been involved in the creation of National Parks in several African countries. The parks, conceived on the American model, are seen as pristine places where wild animal habitats can be preserved without human disturbance. This often happens at the expense of native peoples, who have been living alongside wild animals for countless generations and, in many cases, fought to keep slave traders, poachers and colonialists out of these areas. Without native protection wildlife habitats might be designated for preservation today, but can be eliminated tomorrow at the stroke of a pen or the roll of a bulldozer. The damage could be done before international wildlife groups knew what was happening.

In Kenya and Tanzania, the pastoral Masaai people have protected elephants and other animals from hunters since the beginnings of European colonialism, but are being systematically excluded from National Parks planned with support from U.S. environmentalists. Moringe Parkipuny, a Masaai elder who represents his people in the national parliament of Tanzania, explains: "To us in Africa, the disappearance of the elephant is just one aspect of the major problem of colonialism. . . . The conflict, as we see it, is between indigenous peoples and the policies imposed on them by foreign governments. These policies discriminate against us by making wild animals more important than indigenous peoples. They have also turned our people against wild animals, because they feel that wildlife is now being used as a weapon to destroy us."

By blinding themselves to underlying political factors, US-based environmental organizations become unwitting agents of imperialism overseas, just as they sometimes help to rationalize polluting practices at home.

270

Evaluating Sources of Information

When historians study and interpret past events, they use two kinds of sources: primary and secondary. Primary sources are eyewitness accounts. For example, an African tribal leader's description of how a large-scale irrigation project affected his community would be a primary source. A book on water conservation in the Third World, written by a scientist who used the leader's description, would be a secondary source. Primary and secondary sources may be decades or even hundreds of years old, and often historians find that the sources offer conflicting and contradictory information. To fully evaluate documents and assess their accuracy, historians analyze the credibility of the documents' authors and, in the case of secondary sources, analyze the credibility of the information the authors used.

Historians are not the only people who encounter conflicting information, however. Anyone who reads a daily newspaper, watches television, or just talks to different people will encounter many different views. Writers and speakers use sources of information to support their own statements. Thus, critical thinkers, just like historians, must question the writer's or speaker's sources of information as well as the writer or speaker.

While there are many criteria that can be applied to assess the accuracy of a primary or secondary source, for this activity you will be asked to apply three. For each source listed on the following page, ask yourself the following questions: First, did the person actually see or participate in the event he or she is reporting? This will help you determine the credibility of the information—an eyewitness to an event is an extremely valuable source. Second, does the person have a vested interest in the report? Assessing the person's social status, professional affiliations, nationality, and religious and political beliefs will be helpful in considering this question. By evaluating this you will be able to determine how objective the person's report may be. Third, how qualified is the author to make the statements he or she is making? Consider the person's profession and how he or she might know about the event. Someone who has spent years being involved with or studying the issue may be able to offer more information than someone who simply is offering an uneducated opinion; for example, a politician or layperson.

Keeping the above criteria in mind, imagine you are writing a paper on how certain agricultural practices and policies affect the earth's resources. You decide to cite an equal number of primary and secondary sources. Listed below are several sources that may be useful for your research. *Place a P next to those descriptions you believe are primary sources. Place an S next to those descriptions you believe are secondary sources.* Next, based on the above criteria, *rank the primary sources, assigning the number 1 to that which appears the most valuable, 2 to the source likely to be the second-most valuable, and so on, until all the primary sources are ranked. Then rank the secondary sources, again using the above criteria.*

P or S		*Rank in Importance*
_____	1. An article by a member of the World Bank describing the bank's support of debt-for-nature swaps.	_____
_____	2. An interview with an Indian woman who describes how her organization, the Chipko movement, prevented the destruction of a local forest.	_____
_____	3. A report in an environmental magazine covering the energy policies of a U.S. leader.	_____
_____	4. A newspaper article that relates the research of a scientist studying how chlorofluorocarbons (CFCs) contribute to the greenhouse effect.	_____
_____	5. A report by a biotechnology firm on the development of a new seed that will produce insect-resistant plants.	_____
_____	6. A book by an anthropologist who describes the farming techniques of ancient American peoples.	_____
_____	7. An editorial by a Roman Catholic archbishop describing how large families help Latin American farmers.	_____
_____	8. A documentary on local aquaculture practices in Nigeria.	_____
_____	9. A U.S. government official's analysis of the environmental policies of developing nations.	_____
_____	10. An interview with a Brazilian farmer, who describes how he clears and cultivates forested land.	_____
_____	11. A press release from an EPA official discussing the controversial research of a group of environmentalists.	_____

Periodical Bibliography

The following articles have been selected to supplement the diverse views presented in this chapter.

Anil Agarwal — "The North-South Perspective: Alienation or Interdependence?" *Ambio*, April 1990.

Bobby Ray Brown — "Defining Coal's Future: Growth or Decline?" *Vital Speeches of the Day*, November 15, 1989.

Lester R. Brown, Christopher Flavin, and Sandra Postel — "A Global Plan to Save Our Planet's Environment," *USA Today*, January 1990.

Gro Harlem Brundtland — "Global Change and Our Common Future," *Environment*, June 1989.

Barry Commoner — "Ending the War Against Earth," *The Nation*, April 30, 1990.

Gregg Easterbrook — "Everything You Know About the Environment Is Wrong," *The New Republic*, April 30, 1990.

Hugh W. Ellsaesser — "The Siren Song of Environmentalism," *The World & I*, July 1989.

Herbert London — "Ecotastrophe Again," *First Things*, June/July 1990.

Kenneth W. Piddington — "Sovereignty and the Environment: Part of the Solution or Part of the Problem?" *Environment*, September 1989.

Georgeanne Potter — "Debt Swaps—Buying In Means Selling Out," *Center Focus*, January 1988. Available from Center of Concern, 3700 13th St. NE, Washington, DC 20017.

William E. Rees — "The Ecology of Sustainable Development," *The Ecologist*, January/February 1990. Available from MIT Press Journals, 55 Hayward St., Cambridge, MA 02142.

Rodney B. Wagner — "Doing More with Debt-for-Nature Swaps," *International Environmental Affairs*, Spring 1990.

Martin Morse Wooster — "Covering the Fate of the Earth," *Reason*, May 1990.

Glossary of Terms

acid rain rain made acidic by pollution from car exhaust and industrial processes; acid rain kills microbes in the soil that help provide nutrients to plants

bacterium a single-celled, microscopic organism

biodiversity all of the **ecosystems,** plant and animal species, and genes on earth; the entire spectrum of life and life systems on the planet

biotechnology the use of technology to manipulate microorganisms, cells, or parts of cells to meet human needs

birthrate the number of births per one thousand people in a given year

carbon dioxide CO_2, a gas present in the air; it is absorbed by plants in photosynthesis, and contributes to the greenhouse effect when produced by burning fossil fuels and trees

chlorofluorocarbons (CFCs) a group of gases that contributes to the greenhouse effect; CFCs also damage the ozone layer that shields the earth from ultraviolet radiation

chromosome a body of genetic material present in each cell; chromosomes contain **DNA** that carries the genetic code that determines hereditary characteristics

conventional agriculture agriculture in which modern machinery and chemical fertilizers, pesticides, and herbicides are used to produce high crop yields

crop rotation farming technique in which different crops are grown in succession on the same land to preserve the productive capacity of the soil; for example, alternating a crop of soil-enriching soybeans with corn, which depletes the soil of nutrients

demography the statistical study of human populations, usually with reference to size and density, distribution, and vital statistics

developed countries (First World, the North, industrialized) countries that have higher levels of per capita income, industrialization, and modernization; these usually include Europe, Canada, the United States, Australia, Japan, New Zealand, and the Soviet Union

developing countries (Third World, the South) the countries of Asia, Africa, and Latin America with low per capita incomes and low standards of living

DNA (deoxyribonucleic acid) the molecule that carries the genetic information for most living systems; each DNA molecule consists of two strands in the shape of a double helix

ecology the complete network of relationships among living organisms

ecosystem a community of animals, plants, and the environment that sustains it

exponential growth a constant rate of growth applied to a continually growing base; for example, a bank account increasing at compounded interest or a population growing at 3 percent annually

fossil fuel a fuel (coal, oil, natural gas) that is formed in the earth from plant or animal remains (fossils)

gene the smallest portion of a chromosome that contains the hereditary information for the production of protein; a piece of **DNA**

genetic engineering a technology used to change the genetic material of living cells in order to make them capable of producing new substances or performing new functions; for example, the gene for human insulin has been inserted into bacteria, and these changed bacteria now produce human insulin for diabetics

global commons four global resources that are regarded in international law and custom as shared by all nations: the oceans, outer space, weather and climate, and Antarctica

Green Revolution the increase in grain production in some **developing countries** in the 1960s and 1970s as a result of improved technology, mainly from the development of new seeds, fertilizers, and pesticides

growth rate the rate at which a population is increasing or decreasing in a given time period

hectare a metric unit of land area equal to ten thousand square meters or approximately two-and-one-half acres

indigenous native; having originated in a given area

inorganic composed of matter that is not of plant or animal origin; minerals

intercropping growing two or more crops in alternate rows on the same plot

leaching the removal of nutrients or additives in the soil by passing water through the soil

life expectancy the average number of additional years a person would live if current mortality trends were to continue

low-input agriculture agriculture that uses few outside aids (or inputs), such as fertilizers, pesticides, or herbicides

monoculture the repeated cultivation or growth of a single crop

nitrogen fixing a biological process, usually associated with plants, in which certain bacteria change nitrogen in the air to ammonia, a nutrient essential for plant growth

organic from living organisms, usually referring to the food produced with the use of fertilizers of plant or animal origin without employment of chemically formulated fertilizers, growth stimulants, antibiotics, or pesticides

ozone ground-level ozone is one of the gases which contributes to the greenhouse effect; in the upper atmosphere ozone shields the earth from the sun's ultraviolet radiation

per capita per person; for example, per capita income is the income produced by a nation divided by the number of people in that nation

regenerative agriculture an agricultural practice that allows the soil to replenish what was lost during cultivation; often used synonymously with **sustainable** agriculture

sustainable capable of passing on the earth's natural resources intact to the next generation; using and conserving resources wisely, while providing for the needs of the population

tillage the preparation of land for raising crops by loosening or breaking up the soil

virus a submicroscopic organism that contains genetic information but cannot reproduce itself; to do so, it must invade another cell and use parts of that cell's reproductive machinery

Organizations to Contact

The editors have compiled the following list of organizations that are concerned with the issues debated in this book. All of them have publications or information available for interested readers. The descriptions are derived from materials provided by the organizations. This list was compiled upon the date of publication. Names and phone numbers of organizations are subject to change.

Competitive Enterprise Institute (CEI)
233 Pennsylvania Ave. SE, Suite 200
Washington, DC 20003
(202) 547-1010

CEI encourages the use of private incentive and property rights to protect the environment. CEI advocates removing government barriers to establish a system in which the private sector would be responsible for the environment. Its publications include the monthly newsletter *CEI UpDate* and numerous reprints and briefs.

Council for Agricultural Science and Technology (CAST)
137 Lynn Ave.
Ames, IA 50010-7120
(515) 292-2125

CAST provides information on the science and technology of food production. In July 1990 CAST published a collection of scientific reviews which criticized alternative agriculture. It also publishes the quarterly *News from CAST* and the biannual *SCIENCE of Food and Agriculture.*

Earth Island Institute
300 Broadway, Suite 28
San Francisco, CA 94133
(415) 788-3666

Earth Island Institute is a nonprofit organization that focuses on environmental issues and their relation to such concerns as human rights and economic development in the Third World. The Institute's publications include its quarterly *Earth Island Journal.*

Environmental Defense Fund (EDF)
257 Park Ave. South
New York, NY 10010
(212) 505-2100

EDF is a nonprofit environmental education and advocacy organization. EDF's staff includes attorneys, scientists, and economists who seek solutions to a broad range of environmental and public health problems. The Fund publishes materials on acid rain, air quality, biotechnology, and other topics. *Biotechnology's Bitter Harvest, Developing Policies for Responding to Climatic Change,* and *Chlorofluorocarbon Policy* are a few of the Fund's publications.

Foundation for Research on Economics and the Environment (FREE)
4900 25th Ave. NE, Suite 201
Seattle, WA 98105
(206) 548-1776

FREE is a research and educational foundation committed to building a society of free and responsible individuals. The Foundation promotes relying on the free market to coordinate social, economic, and environmental activities. Its publications include the quarterly newsletter *FREE Perspectives on Economics and the Environment*.

Friends of the Earth Foundation
218 D St. SE
Washington, DC 20003
(202) 544-2600

Friends of the Earth is dedicated to the preservation, restoration, and rational use of the Earth's resources. Some of the specific issues it is working on include: tropical rainforest destruction, global warming, and coastal and groundwater contamination. It publishes the quarterly periodical *Atmospheres*, research reports, and bibliographies.

The Heritage Foundation
214 Massachusetts Ave. NE
Washington, DC 20002
(202) 546-4400

The Heritage Foundation is a public policy think tank which advocates the use of the free market to solve environmental problems. Its publications include the quarterly magazine *Policy Review*, brief *Executive Memorandum* editorials, and the longer *Backgrounder* studies.

Hudson Institute
Herman Kahn Center
5395 Emerson Way
PO Box 26-919
Indianapolis, IN 46226
(317) 545-1000

The Hudson Institute is a public policy research center whose members are elected from academia, government, and industry. The Institute believes in the power of the free market and human ingenuity to solve environmental problems. Its publications include the periodic paper *Hudson Institute Briefing* and the bimonthly journal *Hudson Institute Opinion*.

Institute for Food and Development Policy (Food First)
145 9th St.
San Francisco, CA 94103
(415) 864-8555

The Institute provides research and education on world hunger and ecological issues. It believes that foreign aid is counterproductive and contends that world hunger can be eliminated if First World countries allow Third World countries to take control of their own food production. The Institute publishes books, pamphlets, and the quarterly *Food First News*.

International Society of Tropical Foresters (ISTF)
c/o Society of American Foresters
5400 Grosvenor Ln.
Bethesda, MD 20814
(301) 897-8720

ISTF is a nonprofit organization committed to the protection, wise management, and rational use of the world's tropical forests. The Society provides a communications network for people concerned about the fate of the forests. It publishes the quarterly *ISTF News*.

Monsanto Chemical Corporation
800 N. Lindbergh Blvd.
St. Louis, MO 63167
(314) 694-1000

Monsanto is a major producer of agricultural pesticides and herbicides. Monsanto began a program to reduce air pollution and wastewater emissions from its plants following the 1984 accident at a Union Carbide plant in Bhopal, India, which released poisonous gas and was responsible for approximately eight thousand deaths. Its publications include *Your Right-to-Know, Monsanto Pledges to Reduce Air Emissions,* and *Of the Earth: Agriculture and the New Biology.*

National Institute for Science, Law, and Public Policy (NISLAPP)
1424 16th St. NW, Suite 105
Washington, DC 20036
(202) 462-8800

NISLAPP seeks to influence public policies on food production topics, including sustainable agriculture, food safety, and nutrition. It attempts to unite individuals working to develop sustainable forms of agriculture with consumers concerned about quality food. Its publications include the newsletter *Health Harvest News.*

New Forests Project
731 Eighth St. SE
Washington, DC 20003
(202) 547-3800

The New Forests Project, part of the International Center for Development Policy, directs development projects in the Third World. These projects focus on planting trees that increase soil fertility and provide fuel wood and livestock feed. New Forests Project publishes the quarterly *Newsletter* and numerous information sheets.

Political Economy Research Center (PERC)
502 S. 19th Ave., Suite 211
Bozeman, MT 59715
(406) 587-9591

PERC is a research and education foundation that focuses primarily on environmental and natural resource issues. Its approach emphasizes the use of the free market and the importance of private property rights. *PERC Viewpoint* and *PERC Reports* are PERC publications.

Rainforest Action Network (RAN)
301 Broadway, Suite A
San Francisco, CA 94133
(415) 398-4404

RAN seeks to preserve the world's rain forests through preventing cattle ranching and the logging of tropical timber in rain forests. Its publications include briefs such as *The Rainforests of Southeast Asia, Indigenous Peoples of the Rainforest,* and *Consumer's and Investor's Guide to the Rainforests.*

Rodale Institute
222 Main St.
Emmaus, PA 18098
(215) 967-5171

Founded by J.I. Rodale, the Rodale Institute disseminates information and technology on regenerative agriculture. The Institute seeks to develop and establish resource-efficient farming methods through research and training. It publishes *Ag-Renew* and *International Ag-Sieve* magazines.

Sierra Club
730 Polk St.
San Francisco, CA 94109
(415) 776-2211

The Sierra Club strives to conserve the natural resources of the U.S. and the world. Its publications include the brochure *Tropical Rain Forests: A Vanishing Treasure* and *Bankrolling Disasters: International Development Banks and the Global Environment.*

Wildlife Conservation International (WCI)
c/o New York Zoological Society
185th St. and Southern Blvd.
Bronx, NY 10460
(212) 220-5155

Wildlife Conservation International supports international species survival strategies and ecosystem conservation projects. Its objective is to save endangered habitats, ecosystems, and species. Its publications include the *WCI News* and the bimonthly magazine *Wildlife Conservation.*

World Resources Institute (WRI)
1709 New York Ave. NW
Washington, DC 20006
(202) 638-6300

The World Resources Institute is a research and policy institute that aims to present accurate information about global resources and environmental conditions, analyses of emerging issues, and development of creative yet workable policy responses. It publishes a wide array of materials, including its *World Resources* annual and numerous papers.

Zero Population Growth (ZPG)
1400 16th St. NW, Suite 320
Washington, DC 20036
(202) 332-2200

Zero Population Growth is a nonprofit membership organization working to achieve a sustainable balance of population, resources, and the environment, both in the U.S. and worldwide. ZPG monitors and reports on legislative and judicial activity affecting population-related issues. It publishes *ZPG Backgrounder* and *ZPG Fact Sheet.*

Bibliography of Books

Sartaj Aziz   *Agricultural Policies for the 1990s.* Paris: Development Centre of the Organisation for Economic Co-operation and Development, 1990.

Melvin A. Benarde   *Our Precarious Habitat: Fifteen Years Later.* New York: John Wiley & Sons, 1989.

Henry Bernstein, Ben Crow, Maureen Mackintosh, and Charlotte Martin, eds.   *The Food Question: Profits Versus People?* New York: Monthly Review Press, 1990.

Peter Borrelli, ed.   *Crossroads: Environmental Priorities for the Future.* Washington, DC: Island Press, 1988.

Daniel B. Botkin, Margriet F. Caswell, John E. Estes, and Angelo A. Orio, eds.   *Changing the Global Environment: Perspectives on Human Involvement.* San Diego, CA: Academic Press, 1989.

Barry Commoner   *Making Peace with the Planet.* New York: Pantheon Books, 1990.

John D. Conner Jr. et al.   *Pesticide Regulation Handbook.* New York: Executive Enterprises Publications Co., 1987.

Rudiger Dornbusch, John H. Makin, and David Zlowe, eds.   *Alternative Solutions to Developing-Country Debt Problems.* Washington, DC: American Enterprise Institute for Public Policy Research, 1989.

Alan B. Durning   *Action at the Grassroots: Fighting Poverty and Environmental Decline.* Washington, DC: Worldwatch Institute, 1989.

Clive Edwards et al.   *Sustainable Agricultural Systems.* Ankeny, IA: Soil and Water Conservation Society, 1990.

Cary Fowler and Pat Mooney   *Shattering: Food, Politics, and the Loss of Genetic Diversity.* Tucson, AZ: University of Arizona Press, 1990.

Stephen R. Gliessman, ed.   *Agroecology: Researching the Ecological Basis for Sustainable Agriculture.* New York: Springer-Verlag, 1990.

Judith Gradwohl and Russel Greenberg   *Saving the Tropical Forests.* Washington, DC: Island Press, 1988.

Susanna Hecht and Alexander Cockburn   *The Fate of the Forest: Developers, Destroyers and Defenders of the Amazon.* New York: Verso, 1989.

Sherwood Idso   *Carbon Dioxide and Global Change: Earth in Transition.* Tempe, AZ: IBR Press, 1989.

H. Jeffrey Leonard et al.   *Environment and the Poor: Development Strategies for a Common Agenda.* New Brunswick, NJ: Transaction Books, 1989.

Scott Lewis   *The Rainforest Book: How You Can Save the World's Rainforests.* Los Angeles: Living Planet Press, 1990.

Michael Lipton   *New Seeds and Poor People.* London: Unwin Hyman, 1989.

James Lovelock   *The Ages of GAIA: A Biography of Our Living Earth.* New York: W.W. Norton & Co., 1988.

Marcia D. Lowe	*Alternatives to the Automobile: Transport for Livable Cities.* Washington, DC: Worldwatch Institute, 1990.
Francesca Lyman, Irving Mintzer, Kathleen Courrier, and James MacKenzie	*The Greenhouse Trap: What We're Doing to the Atmosphere and How We Can Slow Global Warming.* Boston: Beacon Press, 1990.
Andrew S. MacDonald	*Nowhere to Go but Down? The International Agricultural Development Game.* London: Unwin Hyman, 1989.
June F. MacDonald, ed.	*Biotechnology and Sustainable Agriculture: Policy Alternatives.* Ithaca, NY: National Agricultural Biotech Council, 1989.
Norman Meyers	*The Primary Source.* New York: W.W. Norton & Co., 1984.
Joan M. Nelson, ed.	*Economic Crisis and Policy Choice: The Politics of Adjustment in the Third World.* Princeton, NJ: Princeton University Press, 1990.
Michael Oppenheimer and Robert H. Boyle	*Dead Heat: The Race Against the Greenhouse Effect.* New York: Basic Books, 1990.
John T. Pierce	*The Food Resource.* New York: John Wiley & Sons, 1990.
Paul R. Portney, ed.	*Public Policies for Environmental Protection.* Washington, DC: Resources for the Future, 1990.
Dixy Lee Ray and Lou Guzzo	*Trashing the Planet: How Science Can Help Us Deal with Acid Rain, Depletion of the Ozone, and Nuclear Waste (Among Other Things).* Washington, DC: Regnery Gateway, 1990.
John F. Richards and Richard P. Tucker, eds.	*World Deforestation in the Twentieth Century.* Durham, NC: Duke University Press, 1988.
John Robbins	*Diet for a New America.* Walpole, NH: Stillpoint Publishing, 1987.
Stephen H. Schneider	*Global Warming: Are We Entering the Greenhouse Century?* San Francisco: Sierra Club Books, 1989.
Julian L. Simon	*Population Matters: People, Resources, Environment, and Immigration.* New Brunswick, NJ: Transaction Publishers, 1990.
Julian L. Simon and Herman Kahn, eds.	*The Resourceful Earth: A Response to Global 2000.* Oxford, England: Basil Blackwell, 1984.
Max Singer	*Passage to a Human World: The Dynamics of Creating Global Wealth.* Indianapolis, IN: Hudson Institute, 1987.
Linda Starke, ed.	*State of the World 1990.* New York: W.W. Norton & Co., 1990.
Jan Wojcik	*The Arguments of Agriculture: A Casebook in Contemporary Agricultural Controversy.* West Lafayette, IN: Purdue University Press, 1989.
World Commission on Environment and Development	*Our Common Future.* London: Oxford University Press, 1987.
World Resources Institute	*World Resources 1990-91.* New York: Oxford University Press, 1990.

Index

abortion, 137
acid rain, 31, 37, 249
  and population growth, 101
  and the greenhouse effect, 65
Ackerman, Bruce, 90
Acquired Immune Deficiency
  Syndrome (AIDS), 82, 91, 101, 144
Afghanistan, 82
Africa
  and population growth, 19-20, 22,
    99, 108, 110
  and World Bank aid, 136-137
  desertification in, 47, 128
  destruction of rain forests in, 47,
    170, 173
  grassland degradation in, 22
  nature tourism in, 178
  need for energy efficiency, 252
  urbanization of, 126
Afsua, Santos Adam, 156
Agarwal, Anil, 243
agriculture
  alternative
    and soil erosion, 191, 200, 201-202
    can be profitable, 194-195
    con, 197, 199-201
    can be sustainable, 188-195
    con, 196-203
    definition of, 189-191, 197
    produces lower crop yields, 199-200
  and air pollution, 18-19
  and irrigation, 244, 255
  animal
    is inefficient, 220-221
  conventional
    and fossil fuel products, 202-203
    chemical use creates hazards, 192,
      194
    increase in crop yields, 189
    is sustainable, 201-203
  in rain forests, 145, 147, 152
  research on, 192-193
  slash-and-burn system, 145, 147,
    152, 208
  sustainable
    and the Third World, 208-209, 266
    biotechnology can harm, 210-216
    definition of, 190, 194, 205
    meat consumption supports, 223-
      229
    needs biotechnology, 204-209
    vegetarianism can promote, 217-222

  use of fertilizers, 198, 200-201
    and biotechnology, 205, 206-208
  use of herbicides, 197-198, 199, 200
  use of pesticides, 199
Ahmed, Iftikhar, 215
air pollution
  and agriculture, 18-19
  and automobile emissions, 248, 249,
    252
  and population growth, 113, 126
  Japanese contribution to, 20
  U.S. contribution to, 20, 251
  Soviet contribution to, 251
Ali, Osman, 134
Amazon
  destruction of rain forests in, 157-
    158
  settling of, 151-153, 155
animals
  in agriculture
    biotechnology in breeding, 207
    is inefficient, 220-221
Asia
  and population growth, 108, 110, 114
  destruction of rain forests in, 47,
    170-173
  tropical tree plantations in, 174
  urbanization of, 126
atmosphere, 63
  and cloud cover, 65, 66, 77
automobiles
  and air pollution, 248, 249, 252
  and fuel efficiency, 90, 248-250

Bangladesh
  and population control, 129, 132-135
Bauer, P.T., 111
Bean, Bridget, 179
Beni Biological Reserve, 268-269
biological diversity, 144-149, 174,
  213, 268
biotechnology
  ethical problems with, 32-33, 214
  is controlled by large corporations,
    211, 212
  will benefit agriculture, 191, 204-
    209
    con, 210-216
  will exploit the Third World, 212-
    216
birth control
  and population growth, 102, 108-109,

282

284

Massachusetts Institute of Technology
  study on ocean temperatures, 62, 63, 79
meat
  as healthy, 228-229
    con, 220
  see also cattle ranching; agriculture
methane
  and the greenhouse effect, 56, 63-64, 88, 227-228, 236
Mexico
  and population growth, 120, 121, 126
  malnutrition in, 121
Meyers, Norman, 76
Michaels, Patrick, 65, 67
Middle East
  and oil production, 248
  wars, 82
Milbraith, Lester W., 29
Mintzer, Irving, 55, 80
Montag, Benjamin, 45
Mooney, Pat, 215, 216
Morain, Mary, 116

Nafziger, Emerson D., 202
Nash, J. Madeleine, 194
National Aeronautics & Space Administration (NASA), 64, 65, 75, 88
National Cattlemen's Association, 223
National Center for Atmospheric Research, 76, 77
National Research Council, 188
Natural Resource Management (NRM), 242-243
Nature Conservancy, The, 155, 177-179, 181
  and debt-for-nature swaps, 263, 268
nature tourism, 176-182
New Forests Project, The, 143-149
nitrous oxide
  and the greenhouse effect, 56, 63, 64, 88
North American Electric Reliability Council, 36-37
nuclear power, 32
  accidents, 38
  politics of, 39, 90
Nugkuag, Evaristo, 158

ocean currents, 62, 63, 67
oil
  costs of, 258
  production of, 248-249
  supply is not finite, 256-260

world consumption of, 248
Oppenheimer, Michael, 81
organic farming
  definition of, 197
  feasibility of, 198
Organization of Petroleum Exporting Countries (OPEC), 26, 36, 258
Ostrov, Janet Ekey, 196
ozone layer
  depletion of, 18, 31, 101, 113, 127

Pearce, Fred, 57
Pease, Robert, 72
People for the Ethical Treatment of Animals, 221
Peru
  Mishana rain forest, 164-166
pesticides, 189, 199, 205-207, 229
Peters, Charles M., 162
plant life
  and carbon dioxide, 69-71, 79
population
  world statistics, 99-101, 113, 125-126
Population Council, 115
population growth, 30-31
  and family planning, 102, 108-109, 114-115, 118-123
  as cause of hunger, 103, 104, 109, 121, 205
    con, 107, 110, 121, 218
  can be positive, 107, 110-111, 128, 133
  control of
    and human rights violations, 108-109, 122-123, 135
    incentives for, 134
    in China, 108, 113, 120
    international programs are harmful, 131-137
      con, 124-130
  effect on the environment
    air pollution, 113, 126
    depletes global resources, 27-28, 30, 98-104, 124-130
    global warming, 107, 113
    species extinction, 113, 127, 144
  in Europe, 99, 110, 128
  in Third World, 99, 107, 108, 110, 113, 114, 120-121, 126, 127, 242
  in United States, 99, 104, 110, 114, 117, 127
  may be declining, 101, 107-108, 114
  rates of increase, 99, 107, 126-127
  see also family planning

Rainforest Action Network, 41

286